Last Out

Last Out

4RAR/NZ (ANZAC) Battalion's second tour in Vietnam

Jerry Taylor

ALLEN&UNWIN

First published in 2001

Allen & Unwin
83 Alexander Street
Crows Nest NSW 2065
Australia
Phone: (61 2) 8425 0100
Fax: (61 2) 9906 2218
Email: info@allenandunwin.com
Web: www.allenandunwin.com

National Library of Australia
Cataloguing-in-Publication entry:

Taylor, Jerry, 1939– .
Last out: 4RAR/NZ (ANZAC) Battalion's second tour in Vietnam.

Includes index.
ISBN 1 86508 561 8.

1. Australia. Army. Royal Australian Regiment. Battalion, 4th. 2. Vietnamese Conflict, 1961–1975—Regimental histories—Australia. 3. Vietnamese Conflict, 1961–1975—Regimental histories—New Zealand. 4. Vietnamese Conflict, 1961–1975—Participation, Australian. 5. Vietnamese Conflict, 1961–1975—Participation, New Zealand. I. Title.

959.70434

Index compiled by Russell Brooks
Typeset in 10.5 on 11.5 pt Garamond by Midland Typesetters, Maryborough
Printed in China by Everbest Printing Co. Ltd

10 9 8 7 6 5 4 3 2 1

Last Out is dedicated to the members of
4RAR/NZ (ANZAC) Battalion
who served in South Vietnam in 1971–72,
and particularly to the memory of:

Pte B.C. Beilkin
Pte J. Duff
Pte K.H. Harding (NZ)
Pte K.M. Kingston-Powles
Pte R.J. Niblett
Pte B.M. Pengilly
Pte M.L. Rhodes
Pte R.J. Sprigg
Cpl A.C.F. Wilkinson

The role of 4RAR is to seek out and close with the enemy, to kill or capture him, to seize and hold ground and to repel attack by night and day, regardless of season, weather, or terrain.

Extract from 4RAR Standing Orders, issued 14 January 1970

Contents

Foreword

Lieutenant General D.S. McIver, CMG, OBE
Chief of the General Staff, New Zealand Army, 1988–89
and
Second-in-Command, 4RAR/NZ (ANZAC) Battalion, 1971

For all of us who served in 4RAR/NZ (ANZAC) Battalion, that period has had a profound impact on our lives. Not only was all of our military experience and training tested in that totally demanding and stressful operational environment, but also we were participants in a unique multi-national military organisation developed solely for operations in South Vietnam, the ANZAC Battalion.

The 4th Battalion, Royal Australian Regiment, from which our Battalion grew, had a core of regular army soldiers and was filled out by conscripts. Their workup was completed in Townsville in an intensive period of training which I was able to join for the last three months. By the time I sailed with the main body of the Battalion on the stately, but almost worn-out old aircraft carrier, HMAS *Sydney*, I had come to know and respect them as soldiers and as friends.

The Kiwi component of the Battalion came directly from the 1st Battalion, Royal New Zealand Infantry Regiment, a regular army unit serving in Singapore. They completed their workup there, physically separated from the rest of the Battalion, but using the 4RAR Standard Operating Procedures as the basis for their training. Brian Monks, Company Commander Victor 6 Company, remained in close and regular consultation with Battalion Commander Jim Hughes throughout that period. The Kiwis arrived in theatre just before the Australian main body and I remember my pride when I met up with them in Nui Dat, looking trim and well prepared, many of them old friends with whom I had served before.

It took a great deal of commitment and dedication from everyone involved to make it all work—and it did! These two disparate elements quickly locked together into a cohesive and effective fighting unit able to deploy immediately onto operations under CO Jim Hughes. Over the period of the 4RAR/NZ (ANZAC) Battalion deployment they faced the enemy together in tough and stressful combat and often provided critical support one for the other; they played together (with the traditional Aussie–Kiwi rivalry that one would expect); they withdrew together as the last operational component of the Task Force in Nui Dat (our ANZAC Battalion was to be the last in the line) and, sadly, they grieve together for comrades-in-arms lost in that unfamiliar, foreign land.

We all owe Jerry Taylor a special debt of gratitude for taking on the role of chronicler of this important and unique period in the military history of our two nations. His research has been painstakingly extensive, detailed and thorough. Not only does his book record the people, places, events and circumstances that are a part of the battalion's history, but it also sets on the record the special ANZAC relationship that was a central part of it—a relationship which saw its first expression at Gallipoli and, today, continues to be at the centre of our mutual commitments to peacekeeping, especially in our Pacific neighbourhood.

Through this book we will refight old battles, relive old experiences, remember old friends and comrades and, maybe, contemplate the reason for it all. I am sure it will become a valued possession for everyone who had the honour to serve in 4RAR/NZ (ANZAC) Battalion.

Don McIver

Introduction

Major General J.C. Hughes, AO, DSO, MC
Commanding Officer, 4RAR/NZ (ANZAC) Battalion 1970–71

In the years 1965–72 sixteen battalions of the Royal Australian Regiment served in Vietnam. Five of those battalions were integrated with New Zealand infrantrymen and had the honour of carrying the name 'ANZAC' in their title. 4RAR was the sixteenth battalion and, therefore, the last to serve in Vietnam, and its title was 4RAR/NZ (ANZAC) Battalion. The unit consisted of 181 New Zealanders and 835 Australians.

The Fighting Fourth, co-edited by Bob Sayce and Mike O'Neill, was published by the Battalion in 1972 and provided a pictorial record of the second tour in Vietnam (1971–72). A second edition was published in 1990, by the Association of 4th Infantry Battalions. Jerry Taylor recognised the need for a narrative military history to complement the pictorial record, and we are indebted to Jerry for his initiative and detailed research that has resulted in this book, *Last Out*.

4RAR moved from Brisbane to Townsville in early December 1969. The move was a Godsend because it resulted in new barracks and good training areas; in addition, by joining 3 Task Force we had access to all supporting units except tanks. Our direct support battery, 104 Field Battery 12 Field Regiment, lived nearby. 2RAR had assisted 6RAR to prepare for Vietnam, and we in turn did the same for 2RAR. Later 6RAR assisted us with training support: umpires for exercises, safety officers, instructors and provision of 'enemy', equipment and ammunition. Each battalion in Vietnam sent home operational reports and intelligence summaries; one-to-one correspondence was encouraged between key appointments. I acknowledge the assistance that I received from fellow Commanding Officers—John Church of 2RAR, and David Butler and later David Drabsch of 6RAR.

The heart and soul of any unit is its people. Other factors are important, but none so much as the people. I was very much aware of the responsibility put on me to train and educate the members of 4RAR in all the skills that eventually result in a unit trained and ready for war. My task was made easier by the assistance of experienced officers and NCOs within the Battalion and at our Army schools, the Central Army Records Officer, the Directorate of Infrantry and Headquarters 3 Task Force. My wife, Jan, gave me great personal support.

1970 was a hard year for all members of the Battalion, and I make no apologies for that. Our training sequence was influenced by a manning policy which stipulated that no more than 50 per cent of the Battalion's strength could be provided by National Servicemen. Consequently I asked for all new regular servicemen to arrive as early as possible in 1970. We sent 380 all-ranks to specialist and career qualification courses in the first six months of that year and the Battalion was also more or less at full strength by mid-1970. Training standards were purposely set high. Weak links were identified and, where possible, every effort was made to re-train people to the necessary levels. But despite counselling and the extra training, some officers, NCOs, and soldiers did not meet the standards required for operational service.

It's said that all work and no play makes Jack a dull boy, but in 4RAR in 1970 members enjoyed a range of social activities as well as inter-company, inter-unit and local Townsville sport.

1970 ended with a month-long course at the Jungle Training Centre, Canungra. As was usual Support Company went through as a rifle company, as did Administration Company, the first such sub-unit to do the JTC course in its own right. The battalion as a whole, and each company, passed the course, but a few individuals failed and had to be replaced. Canungra was a good way to finish the year, and I felt confident that we were functioning well and were prepared for 1971.

January to March 1971 saw the Battalion and its attached troops undertake three separate battalion-level exercises in a variety of terrain and weather conditions. We wrote the first exercise ourselves and 6RAR ran it for us; the second was prepared and conducted by HQ 3 Task Force; and the final one was the HQ 1 Division test exercise. The unit acquitted itself well, improving steadily as time went on. Any remaining minor problems were quickly discovered and corrected. April 1971 was used for administration, packing stores and embarkation leave. 4RAR was ready for war.

Throughout 1970 I had lobbied for the New Zealand Victor Company, who were training in Singapore and Malaysia and would become our fourth rifle company in Vietnam, to attend at least one of the final three exercises. Training apart, I had hoped that we could mix socially and at sport before Vietnam. Agreement was, in principle, given, but in November 1970 I received a message to the effect that no funds were available to transport Victor Company to Townsville. Consequently we were no better off than previous ANZAC battalions. But, as Don McIver recalls in his Foreword, 'It took a great deal of commitment and dedication from everyone involved to make it (the integration) all work—and it did!'. A very effective fighting battalion resulted.

Our advance party arrived in Vietnam on 2 May 1971; Victor Company arrived on 7 May; and the main body joined us on 23 May. After a week of orientation and safety exercises 4RAR/NZ (ANZAC) Battalion was fully operational.

Since November 1970, 1 Australian Task Force had been reduced to two battalions on its order of battle. Our area of operations was the western half of Phuoc Tuy Province and the northern border area astride Route 2, which ran north–south and bisected the Province. We had no responsibility for any city, town or village, those being allotted to the local South Vietnamese Regional Forces. Our two targets were 274 Viet Cong Regiment and 33 North Vietnamese Army Regiment, and our aim was to deny them contact with the civilian popuation. This meant that at all times one-half to three-quarters of the Battalion was out on operations, with the remainder deployed as Task Force Ready Reaction Force or undertaking retraining or rest. During June and July 1971 the entire Battalion was committed to operations.

141 members of 4RAR, mostly officers and NCOs, who went to Vietnam in May 1971 had previously served there either during the Battalion's first tour or with another unit. And among this 141 were individuals who had also seen service in Borneo as well as Vietnam. We were very fortunate to have such a depth of active service experience.

On 21 August 1971 we heard the replay of a statement by the Australian Prime Minister, Mr McMahon, to the effect that the Task Force would be withdrawn from Vietnam prior to Christmas, and the logistic units would leave early in 1972. Someone, an announcer or commentator or spokesman, remarked that members of the Task Force had, or soon would, return to their base in Nui Dat in order to pack up. At the time I thought this was a silly statement to make. As we were the last battalion to arrive in Vietnam it seemed obvious that we would be the last to leave, and that our departure would mean a tactical withdrawal. I resolved that we would withdraw intact and with honour.

By July 1971 we had inflicted considerable damage to 274 Viet Cong Regiment, and they had been forced to withdraw north out of the Province. Now our most dangerous enemy was 33 North Vietnamese Army Regiment (33rd), who had not been contacted since June. Their usual area of operations was east of Route 2 and, in turn, B Company, then C Company, then V Company and, finally, D Company found numerous signs that elements of 33rd had recently returned to Phuoc Tuy. On 21 September D Company attacked an enemy group later identified as 33rd's Regimental Headquarters and their 2 Battalion. Then, some four kilometres south-west of D Company, B Company attacked a second enemy group, which turned out to be the Regiment's 3 Battalion. It was a long day and night, but 33rd was eventually forced to withdraw. Sadly, we lost five men killed and 24 wounded.

As part of the withdrawal in October 1971, 4RAR/NZ (ANZAC) Battalion occupied a defensive position round Luscombe Airfield at Nui Dat. We had become a battalion group with our own cavalry, gunners, engineers, signal and logistic detachments. In direct support were US medium artillery, Australian Army Aviation and RAAF elements. The remainder of the Task Force had departed for Vung Tay and, ultimately, to Australia. I felt very confident that we could repel any enemy attack as our security level was high at all times. Later, in November, we withdrew, in textbook style, from Nui Dat to Vung Tau. In December the main body departed Vietnam, with the New Zealanders returning to Singapore and Australians to Townsville. Left at Vung Tau was our D Company Group of some 200 men, who provided a Ready Reaction Force for the Vung Tau logistic base. The D Company Group returned to Australia in March 1972.

I was fortunate to command 4RAR/NZ (ANZAC) Battalion in Vietnam in 1971. Everyone gave of their best: professionalism, team work, pride in self and unit, self and corporate discipline—these were the hallmarks of the ANZAC Battalion. We were never defeated. We were successful in denying 274 Viet Cong Regiment and 33 North Vietnamese Army Regiment contact with the civilian population. We withdrew from Vietnam cleanly, intact and with honour. The special ANZAC relationship was an added spur to our Battalion. And the mottoes of the Royal New Zealand Infantry Regiment, 'Onward', and the Royal Australian Regiment, 'Duty First', had been well and truly honoured.

Jim Hughes.

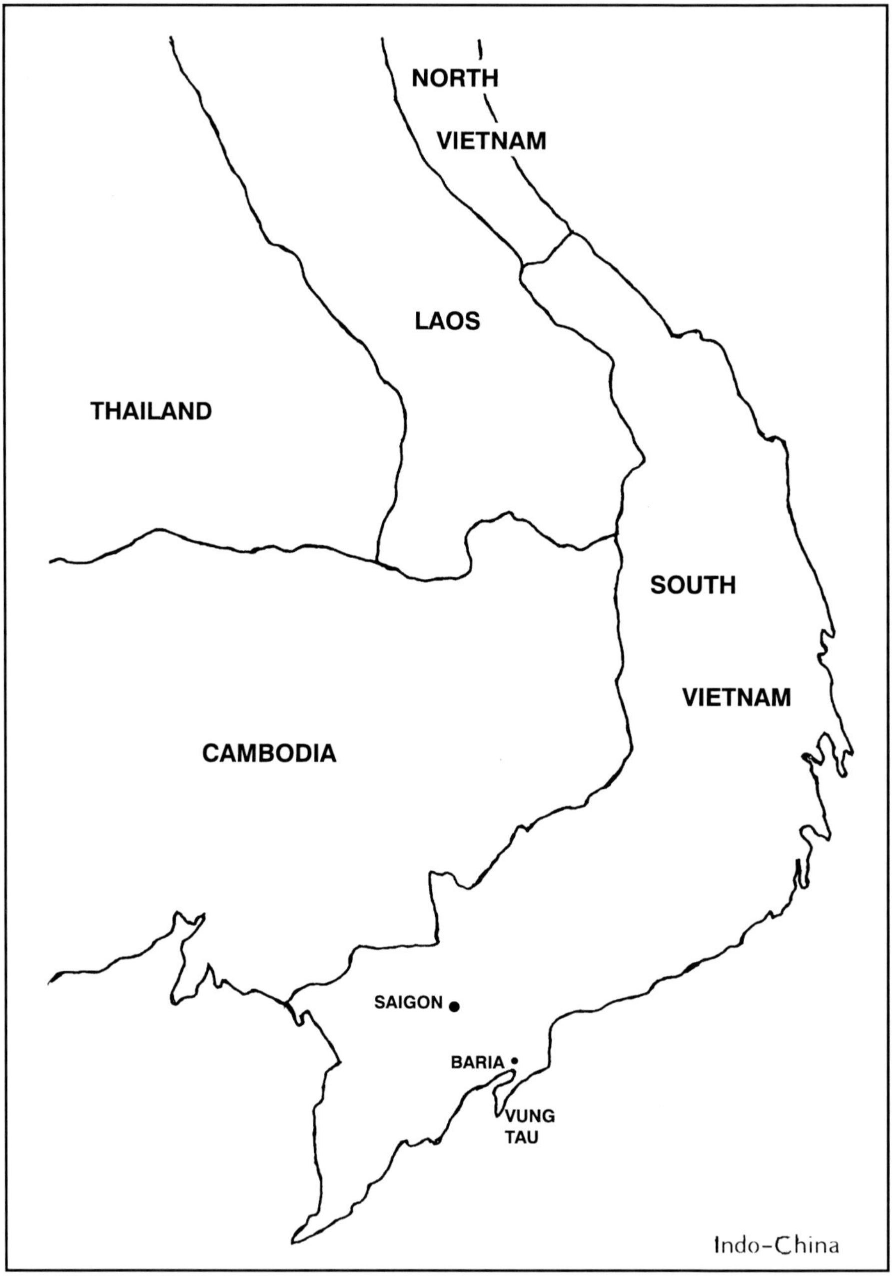
NORTH
VIETNAM
LAOS
THAILAND
SOUTH
VIETNAM
CAMBODIA
SAIGON
BARIA
VUNG
TAU
Indo-China

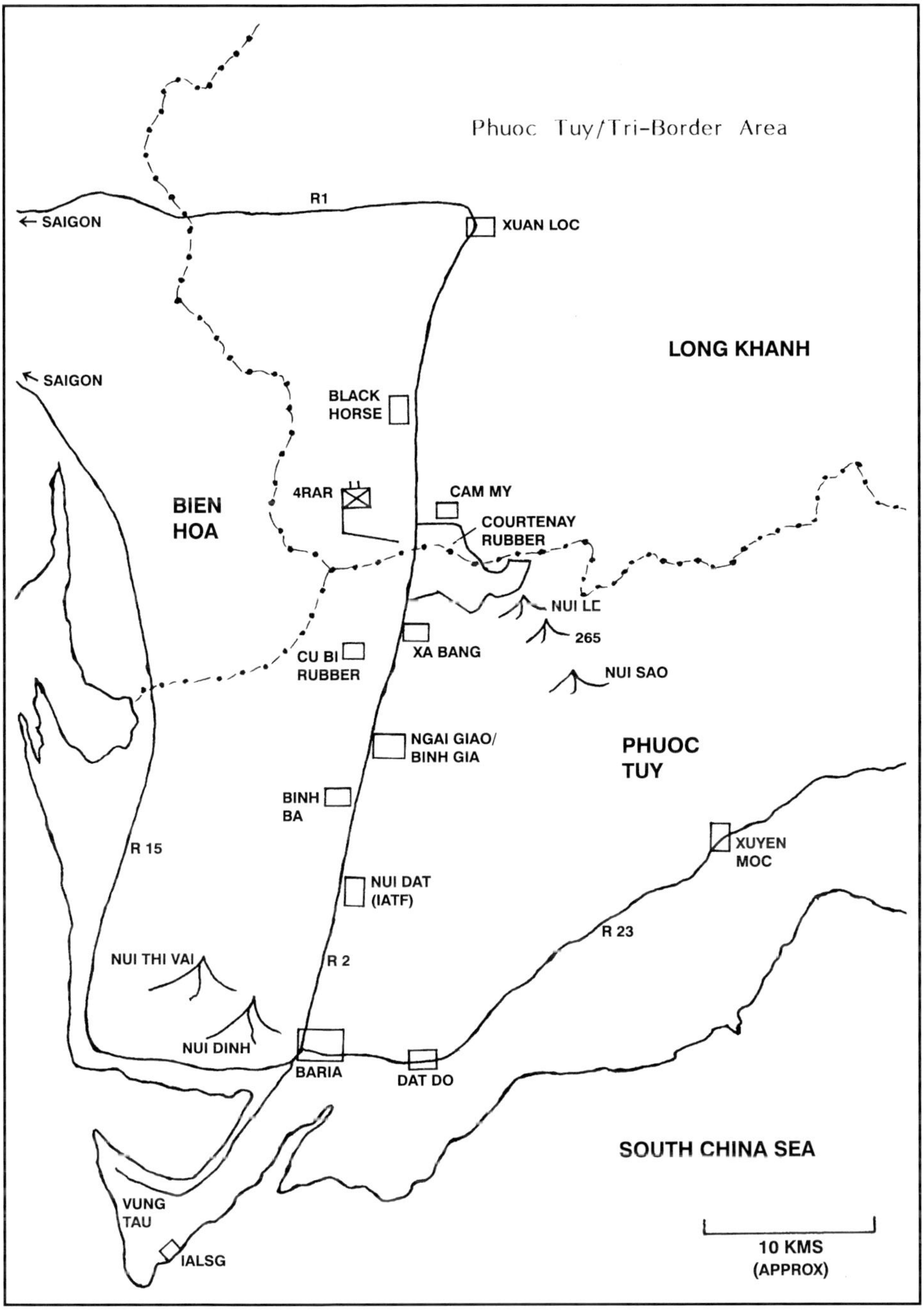
Phuoc Tuy/Tri-Border Area
R1
SAIGON
XUAN LOC
LONG KHANH
SAIGON
BLACK HORSE
4RAR
CAM MY
COURTENAY RUBBER
BIEN HOA
NUI LE
265
XA BANG
CU BI RUBBER
NUI SAO
NGAI GIAO/ BINH GIA
PHUOC TUY
BINH BA
XUYEN MOC
R 15
NUI DAT (IATF)
R 23
NUI THI VAI
R 2
NUI DINH
BARIA
DAT DO
SOUTH CHINA SEA
VUNG TAU
IALSG
10 KMS (APPROX)

Prologue

Night, 21 September 1971
Phuoc Tuy Province, South Vietnam

Even early that morning it was obvious that the ANZAC Battalion was encountering a major enemy force.

At 1128hr, in the south of the area of operations, B Company's 6 Platoon had killed one enemy soldier and wounded a second who escaped, leaving behind his AK47. Continuing on, the platoon located a telephone cable, and then killed another enemy soldier who appeared to be rolling it up. A moment later the platoon came under intense small arms and 60mm mortar fire that caused several casualties.

Meanwhile 5 Platoon was reporting the fresh tracks of a large enemy force; and then 4 Platoon contacted three enemy, killing one of them. The platoon brought artillery and Cobra gunship fire down on the contact area, and the pilots reported seeing 'many' enemy. Then, at 1311hr, B Company confirmed from documents found on enemy bodies that they had encountered 33 North Vietnamese Army Regiment.

Throughout the afternoon B Company continued to contact aggressive groups of enemy and, at 1615hr, 6 Platoon reported that they had been surrounded by an enemy force and had suffered seven casualties. B Company was now struggling to concentrate into a defensive position in order to bring in a helicopter resupply of ammunition and extract the wounded.

Earlier in the day, at 0851hr, D Company's 12 Platoon, four kilometres north-east of B Company, had come under small arms and RPG fire from bunkers, which killed a machinegunner and wounded the platoon commander and a section commander.

For the rest of the morning, and into the afternoon, D Company fought aggressive enemy groups seeking to outflank them. Then, at

1540hr, when the company attacked the enemy position, they were bloodily repulsed, losing four young soldiers 15 metres from the bunkers. Withdrawing so that aircraft could put hard bombs onto the position, D Company forced up against a second bunker system. Now, in the dark, with five killed and nine wounded, and with most of their ammunition expended, the company was surrounded, and awaiting a coordinated enemy attack.

At the Battalion Command Post on Courtenay Hill, the Commanding Officer filled his pipe with Red Amphora, set a match to it and pondered his options.

B Company was not his main worry: company headquarters and the three platoons had now concentrated, and were relatively secure in a well coordinated night defensive position. Besides, the enemy encountered by the company during the day, although aggressive, appeared to be withdrawing. The company would need another ammunition resupply as soon as it got light, and the minor wounded who had stayed on duty would have to be evacuated. But for the time being B Company was probably all right.

It was D Company that posed the major problem. They were now surrounded by a strong and aggressive enemy force who showed no inclination at all to withdraw. Quite the opposite, in fact. Indeed so rapidly had the enemy followed the company when it withdrew from the first bunkers that it was now in a defensive position little better than a ragged circle roughly 35 metres across, and without even shellscrapes for protection. Small arms fire and grenades were being directed onto them from the north, east and west of the perimeter, and more enemy were seen approaching from the south. So D Company was undoubtedly the problem. But how could they be helped?

APCs? wondered the CO. But it was dark, and it would be madness to send armoured vehicles into that terrain at night, even with close infantry protection. Not an option.

More air, then? Same problem: darkness would make it impossible for D Company to mark their position, nor could the pilots deliver their ordnance without visual references. So also not an option.

Well then, what about the New Zealanders of Victor Company? But V Company would first need to concentrate, and once they'd done that they'd still have a significant distance to cover on foot. In the dark. In secondary jungle. Against North Vietnamese regulars. Then, too, it would take the New Zealanders several hours to reach D Company, and even if everything went well they might yet be too late.

But there were still the guns of 104 Battery. With superb commitment the artillerymen had toiled at their guns all day and now, twelve hours later, they were desperately weary. Even so, they were D Company's best chance. In fact, until it got light, the guns were the company's only chance. Beyond that, all D Company could hope for was a bit of luck.

But the CO knew that luck is the portion of the prepared, and he also knew that the ANZAC Battalion, and those who supported them, could not have been better prepared for their task in Vietnam . . .

PART I

Preparing for war

The best form of welfare for the troops is intense training.

Field Marshall Erwin Rommel

1

The sleeping sword

When 4RAR began preparing in January 1970 for their second tour of Vietnam, the Battalion embarked on a training cycle which had already proved its merit many times over against the sharp edge of battle. It was a system of training designed not only to teach individuals and groups the skills and procedures that would bring success in battle, but also to *test* those individuals and groups. It was felt, correctly, that it was better to identify any weak links here in Australia than to have them revealed under the profound pressure of operations in Vietnam.

And so, in the sixteen months ahead, all ranks of 4RAR would undergo prolonged, intense and unrelenting preparation for battle. And, as was anticipated, not everyone would find the professional, physical and emotional resources that were needed to pass successfully through that crucible.

4RAR was a young battalion. It had been in existence for less than six years, being raised at Woodside, near Adelaide, on 1 February 1964. But despite its youth the Battalion had already established for itself an impressive fighting record.

In October 1965, under its first commanding officer, LtCol D.S. Thomson, MC, the Battalion had joined 28 Commonwealth Brigade Group in Terendak Camp, Malaysia, and had been immediately placed on short notice to move to Sarawak in Borneo for operations against the Indonesians. This crisis, which lasted from 1962–66, was known as Confrontation, and 4RAR's tour of duty lasted from April to August 1966.

The Battalion's first tour of duty in Vietnam, under the command of LtCol L.R. Greville, commenced on 13 May 1968, and by 19 May the following year, when the Battalion returned to Australia, 4RAR had taken part in eleven major and five company-sized operations against the Viet Cong and North Vietnamese Army, and now possessed an enviable fighting reputation.

But the Battalion which returned from its post-Vietnam leave in July 1969 looked very different from the one which had returned from Vietnam the previous May. The majority of its national servicemen had gone back to civilian employment. Few officers remained from the tour in Vietnam, and of those the majority already had posting orders. Only two, Capt Bob Sayce and Capt Don McKenzie, would stay with the Battalion for the second tour. Luckily the Sergeants' Mess had survived the new round of postings well, and a hard core of original senior NCOs and WOs with Borneo and Vietnam experience remained. So among a total strength of 200 all ranks there were now many new faces in the Battalion. And principal among them was the Commanding Officer, LtCol J.C. Hughes, MC, the man whose primary responsibility it was to rebuild the Battalion in readiness for its return to Vietnam.

Not many professional infantrymen would deny that the CO was the most influential member of any battalion. This was not just because he was the most senior in rank, or because logically he was the most experienced and knowledgeable. It was because his personality and character, and thence the leadership style he exhibited, had a profound effect on his battalion. This effect permeated downwards so that to a marked degree the battalion itself took on the personality and style of its leader. If the CO was negative and grudging, so was his battalion. If he was positive and enthusiastic, the battalion mirrored those qualities.

A battalion was not just a military organisation. A battalion was people and, moreover, people who would in war be ordered to put themselves in situations of danger which could result in their death or maiming. But no commander, at any level, could expect that commitment from his men just because he shouted orders at them. His soldiers had to respect him as a man and a leader, and to trust his professional ability and judgement, or they'd not work to full capacity for him. He had to earn their commitment—it was not negotiable.

So the CO's character, personality and leadership style were crucial ingredients of the battalion's success or failure in battle. An effective leadership style rubbed off on his company commanders and in turn on the commanders below, all of whom were influenced by it. That ultimately helped to generate those two vital combat multipliers without which no unit or sub-unit could expect to reach its full potential: morale and esprit de corps. Those two elements, more than any other, brought the best out in each member of the battalion, so that every man saw himself as an important part of a winning team. Therefore it could be said that the CO *was* the battalion, and most experienced infantrymen would agree with that statement.

So 4RAR, as they began readying themselves for battle in 1970, were extremely fortunate to have as their CO LtCol Jim Hughes. One of his company commanders describes him this way:

> In my 32 years of soldiering I've been privileged to serve under many outstanding commanders, and each of them has had a particular professional impact on me because they excelled as leaders of men.
>
> But despite the fact that I've served in many outstanding units, there was something unique about 4RAR: a quality that's difficult to put your finger on, but which set it apart from any other unit I've ever served in.
>
> Everything about 4RAR was 'right': the very strong Sergeants' Mess; the fact that all the Australian company commanders and the Operations Officer had been to Vietnam before, and our New Zealand 2i/c, Major Don McIver, and Major Brian Monks, 1RNZIR, who would command Victor Company, both had operational experience in Malaysia and Borneo. And at the apex of this impressive structure was Colonel Jim.
>
> Although not a large man physically, he was immensely robust, and totally untiring and unyielding in the preparation of the Battalion for operations. He had been decorated as a platoon commander in Korea; in the Malayan Emergency he had served with 3RAR as Operations Officer and then as a company commander; and had commanded 2SAS Squadron in Borneo during Confrontation, so he was very much a warrior. He was also a very kind and gentle man, and his intense devotion to his own family flowed across to the Battalion, so there was a very strong sense of family within it also.
>
> I very seldom ever saw him angry, but when he was you knew there was something for him to be angry about. I was only ever on the receiving end twice, and I think each was probably a more terrifying experience than meeting up with 33rd NVA Regiment.
>
> He was a meticulously efficient officer, but he achieved that without appearing to be pernickety; and he always exuded calm self-confidence. I found him to be an exceptionally capable CO in operations. His plans were always simple and straightforward, and he allowed his company commanders maximum initiative to get on with their jobs without constantly breathing down their necks.
>
> He never hassled us company commanders during a contact or battle. Instead he would find an opportune moment early in the proceedings to quietly let you know that he was there if you needed advice, and that any resources you might require would also be there for the asking. He was totally unflappable under pressure.
>
> Jim Hughes was a singular CO by even the highest standards.[1]

James Hughes was born at Rose Park in South Australia in 1929. Having matriculated from Saint Peter's College in Adelaide, he entered the

MajGen Jim Hughes, AO, DSO, MC: CO 4RAR in 1970–71, pictured when he was GOC Logistic Command in 1982. (Courtesy MajGen Hughes)

Royal Military College, Duntroon. After graduating in December 1950 he was posted to 1RAR in January 1951 as a platoon commander, and in July 1951 joined 3RAR in Korea, where he was awarded the Military Cross for his gallantry and leadership during the battle of Maryang San. From July 1952 he served in Japan as the Australian company commander at the 1st Commonwealth Division Battle School at Haramura; and this was followed by an appointment as a staff captain in the Military Secretary's branch at Headquarters Australian Army Component.

Returning to Australia in October 1953, he became a company commander in 16 National Service Training Battalion at Woodside, and in May 1954 became adjutant of the Adelaide University Regiment. Posted back to 3RAR in February 1957, he served the battalion as a company second-in-command, Intelligence Officer, and finally as a company commander.

From November 1959 to May 1960 he was attached to HQ Central Command as GSO3 Training, and in June 1960 was selected to be the exchange instructor at the Royal Military Academy, Sandhurst. From July 1962 he underwent training in the United States and United Kingdom, returning to Australia to attend Staff College at Queenscliff from June 1963–December 1964. He was then posted to the Special Air Service Regiment, where he raised 2 Squadron, which he subsequently commanded in Borneo during Confrontation in 1966. He was promoted lieutenant colonel, also in 1966, and became Director of Army Recruiting, in which capacity he served until he assumed command of 4RAR on 1 October 1969.

His subsequent career was most distinguished. He was promoted colonel in 1972 and appointed Commandant of the Land Warfare Centre at Canungra (formerly JTC) where he remained until 1975. From February to August 1975 he was the Director of Individual Training Policy at Army Office in Canberra and he was then promoted to brigadier and appointed Director General Training and Education Policy. In 1977 he spent a year in London as a student at the Royal College of Defence Studies.

From January to April 1978 he held the appointment of Deputy Chief of Army Reserves, and was then promoted to major general and appointed Controller Organization and Manpower in Canberra. He became GOC Logistic Command in 1981, and retired from the Army on 20 December 1983 as MajGen J.C. Hughes, AO, DSO, MC.

If the Battalion was fortunate to have Jim Hughes as their CO, they were equally fortunate to have WO1 Jim Healy as their Regimental Sergeant Major.

A good working relationship between a CO and his RSM was yet another vital ingredient in the life of a battalion, especially one preparing for war. The RSM was the CO's principal adviser, confidant and sounding board on many matters concerning the battalion, and especially those which affected the daily lives, well-being, careers and morale of the soldiers and non-commissioned ranks.

Almost every aspect of the life of a battalion was regulated by a formal chain of command This was the conduit down which orders, instructions and directions flowed from the CO through the various levels of command to the soldiers. But there was also an *informal* chain of command or, perhaps more correctly, a chain of communication. If it worked properly, information flowed not only from top to bottom but also from bottom to top, and laterally, so that in effect the informal chain was like a ladder: CO to company commanders to platoon commanders to section commanders to soldiers; RSM to CSMs to platoon sergeants to section commanders to soldiers. And then the lateral rungs: CO to RSM, company commanders to CSMs, platoon commanders to platoon sergeants, section commanders to soldiers.

Information on a range of issues flowed back and forth along this chain, so that if it was working properly, commanders at all levels were able to gauge the soldiers' reactions to 'how things were going'. This information was crucial to morale. If, for some reason, an order, instruction or system was impacting adversely or unfairly on the battalion or any part of it, the CO needed to know about it. So sensible COs and RSMs went to great lengths to ensure their working relationship was sound and that both chains of command, the formal and the informal, worked effectively. If for whatever reason they did not, then the battalion was the poorer for it. But in 4RAR from 1970 to the end of the second tour the two chains of command *did* work, and the benefits which accrued to the Battalion as a consequence were immeasurable.

WO1 Jim Healy had been appointed RSM of the Battalion in Brisbane in October 1969, two weeks after the arrival of LtCol Hughes. The two men had liked one another from the start, and the CO had previously served with the RSM's brother, Peter, in the SAS Regiment and the Directorate of Recruiting.

One of eleven children, James Michael Healy had joined the Regular Army on 6 July 1953 at the age of 21 and, like three of his four brothers, had elected to serve in the Infantry Corps. He underwent basic training at 1RTB, and in September that year was posted to the 4th Training Battalion. From there he went to 1 Reinforcement Holding Unit in Japan in May 1954, and in July qualified as a Vickers medium machinegunner at the Battle School in Haramura. On 19 April 1955 he was posted to 1RAR in Korea, where he was promoted to temporary corporal, and he remained with the Battalion when it returned to Australia. Still with 1RAR in 1958, he was promoted to temporary sergeant, and in that capacity served with the Battalion in Malaya from 1959, being promoted substantive sergeant on 10 August 1961.

Leaving 1RAR at Holsworthy in August 1963, Sgt Healy now went as an instructor at the Royal Military College in Canberra, and less than a month later, on 10 September, was promoted to temporary WO2, confirming that rank in April 1964. He next became an instructor at the Northern Command Officer Training Group, in September 1967.

Jim Healy was promoted to WO1 in October 1969 and was immediately appointed RSM 4RAR. He arrived in the Battalion on 17 October. An enthusiastic, skilful and hard-playing rugby forward, RSM Healy had been a member of the Souths and Brothers teams in Brisbane as a young man, and had instantly been appointed captain–coach of 1RAR's team on arrival at Kuala Kangsar in Malaysia. Now, in January 1970, with his impetus behind them, it seemed highly likely that 4RAR's rugby players would also become a force to be reckoned with. But sensibly, at age 38, and with a great deal of work to do in supporting his CO in shaping the Battalion for Vietnam, RSM Healy decided to devote what little time he could spare for rugby to refereeing the game.

So, by happy chance, the two principal figures within 4RAR in January 1970, the CO and his RSM, were both knowledgeable and experienced soldiers, warriors by inclination and training, and highly regarded by the members of their Battalion and by the Army at large. Therefore it was the personalities and strengths of these two men working in close harmony, that were the basic blocks upon which the Battalion would build during the next sixteen months.

But before training could begin it was necessary to get the Battalion fully manned. And manning was the problem.

Australia faced a turbulent and deteriorating strategic situation in South-East Asia in the early 1960s. The Viet Cong were waging a fierce guerrilla war in South Vietnam, which had resulted in the deployment of Australian military advisers there in 1962. By September 1964 there was also the likelihood of war between Indonesia and Malaysia over Borneo. And too, in 1964 it seemed possible that Indonesian troops might begin infiltrating from Irian Jaya into Papua New Guinea.

Facing the strong possibility that Australia might have to send troops to Vietnam, Borneo and Papua New Guinea simultaneously and on a prolonged basis, in November 1964, Prime Minister Sir Robert Menzies announced a major expansion of the Australian Army from 22 750 all ranks to 37 500. The CMF would also increase in number.

As a consequence of this expansion the Royal Australian Regiment more than doubled in size between 1964 and 1965. 4RAR was raised, as we have seen, in February 1964; and 5RAR, 6RAR and 7RAR in March, June and September of 1965 respectively. Finally 8 RAR was raised in August 1966 and 9RAR in November 1967.

But there were insufficient regular volunteers to man this rapidly expanding Army, and so in 1965 the government introduced conscription for eligible 20-year-olds. However, not all who were thus made available for military service were required, and a lottery was devised for selection. Every three months, the birth dates of those eligible were drawn out of a barrel, and they were then liable for two years' national service.

As it turned out, Confrontation with Indonesia was relatively short lived, and the threat to Papua New Guinea was never realised. But the military situation in South Vietnam had worsened, the war had escalated and, by late 1967, the Australian Task Force in Phuoc Tuy Province comprised three RAR battalions and supporting arms and services. All these units had to be fully manned and, when necessary, reinforced. They also had to be rotated sequentially every twelve months; and an additional degree of difficulty arose when the government insisted, in February 1967, that each Vietnam battalion should not have more than

50 per cent national servicemen (NSM) on its strength. Battalions were rigorously audited to ensure that this requirement was enforced.

To achieve these ends, manning policy was formulated by the Directorate of Manning at Army Headquarters in Canberra. It was implemented by the Central Army Records Office (CARO) in Melbourne, assisted in the RAR's case by the Directorate of Infantry. Battalions which were next to go to Vietnam received manning priority, but in January 1970, with Vietnam still sixteen months away, 4RAR did not have this precedence. As a consequence, the Battalion's strength was about 200 all ranks, or less than 25 per cent of the number needed to fully man it.

Before the Battalion left Brisbane for its new home in Townsville at the beginning of December 1969, the CO had arranged to post out all those members who could not be considered for service in Vietnam. Some of these men were due for reposting anyway, others were medically unfit, and a few would not reach the prescribed age for overseas service of nineteen years by April 1971. And to minimise removal costs and family turbulence, single soldiers were posted in, and where possible married personnel joined the Battalion after it arrived in Townsville.

The CO also asked CARO to post in as many Regular Army (ARA) soldiers as were available as early as possible in order to begin filling the more specialist appointments within the Battalion. The CO's policy was that these positions should not be filled by NSM, because they required attendance and qualification at lengthy training courses. Subsequently, however, some specialist appointments were filled by NSM who elected to extend their commitment. Indeed some of these men, finding that soldiering suited them well, later joined the ARA.

As well as regular soldiers, NSM were beginning to arrive in the Battalion in increasing numbers. The October 1969 NS intake completed their corps training in mid-February 1970, and 90 of those arrived in the Battalion at the beginning of March. Ninety more, from the January 1970 intake, would follow them to 4RAR when they completed corps training at the end of April. And another 180, from the April 1970 intake, would arrive in June to be corps trained by the Battalion.

As a consequence of these arrivals, the Battalion's strength increased from 200 all ranks in January 1970 to around 600 towards the end of May. It would, of course, have been far more convenient if all these men, regular and NS, had arrived together. But that was simply not possible, and it meant that the CO, the adjutant, Capt Mike Keating, and the Chief Clerk, S/Sgt Ray Heffernan, were kept constantly busy implementing the manning plan in such a way that useful, progressive training could begin as soon as possible.

As will be explained in a later chapter, all members of an infantry battalion, and especially one destined for active service, must be fully trained in the essential infantry skills. The central philosophy was, and still is today, that all members of a battalion, regardless of rank or task, must first and foremost be able to fight. But in addition to that, BHQ, Administration Company and Support Company also had specialist jobs to do: clerks, drivers, signallers, storemen, mortar crews and many more besides. Those skills took time to acquire, and those undertaking them had to attend specialist courses, some conducted within the Battalion, and others at Army schools. But, just as the Battalion had no manning priority, it also had no priority for attendance on specialist courses. Moreover, many specialist jobs also required the incumbents to have rank, which additionally demanded attendance at promotion courses, for which the Battalion had no priority either. Obviously something very positive had to be done to meet this substantial requirement, and the CO remembers that:

> This took weeks of work by a lot of my staff. Letters, telephone calls, planning, lobbying, and so on. The staff at the Directorate of Infantry also interceded on our behalf with the courses cell at the Directorate of Military Training in Canberra. So we got our own share of courses and every other spare vacancy as well. I recall that 9RAR also gave up some of their vacancies to help us. Every officer and NCO who needed promotion qualifications was given the chance, for morale as well as professional reasons. More important was the training of specialists and then the cross-training that went on. And we also won the battle to use civilian air to get people to and from courses, which saved valuable time. Experienced people now became better trained. I believe this effort paid off in more ways than one: if we hadn't made the effort in the period January–June 1970, we would never have been able to spare the individuals from July onwards because of other training committments.[2]

It was a significant achievement by everyone concerned, both within the Battalion and outside it. And because of it, 380 members of 4RAR attended specialist and promotion courses between January and June 1970.

The CO had already decided to give priority of manning to BHQ and Administration Company, and as a consequence those two organisations were well on the way to being fully manned by February 1970. They also contained more than 50 per cent regular soldiers. This was not only unavoidable but also sensible, because it guaranteed both lengthy tenure and continuity in those two pivotal organisations.

However the CO's policy had an equal and opposite effect on the rifle companies. They had to be manned by more than 50 per cent NSM, although this was quite acceptable within the guidelines laid down by the Directorate of Manning. In addition, each intake had to be evenly spread throughout the rifle companies, so that later in Vietnam, as NSM reached the end of their engagements, the loss of battle–hardened men in sections and platoons would also be evenly spread. As well, regular soldiers who asked to remain in the rifle companies, rather than taking on specialist appointments elsewhere in the Battalion, were allowed to do so, and this maintained continuity and ensured a solid core of experience.

So by February 1970, 4RAR's manning situation was this: the Battalion had a strength of about 200 all ranks. Administration Company, commanded by Maj David Wallis, and BHQ had the lion's share of ARA soldiers, and had all key appointments in place. Support Company, under Capt Don McKenzie, was a mixture of ARA and NS soldiers, many of whom were awaiting priority for attendance at Infantry Centre specialist and/or promotion courses.

B Company had only 4 Platoon, commanded by Lt Greg Dodds, at full strength, because 5 Platoon, commanded by Lt Wally Arndt, and 6 Platoon, which was commanded by a young officer who eventually judged himself unsuitable for military service and resigned, had been sent to C and D Company to form a nucleus for their buildup. Now the three rifle companies, B, C and D, commanded by Maj Bob Hogarth, Maj Ron Boxall and Maj Franz Kudnig respectively, had only framework manning in place, of which the majority were NSM, supported by a core of regular soldiers.

It should be noted here that throughout the Vietnam War the standard RAR battalion had four rifle companies on its establishment. But 4RAR was slightly different because it was scheduled to become an ANZAC battalion—thus when it reached Phuoc Tuy Province in May 1971, its fourth rifle company, Victor, would come from 1RNZIR in Singapore, and would be commanded by Maj Brian Monks, RNZIR. And under the terms of the ANZAC affiliation, the Battalion's second-in-command would also be a New Zealander, Maj Don McIver. As he would not arrive to take up his appointment until January 1971, initially the Battalion 2i/c role was held conjointly by the Operations Officer, Maj Reg Pollard, and OC Admin Coy, Maj Wallis. However, this became an unsatisfactory arrangement as the Battalion achieved full manning and the tempo of training increased. So Maj Keith Houley, who had served in Vietnam throughout 2RAR's first tour in 1967–68, was loaned by HQ 3TF as caretaker Battalion 2i/c until Maj McIver arrived.

In 1970 it was required that officers, warrant officers, senior and junior NCOs be qualified for the ranks, jobs and responsibilities they would have in Vietnam. Many already were, but if they were not, those qualifications would have to be gained before they departed for active service. This was ensured through a system of mandatory courses and by prescribed time-in-rank. For example, a major must have attended a company commander's course at the Infantry Centre at Ingleburn in New South Wales where he studied infantry tactics and techniques of both conventional and counter-revolutionary warfare. He must also have attended the TAC 3 course at the Jungle Training Centre at Canungra in Queensland. This was an all-corps course which also taught conventional and counter-revolutionary techniques, but which emphasised the tactics, administration and logistics to be used by all Arms and Corps working together. Moreover, the major who was to fill the position of Battalion Operations Officer, the 'OPSO', must have attended and qualified at a staff college course, which in most cases was eleven months long.

In many instances the mandatory time-in-rank for both officers and non-commissioned officers had to be foreshortened during the Vietnam years, due to the compelling need to man newly raised units in the expanded Army generally, and the RAR in particular. For example, in 4RAR the commanders of B, C and D Company were all substantive captains who had either been promoted to temporary major on posting to the Battalion, or shortly thereafter. And they either had, or soon would, attend a company commander's course and TAC 3 to fully qualify them for their responsibilities.

Captains, who filled appointments such as company second-in-command, adjutant, intelligence officer and some Support Company platoon commanders, might already have been promoted after reaching the required time in rank as lieutenants. Alternatively, they had been promoted to temporary captain and would acquire the necessary time-in-rank before arriving in Vietnam.

Subalterns (lieutenants and second lieutenants) were trained either at RMC Duntroon or OCS Portsea, if they were destined for the ARA, or at OCS Scheyville, if they were to be national service officers. On commissioning, the vast majority of infantry graduates, regardless of where they had been trained, were posted to battalions as rifle platoon commanders.

Also to meet the manning needs of the Army's expansion, suitable officers of all ranks up to and including major were recruited from the British Army, and given five-year short service commissions in the ARA. These could later be converted to regular commissions if their service proved satisfactory. Members of the Citizens Military Forces, mainly officers, WOs and SNCOs, could also volunteer for full-time duty and serve in Vietnam.

In addition to course and time-in-rank requirements, all lieutenants and captains had to pass written promotion examinations. The usefulness of these had always been hotly debated, for three main reasons. First, an officer could not be promoted substantively to the next rank until he had passed the prescribed exams. Second, studying for them frequently required a good deal of time to be spent on largely theoretical topics. These topics often used unit and formation establishments which bore little relation to those actually in use by the Australian Army of the 1960s–1970s. Therefore, and third, most of the information learned for the examinations was forgotten within a few days of having sat for them. This seemed to many officers, except probably those who had already passed the exams, to make the whole exercise pointless. Thankfully the requirement was discontinued in the mid-1970s.

Warrant officers class 2 seeking promotion attended the Infantry RSMs Course at the Infantry Centre. Of ten weeks' duration, this was one of the most demanding courses in the Army, and certainly one of the most difficult to pass. Moreover, by no means everyone who passed would be selected to become an RSM, an appointment which was widely regarded as the crowning achievement in a non-commissioned soldier's career.

Infantry staff sergeants were specialists who had elected to move into the clerical or quartermaster streams, and they had attended and qualified at a succession of courses to prepare them for those technical responsibilities.

Regular Army sergeants and corporals were also required to attend courses which qualified them for promotion. These were Subjects A, B and C at each rank respectively. Subject A was drill, ceremonial and weapons; Subject B was tactics; and Subject C was military law and administration.

Private soldiers for the ARA continued to undergo basic training at 1st Recruit Training Battalion (1RTB) Kapooka, near Wagga Wagga. But to meet the increased requirement to train NS recruits, two new RTBs were opened: 3RTB at Singleton in New South Wales and 2RTB at Puckapunyal in Victoria. The task of all three RTBs was to provide basic training for soldiers destined for all corps. Having 'marched out' successfully, recruits went on to their allocated corps schools for the next stage of their development, known simply as corps training.

However, many infantry recruits underwent corps training in the battalions to which they were posted after marching out from an RTB. There were two reasons for this. First, the numbers to be trained were too great for the Infantry Centre to absorb. Second, the national service commitment was only for two years. Therefore it was seen as both prudent and desirable to put NSM into battalions as quickly as possible, and thus get maximum value from their comparatively short tenure. In 4RAR they joined a nucleus of regular soldiers, some of whom had already been serving in the Battalion for several years.

It must be emphasised here that all NS conscripts who went to Vietnam were volunteers. They made that commitment during corps training, and were motivated usually by the same impulses as their ARA comrades: a sense of duty, a sense of adventure, the need to test themselves under extreme circumstances, or all of those. Whatever their motivation, NSM gave Australia very valuable service, and often with distinction.

These then were the men of all ranks, backgrounds and experience who joined 4RAR in 1970, and who now, through intense training in Australia, would be welded into an efficient fighting battalion for Vietnam.

While Capt Keating and his BHQ staff battled with the complexities of manning, Maj Pollard began formulating the Battalion's training policy.

The cycle of training for Vietnam was both logical and thorough. It began with individual training, which concentrated on those knowledges and skills which every member of the Battalion needed to live, fight and survive on the jungle battlefield of Vietnam. Individua training, as we have seen, also embraced preparation for specialist tasks needed throughout BHQ, Administration and Support Company. These included clerical assistants for pay, personnel and other administrative aspects, operations and intelligence clerks, signallers, assault pioneers, trackers, mortar men of all kinds, drivers, and musicians for the Regimental Pipes and Drums. Some of these men were also cross-trained in other specialities. For example, it made good sense for operations clerks in the Battalion CP to be competent signallers, and members of the Regimental Pipes and Drums became stretcher-bearers.

In B, C and D Company, individual rifleman training would be followed by collective training in, among other things, the techniques of advance, attack, defence, withdrawal and patrolling at section, platoon, company and, finally, battalion level. Individual specialist training in BHQ, Administration and Support Company would be succeeded by collective specialist training. All these would be completed within the Battalion, although from time to time 4RAR would receive much appreciated training assistance from 6RAR, who had just returned from their second and last tour of duty in Vietnam.

The final components of training would be the attendance by every man with his company at the Sub-Unit Course conducted by Battle Wing instructors at the Jungle Training Centre, Canungra. This would be followed by Battalion workup exercises organised, sponsored and monitored by HQ 1 Division. Invaluable assistance for these would be provided by supporting units from within 3 Task Force, commanded by

4RAR's staunch friend, Brig David Thomson. Those final workup exercises were designed to parallel as closely as possible the operational conditions that the Battalion would face in Phuoc Tuy Province and would draw firmly together the threads of individual and collective training, ensuring that every member of the Battalion was capable of playing his part efficiently even under the severest pressure and conditions.

Throughout this entire cycle, every digger, NCO, WO and officer would be under the closest professional scrutiny. Those who were found wanting would be removed and their places taken by more suitable material.

As Battalion Operations Officer, Maj Pollard was responsible for implementing the CO's training policy. But he would not be going to Vietnam with the Battalion because he had already been cleared for promotion to lieutenant colonel, and would receive that promotion in January 1971. His place would be taken by Maj Ted Stevenson, who had already served in Vietnam. Currently a student at the RAAF Staff College, he would be posted into the Battalion at the beginning of January 1971.

The OPSO was the CO's senior operations staff officer. He translated the CO's intentions, plans and directions into written operation orders which in Vietnam would launch the Battalion into battle. He would also deputise for the CO, when necessary, on any and all operational matters. In addition he would run the Battalion Command Post (CP), and direct and supervise its staff on a day-to-day basis. It was therefore important that the OPSO got to know how the CO thought, and how he would react under any given set of circumstances. For this reason it would have been highly desirable to have Maj Stevenson in the job when the Battalion *began* training in February 1970, rather than arriving as training reached its climax a year later. But this was just one of many inconveniences that the Battalion faced and overcame.

Working on a broad framework issued by the CO, Maj Pollard set about structuring the training plan and writing directives to put it in motion. The CO recalls:

> We discussed in the directives and at coordinating conferences the question of standards. I wanted us to start by aiming high in all aspects of training, and especially in the essential infantry skills such as physical and mental fitness, shooting to kill, individual skill proficiency, navigation, battle drills, leadership and initiative, and self and corporate discipline. Later it might be necessary or advisable to relax a bit. But if you start by aiming low, it becomes accepted practice, and you can never raise the standard.[3]

In fact 4RAR started high and, as it turned out, finished higher. There was never any debate about it: the Battalion came to pride itself on its standards.

From both verbal and written directives the company commanders designed their own training programmes, having in mind the special manning circumstances of each sub-unit. These weekly programmes were submitted to BHQ by midday on the Thursday preceding the week covered, and were vetted, refined and coordinated by the CO and OPSO as necessary. Comparisons were made between the rifle company programmes to ensure that there was a broad similarity in both tempo and quality, but without in any way stifling the individuality of the OCs.

Maj Bob Hogarth recalls:

> I remember having a clear idea of what I had to do and the time I had available for individual, platoon and company training. I also remember a good degree of autonomy but that we discussed what was to be done and how we would do it. As we approached departure time the autonomy decreased and one had the impression that one was in the hands of a centralised and largely bureaucratic training system which required us to achieve a number of ticks from various sources. I felt the intrusions from outside the Battalion were often counter-productive and tended to encourage an inflexible 'cookbook' approach.
>
> I tried to encourage initiative in subordinates and trust from commanders at all levels. I tried not to do the platoon commanders' jobs for them and encouraged them to do the same with their subordinates. I hope I offered my subordinates, at least in training, the freedom to fail and to learn from that failure. In retrospect, I do think that this approach probably helped develop the platoon commanders' judgement in which I always had absolute trust.
>
> I suppose I tried to strike a balance between learning from previous tours and understanding how the war had changed. In some ways those who had a previous tour to their credit were more difficult to train as they had a clear idea of what was done last time and weren't going to change it too readily.[4]

Complete and accurate training records were kept by each sub-unit, and they included the results of tests of elementary training, all small arms grouping and range practices, battle efficiency tests (physical fitness), and promotion, education and specialist qualifications. These were also monitored by the CO and OPSO to ensure parity of results.

In general terms, the training plan for the next sixteen months looked like this:

- January–June 1970: Individual training and specialist skills.
- July–December 1970: Section, platoon, company training, including Support and Administration Company and the Battalion CP. Sub-unit Course at JTC Canungra.
- January–April 1971: Battalion training including three major workup exercises.

The uncertainties of manning meant that training began at a slower pace than the CO would have preferred. And some members of the Battalion had to face repetition in various aspects of training when new men were posted in and subjects had to be repeated for their benefit. But by April training was gathering tempo. Now, throughout the Battalion area, groups of men with their section or platoon commanders could be found toiling along under their loads of weapons and equipment. Dominating the Townsville skyline, Mount Stewart reverberated to the sound of rifle and machinegun fire from the 25-metre and classification ranges. And RSM Healy's crisp words of command echoed across the regimental parade ground as he obliquely reminded squads of men that the foundations of success in battle were always to be found on the drill square.

Already there was a clear sense of purpose. Men of different backgrounds and ranks from all over Australia, regular soldiers and national servicemen alike, were beginning to unite towards a common objective. There was no time for the petty quarrelling that so often besets peacetime armies. Instead there came the realisation that in just over a year the man next to you might hold your life in his hands, and that the key to your survival could well depend on his quickness of instinct and reaction. Day by day the lesson was learned, and reinforced over the next months, that it was teamwork that mattered, and that when the chips were down it was not patriotism that motivated men but the desire not to let their mates down, not to let the team down.

The understanding was beginning to dawn in everyone that there could be no individuals in battle. You fought for the men on your left and right, and they fought for you.

2

The men and the means

The officers and men arriving in 4RAR in 1970 brought with them a wide range of backgrounds, experience, skills and personalities. But although their individuality was welcomed and nurtured, those individuals had of necessity to be formed into sub-units, and then those sub-units had to be shaped and sharpened into close-knit fighting organisations for the task ahead. This would take time, because the skills and techniques of a battlefield like Vietnam were many and varied, and the training for them had to be meticulously thorough. The equation was simple: if a soldier's training was inadequate, his performance in battle would be inadequate.

But by 1970 the training cycle for Vietnam was very effective, and this was principally due to two factors. The first, as we have seen, was the expansion of the Royal Australian Regiment, and the commitment of three battalions at a time to Vietnam. So there was, by 1970, a very effective rotation for Vietnam under which, in a planned and orderly sequence, battalions were either there, just back or preparing to go. Although this presented staff officers in Canberra and other senior headquarters with constant manning problems, it was very convenient at battalion level, because the rotation gave a clear picture of the way ahead, and thus provided focus and impetus to training for war. The second reason that the training cycle for Vietnam was so effective was that by 1970 twelve battalions, and numerous other major units, had already served there.

1RAR, fittingly, had been first to arrive in Vietnam, becoming part of US 173rd Airborne Brigade at Bien Hoa in June 1965. Moving down to Phuoc Tuy Province in late March 1966, 1RAR supported elements of 173rd Airborne in establishing the 1ATF base at Nui Dat. At the end of May the battalion had returned to Australia after being relieved by 5RAR and 6RAR. And by the end of 1967 a third battalion had been added permanently to 1ATF's order of battle.

Thus by the end of Australia's involvement in Vietnam in December 1971, each battalion had served there twice, except for 8RAR and 9RAR, who had completed one tour each. This meant that over time a wealth of operational experience and data had been gained, operational trends had been analysed and techniques to meet them refined and polished. Therefore as 4RAR began preparation in earnest, the Battalion already knew, to within a few days, when it would arrive in Vietnam, the type of war it would fight there, and the terrain and conditions in which it would fight.

The enemy, and the environment in which they lived and operated, will be examined in detail later, but in the main the Battalion understood that it must prepare itself for protracted jungle operations against an elusive, cunning and relentless enemy. But, as had already been demonstrated at the battles of Long Tan, Coral, Balmoral and many others, the infantrymen of the Regiment, and those who supported them, were more than equal to the task.

A Vietnam-bound battalion consisted of about 850 all ranks, organised into a battalion headquarters, four rifle companies, a support company and an administration company. But, as has already been explained, 4RAR was slightly different to the norm because it was scheduled to become an ANZAC Battalion and for the time being the Battalion trained with three rifle companies: B, C and D.

Just as it is widely accepted that Vietnam was an 'infantryman's war', so it was also said that the brunt of the battle fell on the rifle companies, for it was they who provided a battalion with its manoeuvre element, as they still do today. In Vietnam it would be the rifle companies who would initially seek out and then destroy the enemy in the Battalion's area of operations. They would be assisted in this task by various supporting agencies, either from within the Battalion itself, or from artillery, air, engineer or armoured units.

A full-strength rifle company in 1970 consisted of about 120 men, but on arrival in Vietnam its strength would increase to about 135 all ranks. It was subdivided into a company headquarters and three identical platoons of about 35 men each. These would be augmented by attachments, some of whom would join the Battalion in Australia, others in Vietnam.

A rifle company was led by a major, known as the officer commanding or OC. His principal task on operations was to command, control and manoeuvre his three platoons. To assist him he had a company second-in-command, who was a captain. His main tasks were to understudy the OC, initiate and control resupply when it became necessary and ensure the health and welfare of the company.

The third member of the command group was the company sergeant major, who was a warrant officer class 2. On operations he understudied the 2i/c and was the de facto platoon commander of CHQ. When not out on operations he was the OC's chief adviser on discipline, morale and ceremonial.

The operating environment in Vietnam required the OC to control his platoons almost entirely by radio, so there were three signallers in CHQ. Each carried and operated an ANPRC-25 set, one of which was used to communicate with the platoons on the company command net. The second set controlled the use of any administrative traffic or air support to the company on the 'admin/air net'. A third radio enabled the CO or his operations staff at the Battalion CP to communicate with the companies on the Battalion command net.

Because of the likelihood of casualties in Vietnam, each company was allocated an RAAMC corporal medical assistant. These men were trained in combat first aid, gunshot and fragmentation wounds, and in measures which ensured the health of the company on operations. Also for Vietnam, CHQ had a support section of seven men usually commanded by a lance corporal. The support section's role was to provide local protection for CHQ, but they could also undertake close patrolling and small-scale ambushing tasks.

Thus when CHQ went into operations it numbered about 25 all ranks. Although its principal task was command and control of its three rifle platoons, CHQ was fully armed; it occupied a similar–sized piece of ground in defence as a platoon; could fight in its own defence and, when push came to shove, during an attack as well.

Each company had a company quartermaster sergeant, who was a staff sergeant. The CQMS's task was to provide everything that the company required to live and fight, both in and out of operations. During training in Australia he carried out this task from the administrative echelon. In Vietnam he would operate, with his assistants, from the company lines in 4RAR's area at Nui Dat, where he prepared and packed the company's requirements, and ensured their delivery by helicopter or APC or, much less frequently, by vehicle.

The company's three rifle platoons each consisted of a four- or five-man headquarters, and three sections of ten men. The platoon commander was usually a lieutenant or second lieutenant, and his 2i/c and understudy was the platoon sergeant. This sergeant was invariably older and more experienced than his officer, but the sensible platoon commander understood this and, until he gained in experience, he was encouraged to seek guidance and advice from his sergeant.

In training in Australia there was only one ANPRC-25 radio set in platoon HQ which provided communication between the OC and the platoons on the company command net. However in Vietnam it was common to find a second 25-set within the platoon. This was not only a spare, but was also used as a patrol radio, providing communication between the platoon and any patrols or ambushes it might send out. It could also switch frequency in order to communicate with supporting arms or aircraft.

The smallest sub-unit in a battalion was the rifle section, consisting of ten men and commanded by a corporal. However there were yet smaller groupings within the section—the scout group of two men; the machinegun group, also of two men, one of whom was a lance corporal and 2i/c of the section; and the rifle group, which consisted of six riflemen, one of them being the section commander himself.

Although all members of the section were trained as scouts, and could therefore take over that job if necessary, only those with a particular aptitude for the role were selected to perform it in Vietnam. The scout's task was to search ahead of the section to locate the enemy. To do this successfully, a scout had first and foremost to be a superlative infantryman who was comfortable and confident at working day in and day out at the forefront of the battle. His senses had to be finely tuned, for he sought the enemy not only with his eyes, ears and quite often his nose, but also with that indefinable sixth sense for danger that ensured he detected the enemy before they detected him.

These qualities and skills had first to be identified, then fashioned and shaped in training, and honed and sharpened to a razor's edge by repetition. There could be no second chance for the scout on active service. He carried not only the responsibility for his own life, but also, in the first instance, for the lives of his section, and often for the platoon as well.

The machinegun group provided the firepower for the section. When in contact with the enemy, infantrymen apply the technique of 'fire and movement', which means that they only move when their machinegun is laying down aimed covering fire onto the enemy. When the gun group moves, they are in turn supported by the other groups. 'No fire, no movement' was and is the infantryman's golden rule, and he breaks it literally at his peril.

The general purpose machinegun was usually known as 'the gun' or 'the M60'. Although the fire of the gun was controlled by the section 2i/c, it was operated by the gunner, who was always chosen for the particular skill and affinity he showed for the weapon. The M60 was of American design and manufacture, and had numerous working parts and components. All of them needed to be kept scrupulously clean if the gun was to avoid stoppages or breakdowns. In Vietnam, with its mud, dust, rain and humidity, this requirement for cleanliness and maintenance was even more compelling. The gun used 7.62mm rimless ammunition in spring-steel linked belts, which also required constant attention. Moreover the gun, with a belt of 50 rounds, weighed about 12 kilograms, and in operations had always to be carried in the ready position for instant action. Therefore the gunner had to be physically robust as well as being totally dedicated to keeping the gun in first-class working order.

The rifle group was the manoeuvre element of the section. It was the section commander's task to decide and order how and when each component group of the section would move, both in and out of contact with the enemy, and relative to the manoeuvre of the rest of the platoon. But when in contact, the section always had at least 'one foot on the ground' to provide aimed covering fire onto the enemy position. This is the basis and creed of all tactics, even at the highest organisational levels.

The standard personal weapon used in Vietnam was the 7.62mm self-loading rifle, which weighed about 4 kilograms with a full magazine of 20 rounds in place. These were fired as single shots each time the trigger was squeezed. The SLR was a very hard-hitting weapon, though some infantrymen thought it was slightly too long for convenient carriage in thick jungle in the mandatory ready position. So on the move, care needed to be taken to ensure that its muzzle was not fouled by vines and other foliage. These drawbacks were offset by the SLR's robustness, reliability and stopping power, and some scouts carried them for those reasons. In addition the rifle's sear mechanism could be modified to provide automatic fire, though it required a strong man to control the weapon in that mode. This was not an approved modification, however, and was officially illegal. Nevertheless it was done, and if it enhanced a scout's effectiveness and survivability, platoon and company commanders were happy to turn a blind eye.

Each section was also allocated a proportion of M16 rifles, but these, inconveniently though not disastrously in 4RAR's case, did not arrive in the Battalion until late in 1970. They were also of American design and manufacture, and fired lighter, less punchy, 5.56mm rounds in either single-shot or automatic mode. Being shorter and lighter than the SLR, this rifle was favoured by some infantrymen, but its stopping power was not always effective. Nevertheless whenever possible, riflemen were given the choice of using either the SLR or the M16.

The XM203, which the Battalion received on arrival in Vietnam, was a 40mm grenade launcher in an under/over configuration with the M16. But in 1970 it was the M79 which provided the grenade-launcher facility,

Small arms used by the ANZAC Battalion. *From top:* GPMG M60, with spare barrel and 'golf bag'; 5.56mm M16 rifle fitted with the XM203 40mm grenade launcher; 7.62mm self-loading rifle.

and it was a stand-alone weapon which looked like a squat shotgun. Opinion in Vietnam was divided as to the real effectiveness of the 40mm grenade. Some section and platoon commanders swore by it, others not. But it was another tool, and it made a very satisfying 'crump' when it hit something, so it was at least useful in helping to dominate a fire-fight.

The role of the GPMG M60 has already been explained, but once the Battalion arrived in Vietnam it was not uncommon to find that enterprising platoon commanders acquired a fourth M60. This became known as the 'floating gun', and could be deployed in the platoon where it was most needed. The floating gun was especially useful in ambush and defence, and for adding weight to suppressive fire in attack.

The M26 fragmentation grenade provided an area weapon that, if thrown accurately, could get to an enemy who might be behind cover, in fighting pits or inside bunkers. However the M26 had something of a chequered career in Vietnam, and there were several tragedies when safety-pins came out accidentally and grenades detonated. There was also a school of thought which said that it was highly undesirable to have grenades being thrown in jungle, where they might hit a tree or branch

Enemy weapons. *From bottom:* RPG7 with rocket attached; RPG2; AK47 assault rifle. The American equivalent of the RPG, the M72 66mm LAW, is at top.

and bounce back onto the friendlies. At least one company commander in 4RAR forbade the carriage and use of M26s for these reasons. However, they were useful in static defensive positions when they came under attack.

The Number 83 grenade did sterling service in Vietnam. They emitted different coloured smoke, usually fluorescent red, green, blue or orange, and were used primarily to signal to incoming helicopters, or to mark the positions of friendly troops in contact for forward air controllers and pilots.

Each rifle section carried one or two M72 light anti-armour weapons, the 66mm LAW. Although enemy armoured fighting vehicles had not been, and never were, encountered by the Task Force in Phuoc Tuy Province, the value of the LAW lay in its effectiveness against bunkers. It was a shoulder-operated weapon which cocked itself when it was extended to firing mode, at which time the graduated sight also popped up. The disposable tube was destroyed after use, and the complete unit was replaced with another as soon as convenient.

The Claymore command detonated mine was a superlative offensive and defensive weapon, and was used extensively in Vietnam. Again of American design and manufacture, it looked somewhat like a large, convex Polaroid camera with four short folding legs. The body contained a high-explosive matrix in which were embedded 500 ball bearings. Embossed in high relief on its olive green casing was the helpful instruction, 'Front Toward Enemy'. This was good advice, because when initiated by a small magneto, colloquially known as 'the clacker', the ball bearings were fired out at high velocity. Claymores could be used singly or in banks. They were especially useful in ambushes and around night defensive positions, where the clacker always lay at the hand of the M60 gun picket.

The symbol of the fighting infantryman has always been the bayonet, and in training, as well as in Vietnam, every man carried one. However, it was highly unlikely that a bayonet would be fitted to the muzzle of a rifle, the thought being that if the enemy were *that* close they were *too* close. Their usefulness came in prodding for mines, and every soldier was taught a mine-incident drill in case it should ever be needed.

These were the basic organisations and weapons within the rifle companies in 1970. In the months ahead, the members of each company would learn to master them in training in Australia, and then to put them to good use in Vietnam.

But rifle companies cannot carry out their missions in isolation, and must be supported by other agencies within the battalion.

4RAR's other two sub-units were Support Company and Administration Company. Although their role may not seem as glamorous as that of the rifle companies, the part they played both in training and in operations was vital. The reality is that without Support and Admin, the rifle companies of any battalion cannot do their jobs either in peace or war.

Support Company was commanded by Capt Don McKenzie, and his CSM was initially WO2 Darcy Tillbrook. But when he was promoted to WO1 in August 1970 and posted to Papua New Guinea, his place was taken by WO2 Gary Holmes, who had already served in Vietnam with the Australian Army Training Team. The company had four platoons: Signals, Mortar, Assault Pioneer and Tracker.

Communications are the lifeblood of any fighting infantry battalion, and nowhere was this truer than in Vietnam. Commanders at almost every level controlled their units by radio, passing orders and directions over the various nets, and receiving reports and information by the same means. In battle, seconds could be vital and minutes worth a lifetime, therefore considerable care was taken to ensure that signallers were selected for their commonsense and initiative.

The Signal Platoon was commanded by the Regimental Signals

Officer, Capt Greg Shannon, and the platoon was subdivided into two sections, each commanded by a sergeant. The radio section provided trained and qualified radio operators throughout the Battalion. Each rifle company was allocated a Signal Platoon corporal, who was responsible for training and supervising company signallers. Other Signal Platoon operators were assigned to the Main and Rear command posts and to the CO's 'rover' set, which he used whenever he was away from the Battalion CP.

The platoon's individual weapons and equipment were standard issue, but as far as possible radio operators were allocated M16s because they were lighter and easier to carry, which helped to offset the additional load of the radio set.

The Signal Platoon Line Section was responsible for setting up and maintaining telephone lines and manning the integral switchboards. In the operational base at Nui Dat all company areas, offices, messes, command posts and departments were connected by line, and the manual switchboard, nicknamed 'Erudite', was manned by members of the Line Section 24 hours a day.

On Courtenay Hill, which would become the permanent home of the ANZAC Battalion's operational headquarters in Vietnam, line was laid to the CP bunker, strong points and to the hoochies of the CO and other principal personnel. This switchboard was also manned 24 hours a day. Communications from Courtenay Hill to the Battalion's Rear CP and to Task Force Headquarters in Nui Dat, known as the 'Rear Link', was by radio.

The Mortar Platoon, commanded by Capt John Sullivan, provided the CO with his own indirect fire support. The platoon consisted of four sections of two 81mm mortars each, one section being manned in Vietnam by New Zealanders under Sgt Brian Porter. The four sections enabled the platoon to bring fire down onto four separate targets simultaneously if necessary. However, the best effect was gained when all eight tubes fired onto a single target together.

In 1970 the 81mm mortar was capable of putting a projectile out to a range of about 4500 metres when firing on maximum charge. But 4500 metres was the *maximum* range, and was seldom used, and then only in emergency because of the stresses it placed on the barrel and the other components. The *planning* range was 4200 metres, and the minimum range was 75 metres, which gave mortars a valuable role in defence when a position was under close ground attack.

Ammunition types were illuminating, smoke and high-explosive (HE), which provided blast and fragmentation effects and could be fused to achieve different results on different targets. Point-detonating fuses could be set to cause the round to burst as it hit the ground, thus maximising blast and fragmentation. This was most effective when used against enemy troops in the open. A delay setting caused the round to dig in before detonating, and was therefore most effective against enemy in weapon pits or bunkers. Illuminating rounds, as the name suggests, provided powerful and prolonged white light for operations at night, or for signalling purposes. Smoke projectiles, the principal chemical component of which was white phosphorus, provided smoke screens to mask an enemy position from manoeuvre by friendly troops; to indicate a target or the direction of advance; or for incendiary purposes against enemy personnel, structures, vehicles or equipment.

The simple design of the mortar and its ammunition allowed for very high rates of fire to be achieved when necessary. These were: slow, 1–3 rounds per minute; normal, 4–7 rounds per minute; rapid, 8–10 rounds per minute; and emergency: 20 rounds per minute for the first minute only.

Theoretically it took only two minutes from the moment a call for fire was received at the Mortar Platoon CP until the first round was on its way. In reality it might take longer if the platoon had first to come into action, or if ground and air clearances had to be obtained before fire could be brought down.

Theoretically also, the 81mm mortar was man-packable, because each mortar could be stripped down into its three main component parts: barrel, base-plate and bipod. In reality, each of these components was both heavy and cumbersome. The barrel or 'tube' weighed 37 kilograms and was 128 centimetres long; the base plate weighed 12 kilograms and was 55 centimetres in diameter; the bipod weighed 12 kilograms and was 114 centimetres long. Therefore each part required a fit, strong man to carry it, especially if a significant distance had to be covered in thick country. However it was not the mortar assembly itself which posed the problem in the man-pack mode, but the ammunition. Each bomb weighed about 4.5 kilograms and if a platoon of eight tubes was to fire for two minutes at the rapid rate, up to 160 bombs weighing 720 kilograms in total would be expended. In short, man-packing mortars and ammunition was not considered practical in Vietnam.

The platoon had its own Landrovers and trailers which gave it very limited mobility and no protection. But A Squadron 3 Cavalry Regiment, which would be in support of the ANZAC Battalion in Phuoc Tuy Province, had M113 armoured personnel carriers which were specially designed so that mortars could fire from the open cargo hatch when the carriers were stationary.

The fire of the mortar platoon was controlled at the base-plate position by a command post, in a similar way to artillery fire. The fall of shot was corrected either by the troops in contact or, more conveniently and effectively, by a qualified mortar fire controller. He was usually a corporal or sergeant from the Mortar Platoon. It should be noted here that MFCs were also capable of calling in, and controlling, artillery fire.

The biggest disadvantage to the use of mortars in Vietnam was their comparatively short range. It became a cardinal rule in 1ATF that no sub-unit could operate outside gun range, the principal gun being the 105mm M2A2 Gun Howitzer with a maximum range of about 15 000 metres. Even that tended to be restrictive, and with a maximum range of only 4500 metres the 81mm mortar could seldom be used in support of more than just close patrols. However, mortar platoons played an important, and often very gallant part in defending battalion CPs, defensive positions and fire support bases which were deployed to provide artillery fire into the areas of operation.

The Pioneers were the CO's combat engineers. Commanded by Lt Reg Swarbrick, they were organised into four sections, one of which was provided by the New Zealanders and commanded by Sgt J.H.T. Mangakahia.

Besides their standard individual weapons and equipment, the platoon's special-to-task items included chainsaws, drillbreakers, mine detectors, flamethrowers, explosives and a wide variety of hand tools. Their skills included construction and breaching of wire obstacles, laying and lifting mines, neutralising booby traps, breaching obstacles by hand and with explosives, destroying unexploded ordnance, tunnel search and clearance, the construction of bunkers, strong points and other defensive works, water reticulation, and building small above- and under-ground structures such as ammunition bunkers, fuel points and command posts. In fact the Pioneers could turn their hands to just about any task required of them, and they were never limited by ingenuity, only by resources. Indeed, pioneer platoons traditionally seem to attract to their ranks men who, whatever their other attributes, are always cheerful, innovative, ingenious and willing to give anything a go.

The last of Support Company's sub-units was the Tracker Platoon. In a conventional warfare environment there are no trackers on an infantry battalion's establishment, their place being taken by the Anti-Armour Platoon. But in jungle warfare, and especially where there is little or no armoured threat—the Malayan Emergency and Confrontation in Borneo were earlier examples—tracker teams have often been employed to advantage, and Vietnam proved to be no exception.

The platoon, which could provide four tracker teams each of half-section strength, was commanded by 2/Lt Mike Murphy, and his platoon sergeant was Sgt Jack Scott, DCM. The sections were armed and equipped identically to those of any rifle platoon. However, the platoon was also required to maintain its anti-armour skills with the 84mm medium range Carl Gustav and the 106mm long-range recoilless

Tracker Platoon commander 2Lt Mike Murphy (right), assisted by Pte Larry North, guiding a helicopter to their location during operations in Phuoc Tuy Province. (*The Fighting Fourth*)

rifle. In Vietnam these would be used mainly in defence of FSBs. But in the tracking role the platoon's principal weapons were two Labrador dogs with a handler each.

Tracker platoons always occupied a special place in the life and affections of a Vietnam battalion. Perhaps it was the novel method they used to seek out the enemy. Or maybe it had something to do with the Australian soldier's love of dogs through his links with the land. Or maybe it was simply the suggestion of home that the presence of a dog implied. Whatever the case, grins always appeared at the approach of the two intelligent and beautiful creatures.

A handler began his course at the Infantry Centre as soon as his dog was old enough to start training, and the two stayed together until both had graduated, at which time, still together, they were posted as a team to a battalion. Each member of the platoon was required to complete a two-week combat tracker team course and a two-week visual tracking course, both of which were conducted at the Infantry Centre. It was during these courses that the dogs and their handlers joined the platoon. They then all trained together in the tactics and techniques which would be used when tracking with and without the dogs.

As it turned out, the two original dogs did not go to Vietnam. A policy decision was made in Canberra that 4RAR would take over 2RAR's dogs at rotation time; so on arrival in Nui Dat in May 1971, Pte Bluey Cree was teamed with Milo, and Pte Dave Nelson with Marcian.

The dogs were black Labradors. Like most of their breed they were characters in their own right, and had temperaments and personalities that caused them to be greatly spoiled by all members of the Battalion. The dogs were never happier than when accompanying their two-legged comrades into battle. Milo was of a particularly inquiring mind, and in helicopters insisted on sitting between the two pilots where he could keep an eye on altitude and heading. Meanwhile the more relaxed Marcian simply curled up on the floor and went instantly to sleep, from which only the most vigorous shaking would rouse him as the helicopter ran in.

Battalion Headquarters, the rifle companies and Support Company all needed administrative, logistic, maintenance, catering, medical, clerical and musical support to carry out their tasks, and this was provided by Administration Company.

Until August 1970, Admin Company was commanded by Maj David Wallis, and his CSM was WO2 Denny Cook. The platoons were Quartermaster, Transport, Medical, Catering and the Regimental Pipes and Drums, whose members were cross-trained as stretcher-bearers in Vietnam. The Battalion also had a Light Aid Detachment on its establishment, manned by tradesmen from the Royal Australian Electrical and Mechanical Engineers. They were predominantly armourers, motor mechanics and recovery specialists, but like all other members of their Corps they invariably relished and accomplished almost any task required of them.

The QM Platoon was responsible for acquiring, accounting for, storing, distributing and maintaining all weapons, ammunition, equipment and stores, including spare parts and replacements, which the Battalion needed to function, both in its daily life in training in Townsville and later during operations in Vietnam. The Quartermaster was Lt Jack Catton, and he was responsible to the CO for this important task. His deputy was 2/Lt Paul Darby, Royal Australian Army Ordnance Corps, and the Regimental Quartermaster Sergeant was WO2 Wally O'Brien. They in turn directed and controlled the technical work of the CQMS within each company, though the CQs were *commanded* by their OCs. This could have led to a CQMS feeling that he was being pulled in two directions at once; but Lt Catton was not only a very efficient QM, he was also an accomplished diplomat. Moreover, sensible company commanders are always well aware that, after the CO and the RSM, the last person who should be antagonised is the QM.

The 4th Battalion was particularly well served by its Q staff. Many items of equipment were in short supply as the Battalion raised and began training, and it was almost a law of nature that the Q staff would be blamed for these shortages, even though the problem lay much higher up the supply chain. But even in the worst crises, the QM's patient persistence invariably conjured up a solution to seemingly insurmountable problems, and on only very few occasions did the Battalion have to modify its training activities because weapons or equipment were in short supply.

Although the supply system in Vietnam was extremely lavish and there were seldom shortages, the Q staff at every level went to great lengths to ensure that supply in operations was as responsive, uncomplicated and swift as possible. Lt Catton, 2/Lt Darby and WO2 O'Brien, their clerks and storemen, and the CQMSs in the companies: S/Sgts 'Toad' Fletcher in B, Peter Webber in C, Bob Hann in D, Frank Galvin in Support, and Digby Lawrence in Admin, joined in Vietnam by S/Sgt Jim Richardson, Victor Company's CQMS and his staff, earned the respect, admiration and gratitude of all those who benefited so greatly from their consistent good work.

The Transport Platoon was commanded by Lt Mike O'Neill, a CMF officer on full time duty, and his deputy was Sgt Owen Legg. The platoon's task, obviously, was the provision of drivers and vehicles to transport personnel, equipment and other commodities, using predominantly Landrovers and trailers and 3-tonne trucks. The platoon ran its own driver courses, and several members of each company were cross-trained and qualified to handle those classes of vehicles which might be used within their sub-units. The Quartermaster, Mortar, Signals and Pioneer Platoons particularly had members driver-trained, as were the CQMSs and their storemen. Most officers and NCOs held licences for light vehicles and there was no shortage of drivers in that class. Transport Platoon drivers, however, were qualified on heavier categories of vehicles. Most of them had also qualified on cross-country and recovery courses, and all were capable, in emergency, of carrying out minor repairs.

The Catering Platoon, under WO2 John Ploenges, was responsible for feeding the Battalion when it was 'at home' in barracks in Townsville or Nui Dat. The platoon also produced hot-box meals during training in the field in Australia and, whenever possible, to fixed positions during operations in Vietnam.

It's Murphy's Law of military catering that soldiers will instantly forget the 99 excellent meals they've eaten previously to complain about the bad one in front of them now. But it must be recorded here that the meals in 4RAR were almost always very good, whether they were produced at a formal dinner in the Officers' or Sergeants' Messes, or to feed 850 tired, wet and hungry infantrymen at one hour's notice at some impossible time of night.

The Battalion's catering staff were highly skilled, and could cook a juicy steak or produce an exotic ice or butter sculpture with equal dexterity. Their cakes, scones, sweets and other confectioneries figured prominently at all Battalion dinners, buffets, barbecues and parties, and were the objects of much praise. The truth is that 4RAR in Townsville, and the ANZAC Battalion in Vietnam, were magnificently fed by WO Ploenges and his chefs.

There are not many people, soldier or civilian, who can resist the lure of a military pipe band. Nor is it surprising that military history is replete with great deeds of valour being performed under the impetus of this rousing music. So 4RAR was particularly lucky to have a pipe and drum band, and they were even luckier to have Pipe Major Douglas Thoreson at its head. He was himself a champion piper, both in Australia and New Zealand, and he had attended courses at the home of military bagpipe music at Edinburgh Castle in Scotland. The Drum Major was Sgt Ian Fryer, and because the Band was affiliated with the Pipes and Drums of the Irish Guards, 4RAR pipers and drummers wore the ceremonial dress, modified, of that distinguished regiment. Volunteers were drawn from both regular and national service members of the Battalion, most of whom had no previous piping or drumming experience.

Apart from their musical duties, Band members underwent cross-training as stretcher-bearers, and in Vietnam they served the companies with a similar commitment and dedication as their RAAMC colleagues. The stretcher-bearer sergeant was Sergeant 'Dusty' Miller, who had been Mentioned in Despatches as a stretcher-bearer with 4RAR during Confrontation.

The Regimental Medical Officer was Capt Paul Trevillian, Royal Australian Army Medical Corps, and his deputy was Sgt 'Blue' Chapman, RAAMC. The role of the Medical Section was the initial treatment of battle casualties until they could be evacuated; the treatment of minor sick and injured; the maintenance of the Battalion's overall health; and the oversight of the Hygiene Section commanded by Sgt Gary Zikking.

The dedication and gallantry of the members of the RAAMC has been a recurring theme throughout Australia's proud military history, and was highlighted again throughout the Vietnam War. The commitment, skill and bravery of the RAAMC personnel posted to the ANZAC Battalion will always be remembered with gratitude by all those who served alongside them.

The last component of 4RAR, and arguably the most crucial, was Battalion Headquarters. BHQ provided the CO with the organisation to administer, train, command and control the Battalion in Australia. In Vietnam it would be from the Battalion CP that the CO would command his own sub-units, and control those supporting arms which would assist the Battalion in battle. More will be said about the functioning of the CP later in this narrative.

3

The golden key

In 1970 there were two documents which regulated every detail in the life of the 4th Battalion. One was Standard Operating Procedures, which laid down the drills, techniques and systems that would be used by the Battalion on active service in Vietnam. The other was 4RAR's Standing Orders, which governed discipline, daily routine, administration, and some training matters.

Standing Orders had been issued on 14 January 1970, and were signed 'J.C. Hughes, Lieutenant Colonel, Commanding Officer 4RAR'. It's worth quoting the first six lines because they are brief, concise, and no one, after reading them, could be in any doubt as to the CO's requirements.

Introduction

1. The provisions of these orders will NOT be varied, amended or departed from without the concurrence of the Commanding Officer.
2. Any contravention of these orders will be dealt with under AMR 203 (1) (XIX).
3. These orders are subject to amendment or to any other orders issued by a higher authority.
4. Whenever members of 4RAR are within the bounds of another unit, or any other military establishment, they will obey the Standing Orders of that unit or establishment.
5. All ranks of 4RAR and any of its attached and under command troops will be responsible for observing these Standing Orders.
6. 4RAR Standing Orders previously issued are cancelled.[1]

It was a statement of intent, a wiping clean of the slate from whatever had gone before, and a setting of personal and corporate standards from which the CO would not deviate, and from which he would not allow his Battalion to deviate either. It was uncompromising, it was unequivocal, and it was exactly what a battalion preparing for war needed to hear.

And in 1970, in a good infantry battalion, it was entirely usual. Rules back then were not made to be ignored or broken, and whoever did so learned early the inadvisability of repeating such a course of action. Moreover, just as an infant needs the security of being tightly wrapped, so the professional soldier found a perverse satisfaction in the tight binding of regulations. He demanded to know exactly where he stood in relation to the rules and the standards that were required of him, and he needed to know that if he broke those rules, or failed to reach the required standards, he would have to suffer the consequences. That suited him well, for he despised weakness in his commanders, and distrusted ambiguity and indecision because those, in battle, caused casualties.

Nor was the Army as a whole confused or disoriented by the strictures of peacetime soldiering. The Army was commanded by men who had learned their trade during World War II, and they were warriors who fought those seeking to harm their country, or to dilute the standards of their Army, with equal ferocity. Politicians, bureaucrats and the public at large understood this, and they also understood that the way the Army conducted its business need bear no relation whatsoever to the way civilians conducted theirs.

Thus, in 1970, when a man joined the Army, he knew what he was letting himself in for or, if he did not, he very quickly found out, and he either accepted the way the Army did things, or he found a less demanding profession.

Men joined the Army because they wanted to be soldiers. For varying reasons they sought challenge and adventure, and along the way most of them found a fulfilment of their personalities. Most also found a high degree of satisfaction, and a profound sense of comradeship which would never desert them. After a career in the Army, and in the Royal Australian Regiment particularly, a man knew that he need never again be alone.

Soldiering was not just a job: it was both an honourable profession and a way of life. You signed on in your teens or early twenties, and you retired in middle age, having achieved whatever goals you perceived as being important. But it was not a way of life that made a man wealthy. The salary was generous in comparison to the British Army of the same era, but even so there were no extra allowances for spending a night or two in the bush, or for the weeks away from home on exercises, or for a long succession of weekends worked. If his OC and CO approved it, a man might get some small compensation for those weeks by the addition of up to five days' Arduous Duty Leave, which was tacked on to his 20 days' Annual Recreational Leave. When he went to Vietnam, he would receive an additional $1.70 a day Combat Pay, regardless of rank, though he would pay no income tax on his salary.

The Army was a demanding way of life, and the Royal Australian Regiment was even more demanding, because both in training and on active service it was always the infantryman who experienced greater extremes of fatigue, discomfort and danger than the other Arms. And finally, it was always the infantryman who went forward to finish the job. Perhaps that was the attraction of it: at the end of all the hardships and dangers, if he survived them, an infantryman could put his hand over his heart and say with perfect honesty, 'I can hack it.'

Without doubt, for those cut out for it, soldiering was a good life.

Those bound for Vietnam understood that they might be called upon to risk their lives. They had contemplated that possibility, assessed the odds, and found the risk worth taking. But that did not mean they were prepared to waste their lives under inept commanders. They expected high professional standards from their officers and NCOs, and they needed to respect them as men and as leaders and to trust their professional ability and judgement. The diggers could be extremely kind and patient with the mistakes of a new platoon commander, and indeed they expected a young officer to make mistakes. When he did, they laughed with him, but never at him. But they also expected him to learn from those mistakes, and if he did not, through arrogance or stupidity, his soldiers came first to mistrust him, and then to ignore him, and turned instead to their platoon sergeant for leadership.

Indeed it was all about leadership, because in 1970 it was people who were important, and the Army considered its soldiers to be its most precious asset. As a consequence, there was no confusion in a commander's mind between the process of management and the art of leadership. Management was applied to equipment in the quartermaster's stores; leadership was applied to people. Great importance was attached to leadership, because many professional infantrymen believed that battles, in the end, were won or lost at section and platoon level. They held strongly to the opinion that it was the leadership and initiative of junior commanders, and the aggressive optimism of the soldiers, which made even an indifferent plan work. And because LtCol Hughes and RSM Healy were good leaders themselves, they demanded, developed and fostered leadership in the officers and non-commissioned ranks of the Battalion. The subject was studied regularly and minutely in the officer and NCO training sessions, which were usually held on Friday afternoons. RSM Healy wrote a hands on leadership précis, and a copy of it was given to every officer, warrant officer, staff sergeant and sergeant in the Battalion; and the CO directed that the précis was to be the basis for company officer and NCO training as well.

Although from time to time over the years the Army has amended its formal definitions of leadership, in practical terms it is the art of getting subordinates to give willingly of their best at all times and in all circumstances. And, as we have already seen, it was the attitude and example of the man in command that set the standard. Once in place, that attitude, and the standard that grew from it, permeated downwards, so that eventually all members of the Battalion came under its influence. Good standards of behaviour, turnout and bearing, a high level of personal fitness, accurate shooting, hard-played rugby, or any other activity, was demanded. In 4RAR second best was not good enough and was not acceptable. The CO, the RSM, the officers and the senior NCOs set the pace and led by example. And if the CO and the RSM moved about the Battalion area smartly and with purpose, and the company officers sweated under their loads of weapons and equipment, then there was no reason why everyone else, right down to the youngest private soldier, should not do the same. The soldiers saw that the OC and the 2i/c and the CSM and the platoon commanders were prepared to do everything that they did. If there were dirty or difficult jobs to do, and the officers and NCOs shared the load, then the soldiers could hardly complain when their turn came. Moreover, it suggested that if the hard yakka was evenly distributed in training, then it would also be evenly distributed in Vietnam. And these small bonds of shared effort and discomfort began to weld individuals together into groups, gradually and loosely at first, and then with increasing shape and symmetry, and finally with unity and purpose. Little by little the Battalion came to like the feeling it sensed in the air. Even modest achievers began to find previously untapped reserves of energy and determination, and came to see themselves as important members of a winning team.

And it was cumulative. In the same way that an avalanche increases in size, power and momentum, so the 4th Battalion fed and grew on its own achievements. And when that happened morale increased; and when morale had increased to a sufficient level it transmuted into *esprit de corps*, that almost indefinable 'something' that is a corporate sense of identity, harmony and loyalty. And that made the difference between a good battalion and a better one. But it all began with leadership. *That* was the golden key.

Officers of the Vietnam years all underwent similar leadership training, regardless of whether they were graduates of Duntroon, Portsea or Scheyville. Great prominence was given to the subject during officer cadet training, and if a cadet's leadership skills were irremediably flawed, it was unlikely he would eventually be commissioned. So by the time they arrived in the Battalion, all junior officers knew, and had demonstrated, at least a basic understanding of the principles and techniques of leadership.

But there was much more to effective leadership than just applying the doctrinal principles and techniques. By commanding a platoon, which is arguably the most formative appointment in an infantry officer's career, he either rapidly developed his leadership skills and ability, or he demonstrated once and for all that he did not have what it took. He also learned by the example of those around him. He saw how other officers and NCOs led, what tricks of the trade they employed, and how a man's leadership style changed and matured as he grew in rank and experience. And he came to understand that a leadership style that worked for one officer might not necessarily work for another. He saw also that each officer and NCO brought to the art of leadership his own personality, strength of character, knowledge, experience, judgement and sensitivity for people. No two leadership styles were alike, except that all good ones exerted a positive influence which subordinates found attractive and relevant to them, and to which they responded with enthusiasm.

And, by talking to those who had already served in Vietnam, the young officer, if he was perceptive enough, learned that additional positive qualities would be required of him on the battlefield, or perhaps it would be more correct to say that they would be revealed by the battlefield environment. Some of the more important would be confidence and calmness under pressure and in the face of fatigue and mortal danger. And he would also need to display physical and moral courage, which are really only strength of character and determination combined.

He would learn, too, on active service, that an officer or NCO who was unable to get the best out of his men in peacetime was unlikely to do much better in war. And he would see, conversely, that some officers and NCOs reached the height of their leadership powers in battle, and found their real personalities under active service conditions.

He would understand soon enough, in Vietnam, that young section and platoon commanders would frequently be required to use their initiative to make instant life and death decisions, often without recourse to their superiors, and usually under great pressure. This would sharpen their powers of decision making, and imbue them with a willingness to accept responsibility for the consequences of those decisions.

And finally, experience would show them that company commanders who, in training, allowed their subordinates 'the freedom to fail', as Major Hogarth so eloquently put it, would also allow their subordinates freedom of decision and action in Vietnam. That almost invariably brought better results than did the insecure company commander who dominated his subordinates and restricted their initiative, and who never wanted to lose sight of what was going on.

So with time and experience, and with guidance from his platoon sergeant and his company commander, and with the impetus of the CO behind him, the young officer would polish his basic leadership skills, learn others, and would bring them all to a bright practical lustre by the time he came home from Vietnam.

It was always to be hoped that good leadership by the officers and NCOs of the Battalion, and the self-discipline of the soldiers, would generate an atmosphere in which there were few disciplinary infringements. Usually this was the case, but when all else failed there were still Australian Military Regulations (AMRs) to fall back on. This was the publication which set out the military legal system. It was AMRs that listed the many crimes, big and small, which an officer, warrant officer, NCO or soldier could commit, specified the method of trying those cases and laid down the penalties for committing them. And although there were no very serious breaches of discipline during 4RAR's preparations for Vietnam, there were still minor infractions that required at least some sort of retribution. To overlook them was to suggest a weakness in the system, and that invited repetition and eventually the breakdown of good order.

In most cases the soldiers regulated and disciplined themselves, and pressure and action from within the section or platoon often prevented high spirits or thoughtlessness from becoming a misdemeanour. The section would invariably rally round a man who was having difficulty getting out of bed because of alcoholic over-indulgence the night before. His mates would get him up and assist him to shave and dress, a process which often involved a good deal of hilarity. When he fell in for parade, he would be positioned in the rear rank where, it was hoped, the CSM and the company NCOs would be less likely to notice him. And indeed, if he could stand up straight, was not making a nuisance of himself and could undergo the day's training activities without being a danger to himself or others, a blind eye was usually turned to his condition. Most often it was a one-off occurrence anyway, because the pain he experienced while he was sobering up during a hard day's training was enough to dissuade him from a repetition. But he was bound to come under scrutiny if he repeated the performance on a regular basis. Apart from the disciplinary implications and the fact that his mates would eventually become fed up with him, constant drunkenness, or any other unusual behaviour, might suggest that a man was undergoing some sort of emotional upheaval. Platoon staffs always needed to be on the lookout for such signs, so that the man could be helped before his problem got out of hand.

Those who administered the Army's legal system within 4RAR in 1970, principally the CO, the RSM, the OCs and the CSMs, concerned themselves much less with the technicalities of military law and much more with the beneficial effects of justice. They became adept at striking a very satisfactory balance between fairness to the individual and the compelling disciplinary needs of the Battalion as a whole. Indeed they saw the essence of the military legal system as a tool for developing responsible soldiers rather than for punishing wrongdoers. The Battalion generally, and the companies particularly, were close-knit societies in which everyone knew everyone else. Officers and NCOs were paid to know their men: it was one of the precepts of good leadership. They knew who the good soldiers were, and who were not so good but were trying, and who were bad soldiers and lazy. As a consequence, the legal system was far more personalised within 4RAR than it was in the wider civilian community. Therefore military punishment was awarded not so much to fit the crime as to fit the criminal.

For this reason, first-time offenders were usually treated quite leniently. A digger who was late for parade would probably come under the admonishing eye of his platoon sergeant or CSM, and he would be spoken to firmly, though not always quietly. If the digger was usually of good character, and a 'trier', the offence might attract no greater penalty than those few well-chosen words. Even so, no doubt would be left in the offender's mind as to what would happen to him if he was late again. But if the CSM had any doubts about a man's demeanour, and felt he would benefit from a timely sharp lesson, he might impose an unofficial penalty: an extra guard or duty perhaps, or some moderately unpleasant cleaning task during off-duty hours. Such penalties were, in fact, not legal, and the CSM could leave himself open to charges for awarding them. But they were accepted practice, and most sensible soldiers preferred to take an unofficial punishment. It meant that the offender would not be subject to the more serious penalty which his company commander might award, say, loss of pay or privileges. Moreover, nothing would be recorded on his conduct sheet, and that was an important factor when he was being considered for promotion.

However, if the same man offended again, which might indicate the start of a poor disciplinary attitude, he would certainly be charged formally. That would require the preparation of a charge sheet, and he would be marched officially before his OC within 24 hours, or as soon after that time as circumstances permitted. The OC's orderly room was the lowest level of military courtroom, and the procedural format was laid down in AMRs and strictly observed.

Before his trial, the accused man, and any witnesses for or against him, would be briefed by the CSM as to what would occur from the moment they were marched into the OC's office. The CSM would also discuss with the accused soldier the salient points of his case, and would probably advise him on how he should plead, and what he should say in his own defence. This could place the CSM in a difficult situation, because he would already have discussed with the OC the charge, the accused and the likely outcome, including an appropriate penalty. So to some extent the CSM was always torn between his loyalty to his OC, the legal system that the OC represented, and his responsibility to be fair and just, as a good CSM should be, to his soldiers.

When all was ready, the accused, without hat or belt, was placed between two escorts, and marched rapidly to a position in front of the OC's desk. Failure to march smartly enough or to raise his knees sufficiently high while marking time would invariably cause the CSM to march him out again and repeat the process. But once the CSM was satisfied that the initial convolutions had been correctly achieved, the case could be heard. The company 2i/c then read the charge, and when that had been done, the OC asked the accused if he pleaded guilty or not guilty. In most cases the accused pleaded guilty, because usually he realised that he had made a fool of himself, and considered the resulting charge a fair cop. Moreover, pleading not guilty wasted everyone's time, and was generally believed to antagonise the OC, who was judge, jury and sentencing authority as well.

Once the accused had made his plea of guilty, the OC asked him if there were any extenuating circumstances or anything he wanted to say which might mitigate the crime and reduce the penalty. And it was at this point that accused men could become quite inventive. For example, there was a case of a D Company soldier, Pte Garry Sloane, who towards the end of the Vietnam involvement was accused of urinating on his CSM, WO2 Noel Huish. When asked what he had to say for himself, Pte Sloane explained that he had drunk rather a lot of beer the previous evening, had woken during the night and, being in a desperate hurry and unable to get to the toilet in time, had urinated over the balcony. Unfortunately he had failed to notice CSM Huish who, amazingly, just happened to be passing under the balcony at that very moment. It had all been a terrible accident, and he was very sorry.

It must be recorded here that Pte Sloane's protestations of innocence and contrition were considered to stretch the bounds of credibility a whisker too far, and he was awarded 28 days' field punishment. This was probably justice in action, because as WO Huish pointed out afterwards, if one soldier got away with peeing on the CSM everyone would want to do it.

Once the OC had listened to the accused's statement, he would make his finding, and impose a penalty according to the guidelines set out in AMRs. Here again the OC took all circumstances into account, and thus it was entirely possible that two soldiers, on identical charges, would receive very different penalties: previous record, demeanour and intent being the most likely deciding factors.

The first choice of action open to the OC was that of dismissing the charge. He might do this even if the accused was found guilty, but was of exceptionally good character, had obviously made an honest mistake, and was highly unlikely ever to offend again. The other alternatives open to the OC were to award an admonishment, which in layman's terms meant a good telling-off, or to impose a fine, or to confine the soldier to barracks for a specified length of time.

If the charge was particularly serious and required a more severe penalty still, the OC could refer the case to the CO, who had greater powers of punishment. The CO could award larger fines, longer periods of confinement to barracks, and could also sentence a guilty man to detention in the Battalion's cells for up to fourteen days. For a very serious crime, a longer period of detention at a military correctional establishment (MCE) might be awarded. While treatment of prisoners at an MCE was not brutal, it was not pleasant either, and very few who went to these military prisons chose to repeat the experience. Indeed, anyone who did so would almost certainly be discharged from the Army after serving out his second sentence.

On the miniscule number of occasions when a soldier felt he had been unfairly treated, he could seek redress of wrongs. This would be done in writing, and the CO would direct that the whole matter be thoroughly investigated. If it was proved that an injustice had been done, the sentence was quashed, all charge sheets were negated and the entries relating to the case were removed from the man's company or regimental conduct sheets.

But in the main, 'crime' was maintained at a very low level in 4RAR in 1970–71. And most often the misdemeanours which did occur resulted only from the youthful high spirits that are so much part of the Australian infantryman's endearing good character.

By the end of May 1970, 4RAR was taking shape, and it was all going very well. The CO's manning plan was proving highly effective, and because of it the Battalion was building appropriately and steadily. The tempo of training, too, was gathering pace: everyone was starting to look fit, and each man carried himself with a newfound confidence. There was a strong sense of corporate purpose in the air and morale was high.

Each man was starting to feel good about himself, and about this Battalion of which he was a part.

This is not to suggest that 4RAR was all sweetness and light. There were officers and NCOs who, for various reasons, were not up to their jobs, and who subsequently would have to be removed and replaced. And one junior officer discovered, under the intense focus of training for war, that he was a pacifist, and could not, in conscience, give orders to his men that might result in their deaths or the deaths of others. With great integrity, this anguished young man sought guidance from the CO, who not only spent several weeks counselling him on a regular basis, but also enlisted the help of a psychiatrist. But it was not to be. The young officer was eventually posted out and shortly afterwards resigned from the Army.

There were other problems as well. At least one company commander felt uneasy about the attitude of his CSM. This may just have been a slight clash of personalities, or a divergence of opinions concerning professional infantry matters. Whatever the case, the two men came to terms with the problem, and it was resolved reasonably well. But for them there would never be the comfortable mutual ease and confidence that marks the best sort of relationship between a company commander and his CSM.

And there were platoon commanders who, newly commissioned and wearing the single pip of a second lieutenant, judged themselves to be God's gift to a war-torn nation. This opinion was not always shared by their subordinates, and quite often, at the end of a long day, their platoon sergeants were only just able to reach the sanctuary of the Sergeants' Mess without becoming totally apoplectic. Indeed one frustrated platoon sergeant was heard to remark that his officer considered himself to be one in a million, while the rest of his platoon thought he was won in a raffle. But time, and a few sharp confrontations with reality, invariably brought young platoon commanders back to an even keel, and several who had begun shakily eventually performed in Vietnam with great dash and courage.

Many teething problems were, in fact, sorted out in the Sergeants' Mess before they became seriously visible. Indeed the Sergeants' Mess, after the CO and RSM themselves, was without doubt the most powerful influence for high standards in 4RAR, which was usually the case in any good battalion back then. And this was hardly surprising, because in 1970 the 4RAR Sergeants' Mess membership was made up of men who had worked their way up from private soldier, and who were now senior non-commissioned officers and warrant officers. Along the way they had seen and done it all, including several tours of active service. Their corporate knowledge of soldiers and soldiering was vast, and the power which they wielded within the Battalion was immense.

WO1 Digby Lawrence, who is one of 4RAR's most respected and beloved old soldiers, was then the CQMS of Administration Company. He remembers:

> Undoubtedly the Sergeants' Mess was a powerful institution, and this was attributable to the fact that all members of the Mess had gained their experience through successive ranks, and, in the main, had been in the service and held various appointments for a lengthy time.
>
> Problems were either prevented or solved in the Sergeants' Mess. One of the RSM's unofficial roles is to prevent problems that can be solved in the Mess from getting to the CO. Often RSM Healy called the CSMs to join him for lunch, and used that forum to discuss any untidy matters. Jim Healy encouraged Mess members not to use the bar as a place for solving problems, because it wasn't good to let the bar staff hear these discussions. But I don't remember any major problems arising in Jim's time as RSM, and I believe this was because of the fact that 4RAR was of a high standard of morale and discipline.[2]

Administration Company's CQMS, S/Sgt Digby Lawrence, with his mascot, 'Rubber Duckie', in the ANZAC Battalion's lines at Nui Dat. He considered that 4RAR 'was of a high standard of morale and discipline'. (*The Fighting Fourth*)

Sgt Digby Lawrence manning an M60 at a fire support base during 4RAR's first tour of duty in Vietnam in 1969. He would return with the Battalion for its second tour in 1971. (Courtesy WO1 Lawrence)

There was even time for socialising. In the Officers' and Sergeants' Messes formal dinners and informal parties were held to which guests from other Task Force units were invited, and members of the Townsville civilian community as well. The 4RAR Soldiers' Club held barbecues and family days, and Jan Hughes, the CO's wife, knowing well that a battalion's families were a vital supporting pillar in the whole structure, continued her preparations and plans to rebuild the 4RAR Wives' Club. In short, it was all going very nicely.

And then tragedy struck.

On the afternoon of Wednesday 27 May 1970, the Combined Services rugby team was playing Queensland University on the 4RAR sports ground at Lavarack Barracks. RSM Healy was the referee. During the game he collapsed with a massive heart attack, and was immediately rushed to Townsville General Hospital. But despite all efforts, he died early that night.

The death of any one of its members is always keenly felt in an RAR battalion. On active service, casualties were to be expected, and although each one was a cause for sadness, the Battalion mourned and then moved on. But the death of a man like RSM Jim Healy was totally unexpected, and the Battalion felt both saddened and diminished by his loss. The vast majority of 4RAR liked him, and everyone respected him. At 38, and the RSM of a Vietnam-bound battalion, he was at the height of his powers and at the peak of his career. Already, in a few short months, his personality and influence had done much to shape the Battalion and raise it above the norm. Capt Sayce, then 4RAR's intelligence officer, remembered:

> He was a very dignified man; urbane and likeable, but he could be as firm, resolute, and ruthless as any other RSM. He had the knack of being able to talk with equal ease to senior officers or young soldiers alike. In fact I was hard put to it to find anything wrong with him. I'm certain that if he had been alive in the 1980s he would have made RSM of the Army.[3]

Jim Healy's body was taken to Brisbane, where he was given a military funeral. A representative group from the Battalion, led by the CO, attended the service, and the soldiers of 9RAR acted as pallbearers and escorted the gun carriage. On the same day, in Townsville, the Battalion held a memorial service at which the caretaker RSM, WO2 Darcy Tillbrook, recited the ode to fallen comrades.

When the CO, commenting in the *Townsville Bulletin*, said, 'RSM Healy's death was a major loss to the unit. I considered him a gentleman and friend', he was speaking for the whole Battalion.

4

To seek out and destroy

By the time the Battalion was manned to the stage where it could begin useful, progressive training for Vietnam, its members already knew when they would arrive there, who they would fight, the terrain and conditions in which they would fight, and the techniques which would be used.

The type of operations the Battalion would undertake had the collective title of Counter Revolutionary Warfare, but what that meant in practical terms was jungle warfare. And that in turn meant that the men of the ANZAC Battalion would spend most of their tour of duty living and moving in the forested areas of Phuoc Tuy Province. And they would fight there too, applying the principles of conventional war and many of its techniques as well, but modified to suit the jungle environment.

They would take the enemy on at his own game, meet him on his own ground, but with this special difference: the Battalion would have access to a lavish resupply system, highly trained and efficient supporting arms, almost unlimited artillery and air support, and a casualty evacuation system that could have a wounded man on the operating table within a matter of minutes. The enemy enjoyed none of these advantages.

Moreover, the Battalion would be operating on a battlefield for which the Australian and New Zealand infantryman has always had a pronounced affinity. He seems to feel comfortable in the jungle environment in a way that most of his British or American counterparts do not. It must be remembered that it was Australians who, on the Kokoda Track, using the techniques of patrolling that eventually earned them such a fearsome reputation in World War II, were the first to beat the Japanese, themselves masters of jungle warfare. And after that there had been Malaya, then Borneo and now six years of operations in Vietnam.

The Australians and New Zealanders had already brought their own operational methods to Phuoc Tuy Province, and they were different to those used by their allies. By 1970 the troops of the Army of the Republic of Vietnam (ARVN), the Regional Force (RF) and the Popular Force (PF) in the province could virtually be discounted as an effective force. They had already fought long and hard—the French, the Viet Minh, the Viet Cong, and now they were tired and dispirited, and preferred to wait for the enemy to come to them in their fortified posts.

The Americans were the exact opposite—vigorous, vastly enthusiastic, invariably courageous and commanding apparently overwhelming resources of men and material. But it seemed to some Australians who had served alongside their line infantry units that the Americans were uneasy in this jungle environment which, for all their resources and technology, they were unable to use with subtlety.

But 4RAR/NZ (ANZAC) Battalion, and those whose task it was to support them, would go into the forests of Phuoc Tuy Province and would live and operate there, confidently and not uncomfortably, for weeks at a time. They would carry everything they needed to live and fight and survive on their backs. They would be resupplied every five or six days with food and water and other necessary combat supplies. They would seek out the enemy by stealth and, when they had found him, they would use all the skill and resources at their disposal to destroy him.

But first, in Australia, they would have to master those skills, both individual and collective, and learn to use to maximum effect the supporting arms and agencies which would be available to them. From this moment on, the attention and imagination of every man was focused forward, so that now, every shot he fired on the range, every tactical manoeuvre he carried out in the training area and every kilometre he marched in full battle order, brought him that much closer to Vietnam.

As the name implies, individual training refers to the getting of the knowledge and skills that each infantryman, regardless of rank or station, needed in order to fight and survive on the jungle battlefield. Of themselves they were not difficult to learn. But to learn them well, and then be able to call them up instantly and instinctively, often in the face of fatigue and sometimes fear, took time. The list of those skills is a very long one, and this is a biography of a battalion, not a training manual. But because individual skills were so crucial to success and survival in battle, their general thrust needs to be understood. And the best way to do that is to follow a rifle section as it moves through a training area.

The men of this section are moving one behind the other in single file. There are many formations, each for a different purpose and tactical situation, but when on the move and searching for the enemy in Vietnam this would be the most usual, convenient and easily controlled formation. The rifle group and gun group are preceded by the two scouts, who always move in 'bounds'. A bound is normally dictated by the thickness of the going, the shape of the ground or the likelihood of enemy contact. Whatever the case, scouts must keep constant visual touch with each other, and the second scout must be able instantly to support his partner with aimed fire.

The first scout sometimes carries a pair of garden secateurs, which he uses to clear any minor obstructions in his path. Silence is the key to finding the enemy, and wide swathes of jungle hacked down with machetes is a figment of Hollywood, not the reality. The second scout may carry a compass, and at the end of each bound he indicates the direction of the next.

There are three ways that scouts move: caterpillar, leapfrog and trail. Using caterpillar, the first scout completes a bound, halts, goes to ground, and after he has examined the foliage, the trees, and the ground ahead of him minutely for sign of the enemy, he signals his mate forward. When the second scout has closed up, the first moves off again. Using leapfrog, the same sequence occurs, but each scout leads a bound alternately. With trail, the forward scout remains in the lead through each bound, and his mate will take over the lead, say, every half hour or hour. From time to time the two scouts may confer in whispers to check a compass bearing or discuss the next bound. But usually, with an experienced scout group, a steady momentum of forward movement, slow, methodical and careful, is maintained.

Behind them the rest of the section move at an equally slow, steady pace, following the barely perceptible track made by the scouts. The section halts when necessary and goes to ground so that they do not offer themselves as targets, and to ensure that the scouts are not crowded or hurried. Indeed no sensible officer or NCO will ever urge his scouts to a pace beyond their best judgement. To do so is to find oneself unambiguously invited to take over the job. Behind the scouts the section moves with equal care. Each man in the rifle and gun group is allotted an arc of observation, either to the left or right of the direction of advance. The last man in the section, 'tail-end-Charlie', has the responsibility of covering the rear. The muzzles of the mens' weapons follow their eyes as they scrutinise their arcs, so that if an enemy appears in that arc, the weapon can be brought up and a shot fired in an instant. To achieve this response, the trained infantryman learns never to take the master hand off the pistol grip of his rifle. And he also learns to check frequently that a twig or vine has not flipped the rear sight of his rifle down: the second he wastes in contact putting it up again is the second in which an enemy may fire the fatal shot.

And, as the section makes its careful way forward, each man ensures that he maintains the correct distance of not less than five metres from his neighbours, because men in a bunch offer a tempting target. He also scans ahead for a good fire position: a fold in the ground perhaps, or a bamboo clump, to which he can manoeuvre if a contact occurs.

On the move, the men communicate using hand signals, so not only must each man constantly and minutely watch his arc, but he must regularly glance at the man in front of him and behind. If either of those men pass a hand signal it must be repeated back by way of acknowledgement and then passed on to be acknowledged in turn. If a man needs to attract the attention of his neighbour quickly he snaps his fingers, sharply, twice. It's an unmistakeable sound close up, and it carries far enough, but not so far that an enemy will hear. And if the double snap of fingers is followed immediately by the thumbs-down sign, it means that an enemy has been seen or his presence is suspected. That is the imperative of the infantrymen, and few who served with 4RAR in Vietnam in 1971 can recall the sound today without a tightening of the stomach.

Within a well-trained and experienced section all this happened automatically. It was ingrained, as natural and unnoticed as breathing, and each man took pride in playing his part with precision. Indeed it was a pleasure to watch a good rifle section working and, like all professionals, making the job look easy. But it took months of grinding repetition to reach this battle-ready standard, and meticulous section commanders and platoon sergeants were often known to become tired and cranky in achieving it.

The section moves on through the underbrush of the training area, polishing these vital individual skills as they go. They are wearing full battle order, because physical fitness, or in this case physical endurance, is also part of individual training. And the only way to gain the endurance necessary for carrying the infantryman's load day after day in operations is to carry it day after day in training.

Throughout the Battalion's tour in Vietnam there was a good deal of discussion as to whether or not infantrymen carried too much on their backs. The general consensus was that they did, but there seemed no satisfactory solution to the problem. Therefore there was no alternative open to the men of the ANZAC Battalion other than to prepare themselves to face it.

There were two main components to individual load-carrying equipment in 1970, just as there are today: patrol order and field order. Patrol order consisted of a pistol belt, attached to which were two basic ammunition pouches, a small pack, at least two water bottles, and a bayonet. A yoke with broad padded shoulder straps attached at four points on the belt, two front, two rear, supported the weight of this basic equipment and kept it positioned on the hips. Patrol order held everything that an infantryman needed to survive and fight for 24 hours. It thus contained his first line of ammunition (120 rounds in six magazines for the SLR, and 160 rounds in eight magazines for an M16); a 24-hour combat ration pack, a hoochy and mosquito net, weapon cleaning kit, possibly shaving things, a combat shovel, and an empty sandbag beneath the small pack. By itself patrol order was light and easy to carry. But because most of 4RAR's operations in 1971 would be of 30 days' duration, with resupply usually every five or six days, a large pack had to be carried in addition to patrol order, and this was where the hard work began.

The large pack was mass-produced, and by today's ergonomic standards probably left much to be desired. But it was certainly better than the 1937 pattern pack, which battalions were still using in 1966, and which was superseded in early 1967. The large pack used by 4RAR in 1970 was the second-generation model. It was made of rip-proof, water-resistant, olive-green material; it was very robust; and it had a modicum of lumbar padding. The pistol-belt fabric stitched around it provided suspension points for water bottles and other items of equipment, including the combat shovel.

The large pack's most convenient feature was the division of the main compartment into two sections horizontally, allowing it to be accessed from the top by means of a flap, and the bottom by undoing three straps. This meant that bedding could be stowed away in the bottom half and forgotten about during the day, while the top half could be used for rations and other items, including the radio set, that were continually in use. There were large side pockets for other assorted cargo.

Most people used the issue pack and found it well up to the task. Once it was married to an individual's patrol order, and correctly adjusted, the two worked very satisfactorily together. Some men added tape and padding over the various clips and protuberances on the belt to minimise abrasions and discomfort to the hips.

Everything that a man needed to move, communicate, live and fight for a month had to be carried on his back, including rations, hexamine solid fuel and water for five days. In addition there was the folding combat shovel and sleeping gear comprising hoochy, mosquito net, blowups or hammock. However because of the relative warmth of the climate in Vietnam at night, it was not necessary to carry a sleeping bag or blanket as well. There was also no need for spare clothing, and many rifle company members dispensed with socks and underclothes as well. At the end of a 30-day operation, during which there was no opportunity to shower, greens were often in tatters, constant sweat having rotted them out and thick foliage and bamboo having torn them. The red soil of Phuoc Tuy Province, which often came in liquid form, also turned greens dark pink. Everyone stank, but as everyone was the same no one noticed. From time to time CQMSs sent in a change of greens for each man with the resupply. On return to Nui Dat, used clothing was often burned, and fresh sets issued.

However a man did not only carry his own equipment on operations. There were additional items that the section, platoon and company needed to function, and these had to be evenly distributed among individuals in those organisations. Spare radio batteries, Claymores with their electrical leads and clackers, detonator cord for connecting Claymores in banks, smoke grenades, M72s, spare M60 ammunition in linked belts, air marker panels, marker balloons, two machetes per section, a small light-proof sheet to cover the CP when operating at night, anti-malarial tablets and medical kits were some of the more obvious items.

Section, platoon and company commanders also needed maps, compass, protractor, sheep-counter, small plastic folders for radio codes, commodity codes, formats of various types of reports, penlight torches, notebooks and chinagraph pencils for marking maps.

M60 gunners needed the 'golf bag', which contained a spare barrel for the gun, spare parts, and the comprehensive cleaning kit that was essential for keeping the gun in first-class working order. Most machine-gunners augmented these issue kits with items of their own preference to assist in maintaining the gun.

Radio operators probably carried the greatest loads, because the set and its ancillary equipment weighed about 14 kilograms. Some of this could be split between other members of the headquarters, but it made little overall difference to the weight carried by the 'sigs'. In some companies, the signaller's personal equipment, rations and water were spread between his immediate neighbours to lessen his load. Signallers also carried an SLR or M16, though probably not a full first line of ammunition. From time to time it was suggested that signallers should carry pistols instead of rifles, but the general consensus was that there were only two things you could do easily with a pistol: lose it, or commit suicide with it. However some signallers acquired US Alice packs on arrival in Vietnam. These were similar to the old Bergen pack, were larger than the Australian issue, had a plethora of useful subsidiary pockets, and the whole was supported on a robust aluminium frame. The Alice pack enabled signallers to dispense with patrol order, or to attach it to the lower end of the assembly.

One of the principal and inescapable weights that all infantrymen carried in Vietnam was water, and it was a constant problem. The climate was extremely humid, and even the smallest exertion caused heavy sweating. Therefore each man carried six or even eight one-litre water bottles, each of which weighed 1.2 kilograms, and sometimes a waterbag which contained another three litres. The weight of the water alone could be between 11 and 13 kilograms. This water had to last the five days between resupplies, but it was never enough for comfort. Occasionally rainwater could be collected, or a creek might be encountered, which helped to alleviate the problem of dehydration. But thirst was every infantryman's constant companion.

From this it can be seen that even with the most careful distribution of rations, water, weapons, ammunition, equipment, and additional necessary items, rifle company members went into operations with between 35 and 40 kilograms on their backs, and radio operators with up to 48 kilograms. These burdens had to be carried from early morning until just before dark, usually every day for up to 30 days. Physical and mental toughness were therefore vital, and major emphasis was laid on this aspect during training in Australia and Malaysia/Singapore.

One of the most crucial requirements of the infantryman is physical robustness. There is a school of thought among trainers of soldiers generally, and infantrymen in particular, that this aspect may be the single most important building block in the production of a fighting soldier. Moreover the beneficial spin-offs of physical fitness go far beyond the purely physical aspect. Some trainers of men believe that physical fitness, once achieved and then maintained, translates to physical toughness, then leads on to emotional toughness. It is also highly likely that, as he achieves increasing levels of physical conditioning, the soldier will additionally experience an increased sense of well-being and self-esteem. His posture is likely to improve so that he carries himself better and with more confidence.

There were, and still are, two components to physical fitness. The first, aerobic fitness, is the ability of the heart and lungs to absorb oxygen into the bloodstream for use by the muscles to sustain physical activity. The second component is muscular fitness, which means that a man is stronger and more robust, is less susceptible to injuries and usually quicker to recover from them. Both aerobic and muscular fitness take time, energy, and willpower to achieve and maintain. But for the infantryman who must spend his days carrying a heavy pack through inhospitable terrain at imminent risk of death or maiming, physical and mental toughness are investments in survival. Moreover there is little doubt that individuals and units that were physically and mentally tough, performed better, longer, in Vietnam than those who were not.

Although the gaining of physical fitness usually started with runs in shorts and sandshoes, the tempo quickened rapidly to include runs and forced marches wearing boots and equipment, and carrying weapons. But the best form of physical preparation for operations was to carry the infantryman's full load for prolonged periods.

When a heavy pack is placed on a man's shoulders his centre of gravity, and therefore his balance, is altered. Different muscles in the back and legs are called into use, and these must be exercised, conditioned and strengthened. The joints in knees and ankles must be similarly prepared. Correct physical preparation required application and courage, but the aim was endurance, and there were no easy options.

The members of the rifle section we are following are all wearing issue olive-green uniforms, with black general-purpose boots, and a soft olive-green bush-hat, known colloquially as a 'giggle hat'. The giggle hat is a multi-purpose item, although platoon sergeants with an eye for their men's smartness frowned on its use for anything other than a headdress. But it was often used to clean dirt and sweat off weapons; to lift a hot mug or mess tin off a hexamine stove; as a towel or a sweat rag; and for getting dust off boots just before a visit to training by the RSM. Its other uses were only limited by imagination. In Vietnam hats were sometimes not worn at all, particularly in thick going where twigs, infuriatingly, whipped them constantly off heads.

Although all members of the Battalion would be encouraged to use issue equipment in Vietnam, non-issue items would not be forbidden for operational use. For example, American tropical fatigue shirts, and trousers particularly, were popular because they tended to dry more quickly than Australian olive-greens. They were also more comfortable. The side pockets of the trousers were larger, better designed and more convenient for carrying maps and other high use items.

Just before 4RAR arrived in Vietnam there was an issue of 'pixie' shirts and trousers. The shirts, which could be worn inside or outside the pants, were quite well designed, and had angled breast pockets which were easy to access. Small pockets on the outer bicep of each sleeve were convenient for grease pencils and cigarettes. The trousers, however were not universally popular because the legs were very close fitting, and could only be worn comfortably by people with slim calves and thighs.

The Australian issued, but American designed and manufactured, basic ammunition pouches were found to be slightly too small, so that it was difficult to remove magazines from them quickly when reloading, especially when in the lying position, and many men obtained 'bren' pouches, British 1944 or 1958 pattern pouches, or others of more roomy design.

The Australian designed and manufactured general purpose boot was an extremely sound item of equipment and rendered excellent service in Vietnam. They were of good quality black leather, had a full-length sewn tongue, and once broken in were very comfortable and long lasting. However some infantrymen found the eyelets a fraction too small, which, they felt, made the boot difficult to lace up in a hurry. A few overcame this perceived shortfall by having a saddler sew a heavy-duty zip into the inner side of each boot, but these were prone to failure, and usually at the most inconvenient moment. Others decided that the American tropical boots were better, and used those, but although they had bigger eyelets, their canvas tops did not come sufficiently high up the leg, and the support and protection they afforded was not as good as that of their Australian cousins. The American boot also had a small vent just above the sole to provide air circulation and to allow water to drain out. Unfortunately, if damaged, this useful facility also let water in.

The list of individual skills includes 'living in the field': learning to make oneself comfortable in the jungle environment. This 4RAR section will be spending the night in the training area, and the section commander, who has already had one tour in Vietnam, intends moving his men as soon as it gets dark. He will make them go through the process of setting up hoochies and bedding, and packing and unpacking equipment in the blackness of close country. Shellscrapes will be dug, and hoochies will be rigged with quick-release knots in such a way that they can be dropped in an instant. But before it gets dark the section must first have its evening meal.

The rifle companies invariably fed on 24-hour combat ration packs (CRPs) throughout the entire 30 days of an operation in Vietnam and therefore they were used during preparatory training and exercises in Australia. There were five different varieties of Australian CRPs, and most infantrymen agreed that with a little thought and a bit of experience, they were not at all bad. The CQMSs went to great lengths to ensure that a wide variety of ration types was included in each five or six day resupply. For operations in Vietnam, American C rations would also be used on a ratio of three days Australian to two days American, or vice versa, in rotation.

Australian CRPs were scientifically researched and produced to ensure high calorific and nutrient value, while keeping the overall weight as low as possible. Perhaps the only consistent comment about them was that they did not include sufficient sweet items, but American C rations made up for that deficiency.

It took only a short time for individuals to identify their favourite rations, so a lot of horse-trading went on during resupply days. Some individuals also carried small bottles of sauces, curry powders and condiments, which improved flavours markedly, and many diggers prided themselves on their gourmet skills and the excellence of their cuisine.

Each ration pack contained food for 24 hours, and was designed to be eaten cold if necessary. A recommended menu, with instructions for cooking, was included in each pack. There was usually a small tin for breakfast whose contents depended on the type of pack; in one pack there were two oatmeal blocks that could be ground up and, with the addition of condensed milk, sugar, water and jam, made into a kind of porridge, although it was nothing that a Highlander would write sonnets about. Lunch was usually tinned cheese or jam and survival biscuits.

The evening meal was considered the main one of the day. It consisted of a medium sized tin, say about 200 grams, of bully beef, frankfurters, meatballs or something similar, augmented by a packet of precooked rice or potato powder. The tea, coffee, sugar and tube of condensed milk was sufficient for most men, but some carried extra. There were also sachets of powder for making fruit-flavoured drinks, and matches, water-sterilising tablets and toilet paper.

Hexamine solid fuel was used to heat food and water. It was an efficient item in the Vietnam climate, though it had a pungent smell, and some infantrymen found it a little slow to heat a mug of water. However it was discovered that C4 plastic explosive was much quicker, the only drawback being that if the mug was placed too close to its intense flame the base melted. The Americans also produced their own solid fuel tablets, but unlike hexamine they ignited instantly and totally, causing the unwary man painfully singed fingers and barely subdued curses. 4RAR used it whenever hexamine was in short supply, but it did not perform as well and was not as popular.

Hexamine tablets came with their own lightweight folding stove that could be adjusted to heat a mess tin when fully open, or a cups canteen folding (a tin mug) when partially closed. Some infantrymen designed and manufactured their own stoves by cutting the sides out of individual meal tins.

Not everyone used a mess tin for cooking, preferring to carry a second cups canteen, into which a water bottle fitted snugly, thus saving space. The folding handle of the mug was held in place by four rivets which came to have more than just a structural significance. Water to cover the bottom two rivets was sufficient for a brew which could be made and consumed conveniently during a ten-minute halt. A four-rivet brew took longer.

During training in Australia each man carried all his garbage out of the area. In Vietnam the principle of 'burn, bash and bury' was followed. Both ends of the ration tins were opened, the tins flattened, and they were placed in the latrine hole, which was covered before the section or platoon moved off next morning. Paper and plastic wrappers were placed on hexamine stoves and burned. There was no waste, because each man carried only the items he liked, and he was always too hungry to leave anything.

Constipation was commonplace because of continual dehydration and ration pack food. However, it should be remembered that the bodily systems of men carrying 35 or 40 kilograms on their backs for ten hours a day through thick country in high humidity would waste very little of the food consumed. In any case constipation seemed to cause no ill effects at the time. And every cloud has its silver lining: the unused toilet paper came in very handy for writing letters home.

Whenever the tactical situation permitted, CQs placed a frozen carton of milk and a freshly baked roll with a fresh salad or meat filling

Sergeant Panui, 3 Platoon Victor Company, brings in a resupply helicopter during operations in Phuoc Tuy Province. (*The Fighting Fourth*)

per man onto the helicopters or APCs that were delivering the resupply. To men who had been weeks on combat rations, this small kindness was always much appreciated.

There are still a number of important things to be done before the section moves off to its night activities, and prime among them is weapon cleaning. A dirty weapon might fail to function properly, and the result in Vietnam could be catastrophic. So weapon cleanliness was one of the earliest and most fundamental lessons drummed into recruits when they began weapon handling as a prelude to shooting.

On operations there would be a compelling need for all members of 4RAR to be able to handle weapons with effect. This did not just imply that all ranks could shoot quickly and accurately. It meant having an intimate understanding of the component parts of each weapon; how the weapon worked and, if it wasn't working properly, why it wasn't; and how the problem could be fixed rapidly and under the worst conditions. In Vietnam that might mean in the dark, while under attack, during a heavy rainstorm.

All rifle company members underwent intensive weapon and shooting training, which first practised and perfected weapon-handling skills, and then qualified each man in live firing. And, because these were crucial skills and of fundamental importance to survival and success in battle, they were subjects to which the rifle companies returned frequently, thereby ensuring ongoing high levels of competence.

Every member of the Battalion was allocated a personal weapon. In Australia these were in the main SLRs, augmented by an issue of M16s towards the end of 1970. With the exception of the Tracker Platoon, whose task would be similar to that of a rifle platoon, members of Support and Administration Company did not need such high levels of weapon-handling competence as the rifle companies. This was because they would be performing other specialist tasks in support of the Battalion during operations. However they still needed a sound working knowledge of all weapons because they must at least be able to defend themselves, and if necessary to fight as part of a coordinated defence of say, Nui Dat, a fire-support base, the Battalion CP on Courtenay Hill, or some other defended position. Moreover, in training in Australia they would be required to demonstrate weapon-handling and shooting skills during the Sub-Unit Course at Canungra. Therefore as a start they were required to pass the appropriate Tests of Elementary Training and obtain shooting qualifications.

In training, too, each man carried his personal weapon with him wherever he went, even if he was moving only a matter of a few metres, and platoon sergeants and CSMs devised unpleasant and inconvenient penalties for those soldiers who overlooked this basic rule. The objective was that a man should learn to feel undressed, uncomfortable and incomplete without his weapon. In Vietnam a soldier without a weapon was totally ineffective, and he could well lose his life as a consequence. Taped to every rifle butt, and to the bipod of the M60, was a shell dressing. This was a sterile pad designed to cover gunshot or fragmentation wounds. Fixed tightly by means of an integral bandage, it could stem severe blood loss and, as the primary means of first aid in the field, could go a long way toward saving a wounded man's life. To have a weapon always at hand was therefore imperative.

Cleanliness of weapons was also stressed, because in the humidity, wet and dirt of Vietnam a rifle would begin to rust in a matter of hours unless energetic steps were taken to prevent it. Weapons were therefore cleaned at least twice a day, and more frequently if necessary. Most rifle company members augmented the issue cleaning kits supplied with each rifle, especially the SLRs. It was generally found that the small cylindrical oil bottle, designed to fit into the SLR's butt-trap, held insufficient oil for more than just a few days. However, the oil bottle issued with the M16 held just the right amount for a 30-day operation and had a convenient screw-top applicator, so many infantrymen acquired one. The long bristles of the issue shaving brush were also found to be particularly effective for getting at dirt and dust that lodged in the various nooks and crannies of rifles and M60s. While this fastidiousness was first engendered under the steely gaze of section commanders and platoon sergeants, it did not take long for each man to realise that, in operations, the small investment in time that it took to maintain a weapon properly might well save his life.

On their arrival in Vietnam the diggers were fascinated by the manuals which often accompanied the American weapons. The one relating to the care and maintenance of the M16 was particularly prized. It came in comic-book form, each stage of 'preventative maintenance' being described by a ravishingly beautiful and voluptuously bosomed young cartoon woman who, with sensuous mouth and dewy eyes, warned repeatedly of the dangers of neglecting 'PM'.

Training pamphlets laid down the formal sequence of weapon-handling periods and the tests that each man had to pass. It was not uncommon, however, to find section commanders filling in idle minutes while waiting for transport by running impromptu, and sometimes hilarious, weapon-handling competitions. These were aimed at sharpening skills in situations of great stress, the principal one being the threat to the worst performer of having to buy an evening's worth of beer for the rest of the section.

When cleaning weapons in training, as would be the case in Vietnam, the men worked in pairs, so that while one was stripping and cleaning his weapon the other had his ready for instant action. By using this 'buddy' system, the section could never be caught with all their weapons out of commission at the one time. Most careful infantrymen also checked their weapons' cleanliness throughout the day and if in doubt gave them a touch-up. Ammunition, magazines, bayonets and other equipment were checked and cleaned at the same time. And, in training, the section or platoon commanders, or the platoon sergeant, invariably inspected weapon cleanliness and serviceability at random, and woe to the digger who was found wanting.

With the evening meal eaten and weapons cleaned, each man renews the camouflage cream on foreheads, ears and face, paying particular attention to the bridge of the nose, jaw-line and cheekbones, for these especially reflect light, even at night. The fingers and backs of the hands are also carefully 'cammed' to just above the shirt cuffs. Sleeves, regardless of weather, are always rolled down.

The section commander makes a final check of the area and of his soldiers. Pocket flaps are buttoned, pouches securely fastened, equipment is checked for rattles, and straps are tightened. When he is completely satisfied that all is as it should be, he indicates the direction of advance and, scouts leading, the section moves off into the gathering dark.

The Battalion's new RSM had arrived. He was WO1 W.T.C. (Wally) Thompson, born in Sydney in 1932. He joined the CMF at the age of seventeen and a half in 1950, and became a member of the 30th Battalion (The NSW Scottish), where he rose to the rank of sergeant. In 1951 he was called up for National Service with the 45th Infantry Battalion, and on 4 May 1954 he enlisted in the Australian Regular Army. He served with 2RAR in Malaya during the Emergency and was promoted to lance corporal in 1955, corporal in 1956 and sergeant in 1958. He then went as an instructor to the Jungle Warfare School at Kota Tinggi in Malaysia in 1961.

Sgt Thompson served briefly in 1RAR before being posted to the Australian Army Training Team Vietnam (AATTV) on 11 August 1964, where he was promoted provisional WO2. He served with 3rd Battalion 5th ARVN Regiment 2nd Division in the north of South Vietnam, for which service he was awarded the Cross of Gallantry, with Silver Star, by the Army of the Republic of Vietnam.

Following this first tour in Vietnam he was posted as an instructor to the Sydney University Regiment on 14 May 1965 and then, as CSM HQ Company, he assisted in raising 10 Task Force at Holsworthy.

As RSM 4RAR, WO1 Wally Thompson was arguably the second most powerful and influential man in the Battalian in 1970–71. Awarded the OAM in 1977, he became the First RSM of the Army in 1983. (*The Fighting Fourth*)

Reposted to 1RAR in 1968, he returned to Vietnam for his second tour of duty as CSM C Company, and was Mentioned in Despatches.

In 1969–70 WO2 Thompson was CSM Battle Wing at the Infantry Centre. He was promoted WO1 and appointed RSM 4RAR on 1 June 1970. In 1977 WO1 Thompson was awarded the Medal of the Order of Australia (OAM) for services as RSM of the Infantry Centre, and he became the first RSM of the Army in January 1983.

Despite the fact that RSM Thompson had arrived at a comparatively late stage in 4RAR's development, and then had to take over from the caretaker RSM, WO2 Darcy Tillbrook, he nonetheless settled in quickly. He did not make the error of instituting immediate changes just to prove that he was the new RSM, which would not have been necessary in any case, because he quickly sensed that there was a good feel to the Battalion, and that in the main only fine-tuning was required.

The opinions of the CO and WO1 Thompson as to how a good RSM should operate exactly coincided, and the RSM understood that LtCol Hughes considered him a principal member of his personal staff.

The CO also made it clear that RSM Thompson had direct and unlimited access, and was answerable only to him. This effectively made the RSM the second-most influential man in the Battalion, which many professional infantrymen would agree was how it should be. While there were about 35 officers in the Battalion, there were 800 soldiers of all non-commissioned ranks; and it was therefore fitting that the soldiers' interests and well-being should be represented right at the top, and by a distinguished soldier with unlimited access to the CO.

From the start the two men consulted each day, even if it was only for a few minutes. Their relationship quickly became totally open and frank, so that it was not long before a strong bond of trust, loyalty, and respect had been firmly cemented between the two. RSM Thompson also consulted on a regular basis with his CSMs: WO2 Tommy Barnes in B Company, WO2 Toddy Smith in C, WO2 Noel Huish in D, WO2 Gary Holmes in Support, and WO2 Denny Cook in Administration Company. All these men had served in Vietnam before, three of them with 4RAR, and all were long-serving and very experienced infantrymen.

Like Jim Healy before him, RSM Thompson clearly understood that the Sergeant's Mess was the most powerful lobby for good with the Battalion, and he encouraged issues and problems to be discussed in the Mess, and solved at the lowest practicable level. This ensured that what S/Sgt Lawrence referred to as 'untidy matters' were quickly put to rights before they caused damage to individuals or the Battalion as a whole.

The RSM was pleased to find that all the OCs gave him free access to their companies but, as custom and good manners demanded, he always called in at CHQ first to let them know he was in the area. He spent a good deal of these first weeks moving around the Battalion by himself, talking with young soldiers, young NCOs, young officers; getting a feel for what was going on and what the Battalion was thinking and saying.

He was also pleased to find that 141 men who had already served in Vietnam, many of them with the Battalion during the first tour, would be returning for the second. Many of these were WOs, senior or junior NCOs, and soldiers, which gave the Battalion a considerable depth of Vietnam experience, particularly at platoon and section level. But there was a downside to this impressive statistic. The RSM discovered that in some cases young officers were being dominated by these first-tour NCOs, some of whom felt that 'the way we did it last time' was the only way it should be done now, which sometimes resulted in the initiative of young officers being stifled; some of them were becoming hesitant and unsure in the face of this superior practical experience. This attitude was probably inevitable, given that there was such a high degree of pride in unit among the WOs and NCOs of 4RAR, and that they were very protective of the Battalion's good reputation. But it was counter-productive, because it could inhibit the development of young officers and give them insufficient opportunity to learn from their own mistakes. And so with a combination of wisdom and diplomacy, RSM Thompson ensured that the subalterns still benefited from the knowledge and experience of their NCOs without being smothered by it.

And as time went on, RSM Thompson was gratified to discover that senior members of other units in Townsville were starting to pay him compliments about the demeanour of 4RAR and the good standards the Battalion was achieving and exhibiting. He recalls: 'There was a good sense of team in 4RAR, and a high degree of trust, loyalty, dignity and mutual confidence between all members, regardless of rank. And there was a very high level of pride in unit.'[1]

The Battalion was fortunate. RSM Thompson was not only an immaculate parade ground soldier, he was also a decorated warrior who was about to return to Vietnam for his third tour. He also had a profound sensitivity to people, and company commander and private soldier alike felt comfortable and confident of seeking his advice. No battalion could ask more of its RSM.

5

The single purpose

The integration of Australian and New Zealand infantrymen into one battalion was an event both unique and historic, and it coincided with the New Zealand government's decision to increase the size of their commitment to the Vietnam war. So, when LtCol N.R. (Chick) Charlesworth's 2RAR arrived in Nui Dat to relieve the battle-weary 6th Battalion in May 1967, he found that:

> Our first V Company arrived in theatre at about the same time as our advance party, the troops coming from Malaysia and Borneo to serve the final six months of their two years overseas duty in Vietnam. The second V Company replaced them in November and the majority of these soldiers extended their two-year overseas tour to serve six months in Vietnam. W Company joined the Battalion in December 1967 after a short shakedown in Malaysia with 1RNZIR. These soldiers, like the third V Company were on a twelve month tour like our own troops. Shortly after this (on 1 March 1968) the Battalion was regrouped and renamed 2RAR/NZ (ANZAC) Battalion. This would be the first time in our history that there has been an official integration of Australian and New Zealand infantry soldiers working side by side under one name with one purpose. To all of us this was an injection of the live Anzac tradition which we know so well. The integration was and will continue to be a great success and to me, it has been a great honour to command the first Anzac Battalion. I am sure the participation of RNZIR troops with the 4th Battalion will be just as successful.[1]

And indeed it was. As the battalions continued in rotation to Vietnam, 2RAR, 4RAR and 6RAR inherited the ANZAC title, and all the members of each battalion, Australian and New Zealand, benefited considerably from that association.

The Victor Company which would become part of 4RAR for the Battalion's second tour in Vietnam had been formed at Burnham Camp, near Christchurch in New Zealand, on 26 March 1970, and it was due to join 1RNZIR in Singapore on 7 May that year. Its commander, Maj Brian Monks, recounted:

> During the final weeks of 1969 I was told of a posting to 1RNZR in Singapore with the likelihood of taking a rifle company to Vietnam in the process of the usual sub-unit rotation. I was permitted to spend time assembling and training the company in Burnham, and so I had the very good fortune to be in at the start of the creation of a rifle company being raised, trained and dispatched to join 1RNZIR as a routine draft replacement. That this company would end up in Vietnam was not guaranteed, however.
>
> For a variety of reasons the usual training pattern had been disrupted. Rather than that full period of post-corps and collective training, usually somewhat over two months in those days, the period available was only one month. I therefore sought and gained permission to conduct a wholly modified syllabus, training pattern, location and style of training. This was conducted at a new site I located on the West Coast: a mini Nui Dat was what I required.[2]

While the soldiers destined for Victor Company were undergoing their recruit training, Maj Monks gave each of his platoon commanders and their NCOs the responsibility for conducting specific phases of follow-on training. Because of the limited time available, this would be in bullring form, which best enabled the company to cover the priority subjects, including the vital individual skills, and patrolling, ambushing, shooting, contact drills and resupply. Concurrently, all NCOs who were eligible to become section commanders were sent away to the School of Infantry to gain their formal section leader qualifications. They would then join the company in Singapore, and immediately take over their new sections.

Under normal circumstances, once the company was complete in Singapore there would have been a further six months training before deployment to Vietnam. However that period was extended to twelve months when the company was notified in September 1970, that it would not replace Whisky Company 2RAR/NZ (ANZAC) Battalion in November after all, but instead would become Victor Company 4RAR/NZ (ANZAC) Battalion in May 1971. This change was due to the New Zealand government's concerns about its involvement in the Vietnam war, and would lead in late 1970 to the start of their wind-back from it with the withdrawal of Whisky Company, SAS elements and 161 Battery RNZ Artillery. But it was a bonus for Brian Monks:

> When the training period was extended I was again given very much a free hand to conduct the training as I felt necessary, and individual and collective training adapted accordingly. Every opportunity was taken to train with other forces in the Malaysia/Singapore area, including 1RAR and other units in 28 ANZUK Brigade. Current after action reports from 2RAR/NZ (ANZAC) Battalion were the source of sand model and TEWT type exercises. I was held accountable for the standard and extent of training achieved. I bid for the resources, training areas, time and support in accordance with unit and formation priorities, and other commitments in Singapore/Malaysia at the time. Then I created the exercises and training pattern and assembled the resources to deliver it.
>
> Although our possible commitment to Vietnam was recognised, it was nevertheless no guarantee that our requests would be met without reservation. Often they could not be met.[3]

Just as 4RAR had experienced manning difficulties in Australia, so Victor Company experienced similar minor problems now in Singapore. From time to time the company lost officers, NCOs and specialists who were needed as replacements in the two companies already in Vietnam. And although there was a limited form of national service in New Zealand, it was coming to an end in 1970, and conscripts were not being sent to Vietnam. Like their peers in Australia, however, New Zealand conscripts were electing to join the Regular Army, so there was generally no difficulty in obtaining private soldiers for service with Victor Company. These regular soldiers came through the RNZIR Depot, commanded by LtCol Tony Mataira, MBE, who had been 4RAR/NZ (ANZAC) Battalion's New Zealand 2i/c during the first tour in 1969.

But Victor Company was not given free access to the ready pool of replacements already available in 1RNZIR just because they *might* eventually go to Vietnam. Moreover, CO 1RNZIR, LtCol Rob Williams, MBE, had the unenviable task of commanding a battalion in which half his rifle companies were under Australian operational command in Vietnam, and the other half were getting themselves ready to go. As he already had a full training calendar which included commitments to major ANZUK exercises, and a heavy round of ceremonial, sporting and garrison duties as well, he made it clear to Maj Monks that he would not be allowed to strip the rest of the battalion for talent at any level. In practical terms it meant that Victor Company would just have to persevere with any members who were not performing satisfactorily and bring them up to standard.

But although Maj Monks did not have exclusive choice in which officers, warrant officers, NCOs and soldiers were selected to join Victor Company, he did have considerable say in the matter, and because there were always more volunteers for service in Vietnam than there were vacancies, Victor Company, to some extent, could be choosy.

Commanders of Vietnam-bound New Zealand companies were selected on merit, so competition was fierce. Selection was made on the cumulative result of overall performance, qualifications and potential. Successful completion of a staff college course was mandatory.

Brian Monks had enlisted as a Regular Force cadet on 25 October 1951. This was the equivalent of a junior leaders unit, and he graduated as a private soldier into the RNZIR in December 1953. From 1954–56, as a lance corporal and corporal at the School of Infantry, he gained his section leader, platoon sergeant, sniper and intelligence qualifications. At the end of 1956 he was selected for officer training, and spent a year at the Officer Cadet Training Unit at Waiouru. This consisted of an initial four-month officer training course, with the remainder of the year spent obtaining instructor level qualifications. His specialisations were three-inch mortar and anti-tank.

In 1957 he became a basic and corps training platoon commander at Papakura and Burnham; in 1958 he went as the Senior Instructor Minor Tactics Wing at the School of Infantry, which also ran OCTU courses for the Tongan Defence Force. In 1959 he became a platoon commander in 1RNZIR in Taiping, Malaysia, which had assumed long-range patrolling duties from 22SAS Regiment, and were characterised by eight- to ten-week patrols along the Malaysia–Thailand border. Communication schedules to base were twice daily by morse, and resupply was approximately every ten days by airdrop.

From 1961–63 Capt Monks was the adjutant of the Wellington, West Coast and Taranaki Regiment, a Territorial unit; in 1964 he became GSO3 Staff Duties at AHQ Wellington and then, on promotion to major, GSO2 in the Directorate of Infantry and SAS in 1965.

After a year as a company commander at the 1 Battalion Depot in Burnham in 1966, he went as a long-term student to the United States Army Command and General Staff College from July 66–June 67. His last posting before command of Victor Company was as senior instructor and then Chief Instructor at the NZ Army Tactical School in 1967–69.

All Victor Company officers were regulars. One had been trained at RMA Sandhurst, two at RMC Duntroon, four at OCS Portsea and two through the New Zealand OCTU system. All of them had been commissioned for not less than one year, and both of the company 2i/cs had previous operational experience in Borneo, with one having SAS service.

At each rank, New Zealand infantry warrant officers and NCOs required attendance and qualification at full-time courses at an Army school. To become a section leader, platoon sergeant and to qualify for warrant rank, it was necessary to reach the highest grade of rifleman, which was three stars, in special-to-corps subjects, and in shooting and general fitness levels. NCOs were then required to gain instructor qualifications, which carried a one to four star grading. A junior NCO might thus carry for a time a three star grading as rifleman and progressive star grading up the instructor ladder in a range of specialist infantry courses—support weapons, signals, assault pioneer and intelligence. Other specialist positions in the company—clerk, Q stream, medical assistant, cook, signals and so on—would have appropriate qualifications in those trades.

New Zealand soldiers achieved their star grading through a combination of formal courses, experience, time-in-grade, shooting skill, general fitness, medical category and recommendation. A one star grade came with the satisfactory completion of corps training. Two stars were earned through a series of advanced training and specialist skills. Three stars were achieved as a result of broadening the skills already acquired, cross-training into additional skills, standards reached, and general potential as a leader.

The star grading system covered all soldiers, NCOs and warrant ranks, trades and appointments. Appropriate qualifications were required for promotion and eligibility for specific postings. Moreover the star system was directly related to pay, and it was the impetus for individual training and the determinant of the overall capacity of each man. Thereafter, collective training extended, developed and sharpened individual skills.

Many company commanders, both Australian and New Zealand, adopted a central philosophical theme in preparing their companies for Vietnam. Brian Monks' was 'To draw on all lessons learned to date about operations and their conduct in Vietnam; to be ready for anything; to make the most of each individual and collective skill; and to design training to fully develop every member's potential and level of confidence.'[4] To achieve these ends, Victor Company trained, like their Australian comrades, using current ANZAC Battalion Standard

Operating Procedures (SOPs), after action reports, and the wealth of knowledge gained by the previous eight New Zealand rifle companies which had served in Vietnam. Nevertheless, Maj Monks recalls:

> We did not follow the constraints of the typical pattern. The one month in New Zealand, instead of the usual three, required us to accelerate the process. We focused on being able to step off the aircraft in Singapore and immediately integrate with an exercise with 1RAR, which was part of 28 ANZUK Brigade in a major Five Power exercise.
>
> After a short period with 1RAR we were given an independent role against the enemy force, which was a Royal Marine Commando unit and then a Gurkha unit. Towards the end of the exercise we infiltrated the enemy main position, maintained surveillance over it for several days, and then we attacked with 1RAR on a converging axis. Our assault was too successful. We secured the Brigade objective several hours before the VIPs, generals, politicians, and the press could get to the pre-selected viewing sites for the climactic battle. Red faces, but never mind.[5]

That coup not only put the company's morale up another notch, but also enabled everyone to assess their training state, and set priorities for the next six months before departure for Vietnam . . . if it came.

So to satisfy the two competing priorities of 1RNZIR's commitments to 28 ANZUK Brigade, and the company's need to be ready to go to Vietnam, individual and collective training programmes were now drawn up, which:

> avoided the boredom of a pedestrian slog through a gradually escalating level of training. I could mix and match, ensure a range of challenging simultaneous activities, and exercise the flexibility needed to reinforce strengths and reduce weaknesses. And repeat if need be. Our general pattern of activity saw us somewhere in the field from Monday to Thursday, and returning to Singapore for regimental and other duties on Friday and the weekend.[6]

In drawing up these training programmes, Brian Monks relied heavily on the continuous stream of information coming from successive ANZAC battalions, particularly after action reports, and analyses and ideas of the New Zealand company commanders who were either in Vietnam or just back.

After action reports were remarkably informative and useful documents because they were compiled at the conclusion of every operation by battalions and other major combat units. Copies of the report were widely circulated throughout the battalions, and the parts which highlighted enemy tactical manoeuvres, described how they reacted to our manoeuvre, and the lessons learned and relearned from each contact, were especially closely studied.

A typical after action report carried the security classification Confidential. On the front page, under the unit identification and name of the operation, came the references, these usually being the HQ 1ATF operation order issued to the units taking part, and the map coverage of the area in which the operation was conducted. This was followed, in separate paragraphs, by the name and type of the operation, the controlling headquarters, and the units taking part with their groupings for battle.

The next paragraphs were extracts from the orders which had initiated the operation, and included the mission statement for both 1ATF as a whole, and the unit compiling the report. For example: '1ATF. To search and destroy enemy elements in the NUI SAO/CU MY area centre of mass YS5487. 4RAR/NZ (ANZAC) Battalion: Redeploy East of Route 2 and locate 33NVA Regt.'

Next came the concept of operations, which gave a brief description of how the CO had envisaged the battalion executing the mission given to it by the Task Force Commander. All these preliminary paragraphs detailed *what* the battalion had been ordered to do. The rest of the after action report was the narrative of *how* the battalion did it, and the results that had been achieved.

This was detailed in a series of annexes. In a typical after action report the operation map overlay came at Annex A, and detailed the Battalion's area of operations (AO); those AOs and boundaries assigned to each rifle company and/or supporting units; the location of headquarters and fire support bases, and similar information.

The intelligence summary came at Annex B, and gave all relevant detail about the enemy forces which would probably be encountered, and those which in fact were encountered throughout the operation. Its appendices gave summaries of the enemy casualties in dead, wounded and weapons captured, and of munitions, equipment and foodstuffs seized.

The sequence of events came at Annex C. It started by giving the locations of the companies and other supporting units as the operation began, and the tasks each had been given. Then came a chronological account of every significant event which took place during the operation. This was compiled from the Battalion Command Post Duty Officer's Log, itself a minute-by-minute diary of all relevant events as they occurred.

Annex D was the summary of contacts and incidents, and Appendix 1 (the summary of contacts) provided some of the most useful information in the report. It gave the date, time and map reference of each contact, and which platoon and company had been involved. It stated whether the enemy or own troops had initiated the contact; the enemy strength and weapons involved; the range at which the enemy had first been seen; the maximum and minimum ranges of the engagement; how the enemy was sighted; and a brief description of the terrain in which the engagement had taken place.

There followed in narrative form a description of the engagement by the commanders on the ground, together with sketches of the action; details of own weapons used and the approximate number of rounds fired; the supporting agencies employed and the number of rounds they had fired; enemy and own casualties; and lastly, comments by the senior commander in contact, with the lessons learned from it.

Annex E listed the installations, bunkers and caches which had been discovered during the operation, and the weapons, ammunition, equipment and foodstuffs recovered from them. Diagrams showing the construction and dimensions of bunkers, and how they were laid out in relation to others in the system, were also included.

Annex F was the artillery report, and it listed the number and type of rounds, contact mission, H and I missions, and DFs fired during the operation.

Annex G gave the statistics of air support, US, Army Aviation or RAAF, used during any engagement; the types of aircraft used; and the amount and types of ordnance expended. An appendix described how the forward air controllers had handled and targeted the air resources they had called in. The final paragraphs of the report, signed by the CO, highlighted the major lessons learned and relearned.

The distribution of the report was wide, and covered not only all the Battalion's sub-units and departments, but also those exterior supporting units which had assisted throughout the operation. Copies of the report also went to those battalions, and to 1RNZIR training in Australia, New Zealand and Singapore/Malaysia for their next tour of Vietnam. In addition, a copy went to the Directorate of Infantry at AHQ in Canberra.

It should be noted that after action reports not only provided a vital blueprint for training for operations in Vietnam but also, today, provide a precise historical record of each operation.

SOPs gave information to commanders at all levels of the Battalion on the standard techniques, procedures, routines and systems to be used within the unit during combat operations. They stipulated, for example, how often location statements (locstats) were to be sent by companies to the Battalion CP; marrying-up procedures; first lines of ammunition to be carried; how night defensive positions were to be laid out; the formats and scheduling for various types of reports to be submitted, such as contact reports, track reports, casualty reports, and so on. The purpose of SOPs was to ensure that procedures were, in fact, standard throughout the Battalion, and that their use became second nature. However SOPs did not lay down the tactics to be applied in specific situations. Tactics were, and still are, an art in their own right, and their application in specific circumstances always rests with each commander on the ground.

Maj Monks believed:

> On the face of it we had no problems with the content of SOPs or our ability to apply them. It would be fair to say that it was what was not in SOPs where our concepts tended to differ. By the time we got to Vietnam we had been using SOPs for a year, and had started using them during our first training on the West Coast of New Zealand. There was a very considerable level of individual and collective skill cemented in and available, and we had scoured every source for lessons learned.
>
> To be practical and effective on operations, SOPs must be limited in content. Understandably they concentrate on the linkages between unit components, support, and coordination matters. We had the great advantage of time and capacity to refine and develop what we did within the Company. Noting of course that what we did within the Company was expressly developed to inflict maximum impact outside it on the battlefield.[7]

There were a number of examples where the New Zealand procedures differed from the rest of 4RAR, but few of them differed markedly, and then usually only in matters of degree and interpretation.

First, it must be emphasised that there was no such thing as a 'basic' rifleman in Victor Company. Each man was cross-qualified to fill at least one or more other task, such as lead scout, cover scout, backup scout, number one or number two on the machinegun, backup machinegunner, section signaller, section medical assistant and grenadier. And it's worth looking at how this depth of multi-skilling applied in practical terms.

For example, Cpl M.M. Douglas, commanding 1 Section of 3 Platoon, had enlisted in 1965, had qualified on the Junior NCO's Minor Tactics/Section Leaders course of eight weeks; the All Arms Instructors course of twelve weeks; the Shooting Coaches course of three weeks; a Cliff Climbing course of two weeks; a Medical Assistants course of three weeks; and a Signals course of three weeks. He was also a three star rifleman, and had qualified for promotion to sergeant

The section 2i/c, L/Cpl L.J. Charman, had also qualified on the Junior NCO's Minor Tactics course; was a qualified signaller and medical assistant; had attended the six-week Assault Pioneer course, and the three-week Demolition Handlers course. He was also a three star rifleman.

Pte J.N. Kopae, the section's lead scout, was a three star rifleman, had attended both the Tracker and Advanced Tracker courses, Demolition Handlers and Medical Assistants courses. And Pte R.W. Wakely, the M60 gunner, had attended the three-week Machine Gunners course, then the two-week Advanced MG course; had qualified on a two-week Mortar Handlers course; and was a two star rifleman.

A similar depth of skills and experience could be found throughout all Victor Company's sections and platoons, and in CHQ as well. This level of multi-skilling was one of the enviable bonuses of an all-regular army.

The New Zealanders had paid considerable attention, *in training*, to personal load distribution, whereas B, C and D Company tended to modify and redistribute their loads as a matter of evolution once operations in Phuoc Tuy began to assume a pattern. And Victor Company not only used patrol order and field order, but also had the additional 'belt order', which contained everything a man needed to live and fight for several hours.

Like most of his fellow Australian company commanders, Maj Monks permitted his soldiers to individualise their load-carrying equipment. Because each man had a specific job and unique physical build, almost any adaptation was allowed, provided it met operational requirements. He also insisted on the use of the yoke with belt and patrol order to ensure that weight was evenly distributed over the hips. The essence of all load-carrying equipment in Victor Company, full or abbreviated, was that its wearer had to be able to shoot accurately while standing, kneeling or lying.

Victor Company was organised almost identically to 4RAR's rifle companies: CHQ, attachments from supporting arms, and three platoons, each of three sections of ten men. The sections had the usual subdivisions of scout group, gun group and rifle group. Moreover:

> Company manning policy was to ensure maximum bayonet strength in the field at all times. This was achieved through staggered leave, R and R allocation drawn by lot soon after arrival in theatre, medical coverage in the field and minimising rear details in Nui Dat. We found that we could maintain platoon strengths, with attachments, sometimes approaching forty in the field. We observed that Australian platoons were sometimes nearly half this figure.[8]

The tactics and techniques employed by New Zealand and Australian companies were essentially identical. However there were slight variations *in procedure* between companies, to achieve the same ends, but these were simply a reflection of the individuality of their leaders. Nevertheless, by the time Victor Company joined 4RAR in May 1971, it would have been entirely possible for a New Zealand rifle platoon to be placed under operational command of an Australian rifle company, or vice versa, with immediate cohesion.

The weapons and equipment carried by the New Zealanders were identical to those of their Australian counterparts: they had to be for the purposes of resupply and replacement. But Victor Company in Singapore had been equipped with the British General Purpose Machine Gun, which they much preferred to the American M60. It had better balance and was generally more reliable and less prone to stoppages. It's tempting to suggest here that if the Australians had been given access to the British GPMG (it had in fact been formally trialled by the Australian Army) they would have preferred it to the M60 for the same reasons. All Victor Company machinegunners were fully qualified on both weapons, including their use in the sustained fire role, but they used only the M60 in Vietnam.

The New Zealanders also preferred the SLR for its reliability and stopping power, and it was standard issue to their riflemen. Like the Australians, they felt that a few centimetres taken off the barrel would have made it more convenient to handle in thick country. In fact, trials were carried out by RAEME at Vung Tau to see how the ballistics would be affected by shortening the barrel by about 15 centimetres. It made almost no difference, and certainly nothing that would have mattered over the usual contact ranges of 20–50 metres, and little more up to 300 metres that could not be remedied by re-zeroing. But eventually nothing came of the trial, and everyone had to persevere with the production barrel. Scouts were given the choice of SLR or M16, as they were in 4RAR's companies.

Victor Company carried considerably more ammunition than the first lines specified in SOPs. Everyone in the company carried at least one 50-round linked belt for the M60s. Extra smoke and HE grenades and Claymores were also carried. But the first lines set down in SOPs were only a guide anyway, and were almost always exceeded within Australian companies too.

The Australians stipulated an interval of not less than 5 metres between men in order to avoid offering temptingly bunched targets while moving and patrolling. VC and NVA units used an interval of

7 metres. But the New Zealanders specified that the interval should be 'maximum visible separation', which would usually be 5 to 10 metres in the forests of Phuoc Tuy. This obviously lessened the chance of taking casualties in an enemy ambush, but it placed more demands on navigation, recognition of own troops and the use of field signals, or what Victor Company referred to as 'silent communication skills'.

The New Zealanders placed considerable emphasis on shooting, and everyone in the company was a first-class shot or better. This emphasis was probably a carry-over from the era of the 303 bolt-action rifle, with its very sensible and necessary axiom of 'one shot, one kill'. Victor Company extended and refined this to the capability of aimed fire from the shoulder, including by machinegunners, as the first reaction on contact. The extreme opposite was the American technique of letting fly with everything you'd got, the theory being that if you fired enough rounds into the target area you were bound to hit something.

Victor Company stipulated ten-minute 'look and listen' halts at least hourly, and section and platoon commanders often incorporated them more frequently. Although the Australians also used this look and listen technique, it tended to be included as part of the ten-minute hourly halt to check navigation and send locstats. It was not used on a scheduled basis, but rather depended on the likelihood of enemy contact, the tactical situation, and the 'feel' of the area. At every halt, Victor Company went into the immediate ambush drill, including Claymore layout.

There is no doubt that the New Zealand Army generally, and those of its members who served in Vietnam particularly, would have preferred to deploy their own battalion group with its own supporting arms and services. They could then have operated as a national entity, under New Zealand commanders, and evolved their own systems and procedures which took into account the special and unique qualities of the New Zealand Army and its soldiers.

Unfortunately this was just not feasible. In the years 1966 to 1971, the population of New Zealand held steady at about 2.7 million people and the Army was correspondingly small. It did not have the numbers to support a battalion group and rotate it on an annual basis over the four years of the country's commitment to the war. Nevertheless New Zealand's Army achieved a commitment from 1967 by sending two rifle companies, support weapons and administrative personnel to the ANZAC battalions, and other arms and services personnel to be integrated with 1ATF and 1ALSG. Although it might have been a relatively small contribution in terms of numbers, it was still a significant one in terms of skill and results. And those Australians who served alongside the New Zealanders very quickly found out that what they lacked in quantity they more than made up for in quality.

The affiliation of Australian and New Zealand troops into one battalion for service in Vietnam required, obviously, special command arrangements. While the CO would have *operational* command and control over Victor Company, if any contentious operational issues arose OC Victor Company could, in the first instance, make representation to the ANZAC Battalion's New Zealand 2i/c, Maj Don McIver. Maj McIver did not have the power of veto over the operational employment of Victor Company, but if an issue could not be resolved by consultation between the CO, Maj McIver and Maj Monks, and it was serious enough, representation could be made to the senior national commanders in Saigon, who would in turn consult with Commander 1ATF. As it turned out, this was never necessary. And, when the withdrawal of Australian and New Zealand troops was announced in August 1971, these command arrangements did not need to be modified.

Victor Company's deployment into battle was handled as a normal operational decision taken by the CO in exactly the same way as it was with his other companies. There were never any political implications or ramifications as to how Victor Company could be deployed or employed. The New Zealanders were also resupplied both on operations and in Nui Dat using the same procedures and logistic systems as their Australian counterparts.

The only divergence came in personnel administration and discipline. Personnel administration, being those matters of a peculiarly New Zealand nature, were handled by the New Zealand Component staff, headed by Capt Murray Winton and WO2 Allan Nixey. Minor disciplinary infractions at company level would be dealt with by Brian Monks, and more serious matters by Maj McIver or, in exceptional circumstances, by the New Zealand staff in Saigon. In the most serious cases, New Zealand personnel could be returned to Singapore for disciplinary processing.

These arrangements worked extremely well, and the relationship between the CO and his New Zealand 2i/c was always efficient, friendly, courteous and trusting. LtGen McIver, as he is now, recalls that:

> The second tour of 4RAR/NZ (ANZAC) Battalion was operationally successful. The command relationships which had been established previously and were employed successfully on this tour of duty have provided the basis for more recent deployments of military forces from our two nations on a range of international commitments. As always, there were

> circumstances which, at times, conspired to make the association less than ideal, but it would be hard to expect otherwise in such a deployment from two sovereign nations; eg,
>
> - The two components trained and worked up separately. Their first association was after arrival in SVN when they were required to move immediately into combined and cooperative operational deployment. There was little time to develop the command and tactical interrelationships which one would normally expect in a battalion before deployment.
> - The Battalion itself faced additional and unusual challenges. There was the clear expectation that one or more governments would make the decision to withdraw and in my mind it was fortuitous that they consulted to make almost concurrent announcements. Nevertheless when the decision was taken the remainder of the tour was made the more complicated by that fact itself, and by the enemy pressure to reinforce the decision.
> - Not surprisingly, from the perspective of the New Zealand troops, there had been disappointment in the fact that our contribution was not of such a size as to allow an independent national structure.
> - Given all these factors I believe that the association worked well and the Battalion as a whole has every right to be proud of what it achieved and the way it set about those achievements.[9]

The ANZAC Battalion was extremely fortunate to have Maj Don McIver as its New Zealand 2i/c. He was an easy man to like and respect, and when he joined the Battalion at the end of January 1971 he settled in quickly and was well accepted at every level. And if, later in Vietnam, there were small rufflings of the two sets of national feathers, they were quickly put to rights by his wisdom, good humour and sound commonsense.

Donald McIver was born at Epsom, Auckland, in New Zealand on 22 February 1936, and joined the Army as a Regular Force cadet in 1952. After two years at OCTU in Waiouru, he went to RMC Duntroon as an officer cadet from 1954–57.

In 1958–59 he served as a platoon commander in 1RNZIR in Malaya during the Emergency; in 1960 he became an instructor at various Army schools at Waiouru until 1962. From 1963–65, as a company 2i/c and adjutant of 1RNZIR, he served in Malaysia during Confrontation; and was then posted as a staff officer to Army Headquarters in Wellington. In 1968 he attended the Royal New Zealand Command and Staff College as a long-term student, after which he returned to Defence Headquarters in Wellington as a staff officer. Maj McIver joined 4RAR in Townsville on 25 January 1971, and served with the ANZAC Battalion until the final withdrawal in December that year.

Maj Don McIver, the ANZAC Battalion's New Zealand Second-in-Command in 1971. His distinguished military career finished in 1991, when he retired from the New Zealand Army as LtGen D.S. McIver, CMG, OBE. (*The Fighting Fourth*)

His subsequent career was extremely distinguished. Promoted to lieutenant colonel in 1973, he received an exchange posting to Army Office in Canberra as SO1 Material Requirements, and remained in that post until 1975. He attended Joint Services Staff College in Canberra in 1978, and in 1979 was promoted to brigadier and became Commander 1 Brigade at Papakura from 1979–81. In 1982–83 Brig McIver was the Deputy Commander New Zealand Force, South East Asia; in 1984 he attended the Royal College of Defence Studies in London. Then in 1985 he became Deputy Chief of the General Staff, and Assistant Chief of Defence Staff (Operations) in Wellington.

In 1988 he was promoted to major general and became Chief of the General Staff (CGS). Promoted lieutenant general in 1989, he became commander Multinational Force and Observers in the Sinai, a peace-making operation set up independently of the United Nations to observe and report on the compliance of Israel and Egypt with the 1979 Peace Treaty, which both nations had signed.

LtGen McIver retired from military life in 1991, and became Director of the New Zealand Security Intelligence Service, a post he held until 31 October 1999.

Obviously it was less than ideal that 4RAR's Australian companies trained for Vietnam in and around Townsville in 1970–71, while Victor Company trained in Singapore/Malaysia. The CO remembers that:

> I visited 1RNZIR and Victor Company in Singapore in December 1970, and I had tried very hard throughout that year to get Victor Company to Australia for the three Battalion exercises (or two, or one). I failed. So I tried to get Victor Company 'O' Group, and failed. Then I tried to get Victor Company 'R' Group: also failed. There were arguments (at staff level) about cost and aircraft availability.[10]

The opportunity to train together would certainly have made a difference to that very important element of mutual understanding between the two parts of the Battalion. Later, because of the tempo of operations in Vietnam, there was almost no time to get to know one another even socially. After sixteen months of training in Townsville, the CO and the Australian company commanders understood each other well, but that close association was just not possible between the CO and Maj Monks under operational conditions. An opportunity for Victor Company to take part in even one Battalion exercise in Australia would have been beneficial. But it had not been possible with previous New Zealand companies either, and experience over the years had shown that it had not created any significant adverse effects subsequently in Vietnam.

In any case, when the chips were down, tradition and professionalism always rose to the top, and combined once again to achieve the single purpose.

6

A duty to be careful

Over the years in Vietnam, the type of operations to which Australians and New Zealanders were most frequently committed were known variously as search and destroy, search and ambush, search and fix, or search and kill. It all meant the same thing: first the enemy had to be found, then he had to be killed or captured, and his camps or bunker systems had to be destroyed. If usable food stocks were also captured, they might be back-loaded to Nui Dat and subsequently redistributed to the civilian population. But this seldom happened because captured enemy food stocks were most often in a highly unpalatable state.

Weapons were also back-loaded. Those in a reasonable condition were first rendered harmless, and then they made an onward journey to Australia or New Zealand, eventually finding their way into museums or onto the walls of military establishments. Others might be kept at Nui Dat to decorate the various messes and canteens, and would be taken home when the unit was rotated. Weapons in poor condition, and all captured ammunition, were destroyed by being blown up or dumped at sea. Captured personal equipment was burnt.

But first the enemy had to be found, and this was done by aggressive patrolling by the rifle companies. In 1971 most operations were conducted at company level and controlled at battalion level. Each rifle company was, in fact, a big fighting patrol whose task was to dominate the AO by its aggressive presence. And when the enemy was encountered, every resource available to the Battalion was used to destroy them.

Patrolling was the basis of all infantry operations in Vietnam, and therefore it was the basis of all training in Australia and Singapore/Malaysia. And since all the Australian company commanders, and most of the senior and many junior NCOs, had already served in Vietnam, training exactly duplicated the operations which would be undertaken. So, just as we have followed a section as it polished its individual skills in training, it's now time to follow a rifle company as it trains at Mount Spec just north of Townsville.

On this occasion the company has been taken to the training area by vehicle. But in Vietnam they will either be carried into battle by APCs or flown into a landing zone (LZ) by Iroquois helicopters. The LZ is always assumed to be occupied by the enemy, and so its margins are prepared, or 'prepped', by artillery fire or air strikes. This preparation cuts out as the helicopters run in, and the task of providing suppressive fire is taken over by the accompanying helicopter gunships. These may be either American Cobras or Australian Iroquois, whose radio callsign was prefixed 'Bushranger'.

Most infantrymen found the approach flight to the LZ exhilarating because the helicopters normally flew at treetop level. This tactic not only made them difficult to hit from the ground, but also accentuated the impression of speed and dash, which in turn engendered a feeling of elation and aggression. And those who took part in a helicopter assault will never forget the distinctive thrash of the whirling rotor blades: it's probably the most emotive sound of the Vietnam war.

If the enemy were present around the LZ, the helicopters might take ground fire on the way in. Depending on the weight of this enemy fire, the air commander, who was usually the senior pilot commanding the flight, made the decision either to land and discharge the infantrymen or to abort the fly-in.

If the infantrymen landed under fire, they would have to fight their way off the LZ by using fire and movement, and employing any gunships on station or the artillery which had prepped the LZ. If the air commander aborted the landing, the helicopters might proceed to an alternative LZ or return to Nui Dat so that the operation could be remounted. By 1971, however, it was highly unlikely that any LZ would be occupied by the enemy, and companies invariably landed unopposed.

Once on the ground, CHQ and the platoons made for their initial rallying points, which were always just inside the treeline. Here sections and platoons shook out into formation, compass bearings and radio communications were checked, and then each sub-unit moved off to begin the slow, careful task of searching out the enemy.

It must be remembered that there were no frontlines in Vietnam as there had been in World Wars I and II. In Vietnam the enemy could be anywhere, and they could be above or below ground. And although air reconnaissance was carried out extensively, the thick tree canopy hid enemy installations and movement. The only really reliable way of finding the enemy was to send ground troops into an area, and even then there was no guarantee that contact would be made.

Searching ground in the tropical terrain of Phuoc Tuy Province was a painstaking and physically demanding business. With visibility at around 15 or 20 metres, enemy soldiers or their bunkers were difficult to see. Nevertheless camps, and bunkers especially, required timber for overhead protection, and the stumps of felled trees were difficult to conceal. And when the enemy moved, he left tracks: broken twigs, footprints or marks where his weapons and equipment had grazed the saplings. If the ground was damp, his tracks were easy to see, and by counting the footmarks contained within one metre, the number of enemy soldiers in the group could be fairly accurately estimated. The age of the footmarks was also assessed, and the direction of travel was obvious. Whenever these signs were encountered the platoons reported them to CHQ by radio.

In order to obtain a high degree of search, the company and its platoons adopted logical and somewhat geometric search patterns. There were several patterns which might be used, each for a different type of terrain and going. But as Phuoc Tuy Province was essentially flat and heavily timbered, searching was usually done by moving on a compass bearing from point to point.

Each company had an AO allotted to it, and the OC 'owned' everything inside its boundaries. This gave him great freedom of initiative, decision and action. He might, for example, decide to allot sub-AOs to his platoon commanders, and allow them to roam at will, and go where their instincts and initiative took them. But there was a problem with that. If the company was too wide-spread, and one of the platoons hit a major force, it could take a considerable length of time for the rest of the company to come to their assistance. Besides, Battalion SOPs laid down that a company must be able to concentrate within 30 minutes. Therefore to achieve the two imperatives of wide search and rapid concentration, some companies used a 'two up, one back' formation when searching. This enabled the company to move through a relatively large area in a relatively short time, while allowing platoons to examine the ground minutely for enemy sign. And, importantly, the company could still concentrate within 30 minutes in any direction if contact was made.

The two leading platoons, separated for safety by a grid square, moved at their own pace. When they had each gone 500 metres they halted, and might send out two sections, laterally, for up to 500 paces. Meanwhile platoon HQ and one section remained stationary, forming a firm base. When the two sections had returned, the whole platoon moved on again for another kilometre, and repeated the sequence. CHQ and the rear platoon, using the same technique, searched the inside grid squares as they passed through them. Using this method, one company could examine a relatively large area in a day, and enemy sign, if it existed, would inevitably be found.

The company moved in this formation either as a complete entity or as separate sub-units, but whatever the case the OC carefully monitored progress to ensure cohesive forward momentum and the necessary safety separation. Thus if one of the searching platoons made contact with the enemy, the rest of the company were well placed to render rapid assistance.

Whichever search technique a company adopted, it required accurate navigation. It was a vital skill, and one demanded not only of the OC, his FO, the platoon commanders and NCOs, but also every man in the company. Apart from the fact that it was extremely embarrassing not to know where you were, there were more compelling reasons on operations. Some commanders chose to bring down artillery fire immediately on contact in order to secure their flanks and to cut off the enemy's line of withdrawal or reinforcement. In order to get that fire down quickly it was necessary to be absolutely certain where you were at all times. But in 1971 there were no global positioning systems available to infantrymen, and because visibility in most areas of Phuoc Tuy Province was so restricted, navigation was by dead reckoning.

This required the use of a map, prismatic compass, protractor, and a sheep-counter taped to the forestock of the rifle. This last kept tally of the number of paces covered. Commanders at all levels were also issued with utility wrist compasses that were worn on the watchstrap. With the hand supporting the stock of the rifle, the wrist compass was always uppermost, and could be constantly checked with a quick glance.

It was not unusual to find that four members of CHQ navigated simultaneously: the OC, 2i/c or CSM, the FO and the i/c Support Section. Starting from a known point, sections, platoons and CHQ moved off on predetermined bearings. Each time a navigator covered, say, 30 inches (which at that time was the regulation military pace), he pressed once on the sheep-counter. It should be noted here that sometimes in particularly thick country, or when the tactical situation demanded very slow movement, it might take up to three small paces to cover 30 inches. However navigators quickly became adept at judging how many part-paces constituted one full one.

It was found most convenient to wear the prismatic compass on a lanyard round the neck and resting against the breastbone. In that position it was easily and quickly get-at-able, and the precise bearing could be frequently checked without the necessity of undoing pouches or rummaging in pockets.

Under normal circumstance, companies moved for an hour, and they would seldom cover more than a kilometre in that time. At the end of that hour they halted for ten minutes. In CHQ, those navigating would then work out individually where they were. This was done by converting the number of 30-inch paces into metres (maps of Vietnam being metric) and marking off that distance along the bearing. A dot was placed on the map at that point, and individual maps were then compared. It was normal to find that all four dots were within a 50-metre circle. The mean point was converted into a six-figure grid reference, and the whole procedure seldom took more than two or three minutes.

Using the same method, the platoons would be establishing their locations, and each passed their encoded grid reference to CHQ. When CHQ had received, decoded and logged all three platoon locations, they sent them on by radio to the Battalion CP. There they were again decoded and placed onto the Master Operations Map, so that the CO and his operations staff were able to keep constant track of the movement of all companies, platoons and, if they were deployed, any section patrols as well. Using the same information, the battery commander and his staff in the Fire Support Control Centre updated their artillery and mortar fire planning maps.

Company commanders always placed this new information onto their own maps, together with the locstats of any other sub-units in proximity to the boundaries of their AO. When all this had been done, the company advance continued, and the process would be repeated every hour throughout the day while the company was searching. Once learned and perfected, it was a simple and efficient procedure.

Sometimes OCs just manoeuvred their companies to criss-cross their AO randomly, which was also an entirely valid way of searching out the enemy. Alternatively, careful study of the map might give commanders a clue as to where the enemy might be found. For example, the enemy always needed water, so the search of a creek-line sometimes revealed tracks and other signs of a watering point. These could be ambushed by day or night.

The enemy tended to put his bunker systems on any high ground, and although 'high' was a relative term in most of Phuoc Tuy, any pimple adjacent to a creek was well worth a look. Tracks or footpaths leading from villages into the forest were frequently ambushed, particularly at night, because they could well be the conduit for enemy resupply. Points at which the forest abutted a working rubber plantation like Courtenay also came under regular scrutiny and ambush. Over the years the Task Force intelligence staff had amassed vast quantities of information concerning the locations of enemy installations. These could be revisited on a regular basis to see if the enemy had re-established them.

Each time a company, platoon or section halted to verify its position and send locstats, it went into a quick halt drill. A quick halt was defined as being up to and including ten minutes in duration. More than that became, obviously, a long halt. In either case it was essential that the sub-unit should not be surprised by an enemy force. Therefore a short halt in close country required a sentry with an M60 to be placed at each end of the line of march, and others at points along it to cover any likely axes of enemy approach. If contact with the enemy was imminent or suspected, Claymores might also be deployed. Each man faced outwards covering his arc of responsibility and, although he could rest, he could not relax.

Halts of longer than ten minutes required the sub-unit to form a quick harbour, which was circular in shape, divided into three sectors, each occupied by a section or, at company level, by a platoon. Sentries, machineguns and Claymores would always be sighted and, depending on the enemy situation, the commander might ask for an artillery or mortar DF to be silently registered. More will be said about the use of artillery, mortars and air later, but silent registration simply meant that target data were calculated and placed onto the guns so that in an emergency fire could be brought down almost instantly.

The hallmark of a good sub-unit was its ability to move noiselessly through close country. How this was achieved at section level has already been explained, but exactly the same procedure applied to platoons and companies as well. The forests of Phuoc Tuy Province were filled with the incessant high-pitched whistle of insects, which sounded like thousands of miniature jet engines, and to some degree this helped to mask the noise of large groups of men as they moved. Nevertheless everyone learned to move about carefully, and to do everything, from stripping a weapon to opening a tin, quietly. Radio operators acquired the knack of speaking low, and at night they murmured into their handsets. In fact the ANPRC-25 set had a 'whisper' facility built into it, so that even when signallers whispered at the transmission end they were clearly audible at the receiving end.

Although any sort of idle chatter was forbidden, anyone who needed to talk during a halt or on the move could do so either by speaking low or using field signals. Field, or hand, signals were learned and perfected during individual training and were essentially identical throughout the Battalion. For example, if the platoon commander placed three fingers, signifying three stripes, against his bicep, and then put the flat of the hand on top of his head, it meant he wanted to speak to his sergeant. The first two fingers extended and placed on the shoulder to signify a lieutenant's rank badges, followed by a circled thumb and forefinger held up to the eye, meant that the platoon commander was going on a reconnaissance.

The first two fingers extended, placed over the lips, and drawn away several times, followed by five fingers held up twice, meant a ten minute halt. Field signals were always logical and unambiguous, and they could often be witheringly cutting as well. If an individual acted in a way which his peers considered to be particularly inappropriate, his nearest neighbour would probably place an extended forefinger into his own ear.

But everyone understood the vital importance of field signals, and always obeyed the infantryman's golden rule of acknowledging and passing them on.

If a recently used foot-track, or a cache, was located, the platoon commander immediately notified CHQ and might ask permission to ambush it. Usually this request was granted, and the OC might also decide to deploy the whole company into an area ambush. This might be necessary if there was no obvious enemy approach into the ambush site, which was often the case in a rubber plantation. Ambushing in rubber was extremely difficult. Visibility between the rubber trees, which were always set out in precise ranks and files, could be several hundred metres in every direction. The approaches to a cache in rubber could also be from any direction. In unworked rubber there might be uncleared vegetation up to waist level, which provided the ambushers with at least some modicum of cover. Therefore the best way for a company to ambush in a plantation was to establish a modified platoon defensive position around or near the cache itself and deploy the other two platoons and CHQ in depth positions. These would typically be about 500 metres out from the cache itself, and in the 12 o'clock, 4 o'clock, and 8 o'clock positions relative to it. With this layout it might be possible to contact the enemy as they headed in towards the cache; at the cache itself; or as they withdrew from it. Entrance and exit routes not covered by troops on the ground could be attacked by bringing down artillery or mortar fire onto them.

Vietnam yet again reinforced the old lesson that successful ambushing is one of the most difficult operations of war. Deciding to sit on, or back from, the ambush site; assessing the direction of the most likely enemy approach; calculating the best killing ground, and siting weapons onto it to achieve maximum effect; leaving the enemy no visible signs that an ambush was in place; and minimising fidgeting and noise by the ambushers, who may have been in location for hours and sometimes days, were just some of the problems. But perhaps the most crucial issue was who, when and how to spring the ambush. Timing was everything. Normally it was sprung by the senior commander present, and typically he sprang it himself by silently ordering the firing of a bank of Claymores and/or an M60. When that happened every weapon overlooking the killing ground opened fire at the rapid rate, because experience had taught that if you didn't hit the enemy in the first five seconds, you didn't hit him at all.

But some of the areas in which the ANZAC Battalion would operate were free fire zones, which meant that civilians were forbidden to enter them at any time. Theoretically anyone found in such an area was assumed to be enemy. Even so, rules of engagement applied, because it was not unknown for civilians to stray into free-fire zones. Whether they were bona fide civilians, or VC sympathisers trying to look innocent, will never be known, but unless they were visibly carrying weapons they could not be engaged out of hand.

The rules of engagement stipulated that fire could not be opened on individuals or groups unless:

- They are positively identified as enemy.
- They open fire first, and are not obviously friendly.
- They fail to stop when challenged and are not obviously friendly.
- By night, they approach a position and are not obviously friendly.

All members of the Battalion had to know, and be able to recite verbatim, these rules. Some felt that they were unrealistic and might well give the enemy the initiative in the crucial first seconds of a contact, or make junior commanders unduly cautious about opening fire at all. It's possible. But in the main they seemed to work fairly well, and undoubtedly helped to avoid unnecessary tragedies.

By May 1971 the enemy in Phuoc Tuy was primarily interested in staying alive: peace talks were under way and the war might soon begin scaling down. Moreover the Australian and New Zealand operations in the province had taken a heavy toll on enemy units. So most contacts with the enemy during search and destroy operations were now usually over in a matter of seconds, and if they were not hit in the first exchange of fire the enemy typically withdrew and lived to fight another day. This was not always the case, however, as will be seen in Part II. Thus a battalion preparing for operations in Vietnam needed to learn, practise and perfect the four 'conventional' phases of war: advance, attack, defence and withdrawal.

There was always a good deal of debate about the wisdom of using conventional techniques in Vietnam, which was considered to be an unconventional battlefield. However the point was that whatever the environment—jungle, open plains, mountains or built-up areas—the *principles* remained the same, and only the *techniques* needed to be modified to meet the special circumstances of each situation.

Searching for the enemy in Vietnam was the equivalent of the advance to contact in a conventional war setting. In Vietnam, contact would normally be initiated by whichever scout saw the other first, which is why most scouts on both sides preferred to use automatic or semi-automatic weapons: the unexpected shock effect of a blast of fire instantly gained a moral ascendency over the opposition. But the Australians and New Zealanders were also taught to follow up the initial opening burst of aimed fire with an immediate action drill. Using this, every man in the contact section swung into extended line, and moved forward to a position from which they could see and bring aimed fire onto the enemy. At the same time, the machinegun group moved to the right of the section, or to the high ground if there was any. This initial manoeuvre by the section took place instantly, and probably needed only a few moments to complete. Its object was twofold: first, to get every man moving *forward*; and second, to bring a heavy weight of aimed fire down onto the enemy as quickly as possible in order to 'win the fire-fight'.

As soon as the immediate action drill had been completed, the section commander, and behind him the platoon commander, began assessing the situation. Commanders at all levels within a company became adept at recognising the sound made by each type of enemy weapon, and to distinguish them from our own. It was therefore not too difficult to gauge, from the volume of fire and its distinctive sound-signature, how many enemy had been contacted and their positions relative to ours. The diggers in the contact section also began passing information, either verbally or by field signals, as to the numbers and locations of the enemy. A good deal of time was spent, in training, in perfecting the immediate action drill. It was also vital to get the diggers to pass information back to the section commander, and to pass his orders and instructions forward, left and right. Nevertheless it came as something of a surprise, during a company's first contact, to discover just how much noise was generated, especially if a full-blown battle developed. It was something that could not be replicated in training. Under the tree canopy of Phuoc Tuy, the blast of rifles and machineguns was greatly intensified, and to these was added, as the battle built, the crump of M79 rounds, the detonation of RPG2 or RPG7 rockets, and the impact of artillery rounds or air-delivered ordnance. If to these basic noises was added the thump of 30- or 50-calibre APC machineguns and the tooth-rattling blast of Centurion tanks' main armament, speech became impossible. Most often those wanting to communicate had to do so either by hand signals or by crawling forward and shouting into an ear.

But the passage of information, however it was achieved, was vital. Pieced together, sifted and evaluated, snippets of information enabled a section commander to make the decision to either attack the enemy himself or to wait for the rest of the platoon or company to come up.

At whatever level it took place, an attack had to be carried out with sufficient numerical superiority to ensure its success. There was nothing foolhardy or 'gung-ho' about an attack, and even the most aggressive leader was first cautious in thought, because there was always a duty to be careful. The attacking force needed numerical superiority of not less than three to one. This meant that three Australians attacked one enemy; a rifle section attacked three or four men; a platoon attacked an enemy squad; a company attacked an enemy platoon; and a battalion attacked an enemy company. To these numerical ratios could be added 'combat multipliers'. A combat multiplier was, and still is, anything that added to one's own numerical superiority. For example, a company which attacked an enemy platoon position while supported by artillery and tanks would be far more likely to win the day than a company attacking without that support. Moreover, the availability of such support might make it possible to carry out a successful attack with a man-to-man superiority of only 2:1 instead of 3:1, although such a solution is not recommended to students attending staff college.

While such factors as a responsive and efficient resupply system, the element of surprise, and the high morale and aggressive optimism of one's own troops are all combat multipliers, firepower is by far the most significant. The ANZAC Battalion used artillery and air support regularly and extensively in Vietnam. APCs and tanks were also used whenever they were available and circumstances allowed.

But it was the contact battle which, as we have just seen, was most often initiated by two opposing scouts, that was by far the most usual occurrence in Phuoc Tuy. They were not always textbook affairs; and quite often, if care was not taken, they degenerated into what was known as a 'shit-fight', the day being won by whoever had the determination to hang on five minutes longer than his opponent.

Less common was the mounting by a battalion of a formal attack onto a known enemy position. But it did happen, as will be described later. But before they could be used in Vietnam, all these skills and techniques had to be learned, practised and perfected in Australia and Malaysia.

Sub-units of the Battalion advanced every day; ambushed regularly; took part in contact battles from time to time; carried out formal attacks seldom; but went into a defensive position almost every night. The forward operational base at Nui Dat and the Battalion CP on Courtenay Hill were continually in a state of defence, as any static installation in a theatre of war must be. But this is not to suggest that the personnel within those installations cowered behind their wire and machineguns or hid in their bunkers. There was nothing passive about the defence of Nui Dat or Courtenay Hill.

By day air reconnaissances scoured the surrounding country for enemy sign; snap road-blocks were set up and passing civilians were stopped and searched; if they were found to be carrying an unusually large quantity of food or money, or any suspicious items, they were detained and handed over to the national police, RF or PF for interrogation.

Each night patrols went out and ambushes were deployed; and the Mortar Platoon or 104 Field Battery fired harassing and interdiction missions. The aim of this aggressive defence was to keep the enemy off balance and on the move, and to make it impossible for them to get close enough to launch either a ground attack or an attack by fire.

After a day's searching for the enemy, rifle companies occupied a night defensive position (NDP), either as a complete concentrated sub-unit or as individual platoons. The purpose of the NDP was to provide the company and its platoons with a secure area in which to spend the hours of darkness, and within which they could eat and sleep. But whatever area was chosen it had to be put into a state of defence, because in effect it also became an ambush position, into which an enemy force, moving by night, might walk.

As has already been explained, the rifle companies tended to search with two platoons moving relatively independently of CHQ, with the third platoon and CHQ either moving together or almost so. Therefore it was also normal practice for the company to occupy NDPs based on those groupings.

There were no set timings for moving into an NDP. They might be occupied at any time in the late afternoon, from 1600hr until after dark. And in fact most OCs preferred to vary the times of occupation in order to avoid any suggestion of routine, which might become complacency and then carelessness. But most OCs and platoon commanders were very conscious of the fact that after a hard day's work their men needed the opportunity for a hot meal, and it made most sense that it should be the evening meal. Therefore depending on the enemy threat, a platoon might halt for an hour at, say, 1600hr and carry out the long-halt procedure, which might take 10 to 20 minutes. Once secure, a meal could be prepared and eaten, weapons cleaned and other routine tasks completed. After a specified length of time, the platoon might saddle-up again and continue searching for perhaps another hour. It would then be getting on towards dusk, and the platoon commander would give the order to 'harbour'.

Alternatively the platoon might put in its NDP an hour or so before last light, cook and eat, and then stand-to, and remain in that location for the rest of the night. Occasionally platoons might stop to eat just before last light, and put in an NDP in the dark. Sometimes this was forced on them by tactical necessity or enemy activity. But most commanders regarded it as unnecessarily risky, because an NDP that was occupied in the dark was never as well coordinated as one put in during daylight, and was therefore less secure.

It was always preferable to get CHQ into an NDP with plenty of daylight remaining because there was much to be done before dark. If radio communications to the Battalion CP were difficult, it would be necessary to put up a 292 aerial. The OC needed to prepare radio orders for the platoons or, alternatively, to find out from the platoon commanders if the day's search had thrown up any leads they might want to follow next day. The grid references of platoon night locations had to be encoded and sent to Battalion HQ, and the FO had to plan a DF for each platoon and CHQ. In addition, the CO would want a report from his company commanders, and to know their intentions for the following day, or he might want to issue orders. It all took time, and it had to be precise. Then, too, the members of CHQ also needed to carry out routine tasks like weapon cleaning and eating. And finally, about 20 minutes before last light, CHQ and the platoons went through the vital procedure of stand-to, which marks the change on active service between day and night. Clearing patrols went out to ensure that no enemy was close. When the clearing patrols were in, every man, with his weapon and equipment, watched the light fade, and listened to the night noises, any of which might indicate the approach of an enemy.

All NDPs had to be sited in such a way that they could repel attack from any direction. 'Depth' and 'mutual support' in defence were the vital principles to be achieved, and the NDPs were always set up so that an enemy attacking from any direction would first have to pass through banks of Claymores, then interlocking machinegun fire, and finally rifle fire. Superimposed on this would be artillery fire, and if the enemy did not pass through that on the way into their attack, they would certainly have to do so on the way out.

The siting, defence and conduct of NDPs in Vietnam raised a number of questions which were never completely resolved. The first concerned the digging of weapon pits, or at least shellscrapes. A weapon pit was six feet long by two feet wide by four feet deep (1.8 m by 0.6 m by 1.2 m), and it was occupied by two soldiers who would fight from it if the NDP was attacked. Even without overhead cover, weapon pits provided effective protection from indirect fire. With OHP in position only a direct hit might cause casualties. The problem was that a hole that size took a lot of digging, even with picks and shovels, and infantrymen on search and destroy operations in Vietnam carried only combat shovels. So even the most energetic pair of soldiers would only just complete a weapon pit in time to fill it in and move on next morning. Clearly it would be a pointless exercise. Shellscrapes were a different matter. Their dimensions were six feet long by two feet wide by eighteen inches deep (1.8 m by 0.6 m by 0.45 m), and they were obviously much quicker and easier to dig. Each afforded one soldier a good degree of cover from direct fire, though not much from indirect.

In either case, weapon pit or shellscrape, the digging made a fair amount of noise, though with practice it was possible to work quietly. Inevitably it was a judgement call by the OC or platoon commander: if you dug shellscrapes you made a noise, so the enemy might find you. But if he did find you, you had a hole to protect you and to fight from. If you didn't dig, the enemy might not find you, but if he did . . . and so on. The permutations are various and, as is usually the case, it came down to the senior man present making the decision. If it didn't work out, he also took responsibility and had to live with the consequences of his decision.

Another decision that company commanders had to make was whether or not to allow the use of hammocks on operations. On the one hand hammocks got men off the ground, and the ground was often inundated by heavy rains and frequented by snakes, scorpions, spiders and other unpleasantnesses. So for physical and psychological comfort, as well as general good health, hammocks made a lot of sense. Moreover, the issue blowup mattress, though generally efficient, tended to squeak loudly under the movement of its occupant at night. Blowups had three independently inflatable tubes, and there was an immutable law pertaining to them: it was always one of the outside tubes which punctured in the night and, unless you were extremely thin, it was impossible to balance on the other two.

But a man in a hammock could be two feet above the ground, whereas a man on a mattress was flush with it, and if he was particularly careful, and put his mattress in a shellscrape, he would be below ground as well. So while a man in a hammock slept better, he was more vulnerable to direct or indirect fire in the first seconds of an attack. Some company commanders in the ANZAC Battalion forbade the use of hammocks because of this added vulnerability. Others believed the comfort factor outweighed the safety considerations. Both arguments were valid.

Hammocks also took some getting used to. Gauging the right tension and obtaining cord of the correct breaking strain were important factors to consider. Not everyone got it right first time, as was evidenced by the intermittent twangs and thumps for a night or two after hammocks came into use. Such occurrences seldom provoked sympathy, particularly when they overtook an officer or the CSM. When that happened the NDP would be filled by the sorts of noises that diggers make when they're trying not to laugh.

Communication between the company commander and his platoon commanders on operations in Vietnam was almost always by radio. This did not mean that CHQ and the platoons were necessarily remote from each other—as we have seen, there was a compelling need for a company to be able to concentrate within 30 minutes. But even if the sub-units were separated by only a few hundred metres it was usually impractical for the OC and his platoon commanders to meet face to face to discuss plans and orders. Indeed the less movement between sub-units the better. First, noise and movement might alert a nearby enemy. Second, it was easy for small groups or individuals to miss each other in thick undergrowth. And third, to go blundering about in potentially hostile country might well cause a friendly clash resulting in own casualties. Therefore it was quicker, easier and safer to just get on the radio and talk.

Great care was exercised when using a radio, nonetheless. It had to be assumed that the enemy had monitoring facilities staffed by English-speaking operators, and therefore orders, intentions, grid references, and any other information that might be of use to the enemy had to be encoded. Pads of codes were issued to all radio operators and commanders and their 2i/cs. These had only a finite life, after which they were destroyed and new sets of codes replaced them. Codes were always classified SECRET, and when not out on operations they had to be accounted for and locked safely away. The loss of even one pad, either through carelessness or enemy action, meant that the whole set, in every unit in the Task Force, had to be withdrawn and destroyed, and a fresh set issued. It was a procedure that was tedious and time consuming and which guaranteed the wrath of the Chief Signals Officer.

Once the complexities of the codes had been mastered, they were used by all members of the ANZAC Battalion with remarkable speed and accuracy. OCs and platoon commanders became adept at passing orders and intentions back and forth rapidly, even though some encoding and decoding might be necessary. Most OCs briefed their platoons for the following day's activities in this way. This system was introduced by the CO, who used it regularly to brief the company commanders quickly and securely.

A platoon commander who was required to ambush a specific location would receive an encoded message from his OC which simply said 'AMBUSH', gave the date and time from/to, and specified the grid reference. This was all that was necessary to enable the platoon commander to plan his ambush from the map and brief his platoon in detail for the task. He could then, using codes, ask the OC for any support he might need. This might be the placement of a silently registered DF for contingency purposes or a request to have a tracker team stood-by for air insertion in case the ambush was sprung and follow-up of the enemy might yield further results. When the platoon commander reached the ambush site, he would carry out a close reconnaissance and either confirm his plan or adjust it as the situation demanded. He might, for example, find a much more promising ambush site elsewhere, and decide to sit on that. All he needed to do in that case was advise the OC in code of the new location and alter the grid reference of the DF task. It was quick, it was simple, and it worked well. But it required good radio communications.

The Battalion's workhorse radio was the ANPRC-25 set, a short-range, man-pack, portable, frequency-modulated receiver/transmitter, which could also be operated from a vehicle or a fixed location. Its frequency coverage in the low band was 30.00–52.95 megacycles, and in the high band 53.00–75.95 megacycles, each of which was spaced 50 kilocycles apart.

The set provided voice communication on all the Battalion and company nets. It was also used by artillery FO's, and it was compatible with sets carried in APCs, tanks and aircraft. Thus it provided great communications flexibility.

The 25-set and its basic ancillary equipment was relatively light, around 14 kilograms with a battery installed. The battery had an average life of about 20 hours when using a 9:1 receive/transmit ratio. It was a very-high-frequency set, which meant it would work well in most operational environments if line of sight between stations could be achieved. At company level this seldom caused a problem, because the sub-units were always close enough to get that line of sight, and a strong signal was usually achieved on a battle-whip or rod antenna. But signal strength and clarity sometimes diminished between the Battalion CP and companies which might be widely dispersed or in dead ground.

Indeed, part of the reason for deploying the Battalion CP to Courtenay Hill was its relative height above most of Phuoc Tuy Province. High-gain 292 aerials on telescopic masts achieved added height, and thence clearer communications. However helicopter pilots were seen to age visibly when trying to land on Courtenay Hill LP, which was surrounded by eleven of these aerials.

The rifle companies also carried the basic 292 aerial, but with none of its lavish accessories and telescopic masts, which were too heavy and cumbersome to be carried in a man-pack role. Instead, the 292 was suspended from a suitable branch of a convenient tree. This was done by throwing a nylon line over the branch and hauling the assembly into the air. But it was never as easy to do as it might sound. The nylon line was connected to a metal weight called a bobbin, which was somewhat longer than a thick pencil. The bobbin had probably been designed by a staff officer, because while it was very useful as a winder for the line, its ballistic properties were hopeless, and it seldom, if ever, hit its target or indeed went anywhere near it. In one rifle company the problem was solved by substituting the bobbin with an unopened 200-gram ration tin, which proved to be a more accurately thrown missile. However it was not always possible to retrieve the tin afterwards, and its owner might be faced with the depressing sight of his now unreachable evening meal swinging gently in the breeze.

The fact that young platoon commanders and their NCOs regularly operated in comparative isolation from their OCs demanded a high degree of mutual trust, a fact that reinforced Maj Hogarth's wise axiom of giving subordinates the freedom to fail in training. That was what training was for. The training area was the place where ideas were first floated and then tried. If they worked they would be salted away and recalled for use later on active service. If they didn't work, no matter: there was always another day and a better idea. For this reason company commanders who demanded immediate perfection in training were their own worst enemies, because they so intimidated their subordinates that they subdued their natural dash and initiative, which might not reappear when it was most needed. The point of training for war was not simply to perfect systems and techniques. It was also to give young commanders room to develop, and to enable the CO and the OCs to assess their subordinates' quality and reliability. The corollary was that when this had been done, the company commander knew which of his officers and NCOs he could trust to get the job done well. And if he couldn't trust them, there was still time to sack them before they became a liability and replace them with men who could be trusted.

OC B Company, Maj Bob Hogarth, had already served in Borneo with 3RAR in 1965 and Vietnam with 2RAR in 1967–68. He believed strongly that subordinates should be allowed 'the freedom to fail' in training.
(Courtesy LtCol Hogarth)

Moreover, when an OC trusted his people completely he could let them get on with their jobs without the need to drive them or constantly look over their shoulders.

Most experienced trainers of infantrymen of all ranks would agree with Maj Hogarth when he says:

> I would like to think that I tried to provide an environment in which my very able subordinates could achieve their considerable potential. I tried to limit my involvement to directing what was to be done rather than how it was to be done. I also thought I should equip everyone with the essential skills to do their job. I do recall thinking that as one of the last battalions to be prepared for service in Vietnam we ought to be extremely well prepared, given the experience we had as an army and the experience we had in the company.[1]

So the training in Australia and Singapore/Malaysia progressed. Mistakes were made, at first many mistakes. But each time a drill or technique was practised a few more wrinkles were ironed out. Then fewer mistakes were made, and each separate technique became slicker and more automatic in its conduct, but without ever becoming mindless. OCs and CSMs and platoon sergeants were finding less to criticise, more to praise. There was still work to be done, but everything was going to schedule.

What remained now was to learn the use of, and the problems associated with, supporting arms.

7

United we stand

If the Royal Australian Regiment made demands on its officers and men in 1970–71, it made equally heavy demands on their wives. Some of the more mature and experienced wives tended to be philosophical about the amount of time their husbands spent away from home. Many of them had already survived prolonged separations during the Malayan Emergency and Confrontation and the Battalion's first tour in Vietnam. Having a house to run, and children to be cared for, tended to take their minds off the ominous approach of active service and the exacting preparations leading up to it.

But a newly married young woman had neither of these distractions, and sometimes no idea that her husband's profession would make so many demands on them both: demands which, in the end, not every marriage could withstand. She may not have anticipated these pressures or not heeded the warnings that her soldier husband had tried to give her. She may just have thought that he was exaggerating, and that it would all be all right in the end. But now she was in Townsville, and Townsville possessed none of the comforting bustle of the Melbourne streets or the luminous greens of the Tasmania she was used to. The family that she had grown up in, and which she might now have left for the first time in her life, was hundreds of kilometres away to the south. She could phone or write, but it wasn't the same.

Some wives had worked before getting married, and that had filled and regulated their days. And if they lived with their families they could go home each evening to their nurturing warmth. But here in Townsville jobs were difficult to find. Not unnaturally, employers preferred to engage local women, and there was also a reluctance to employ army wives who, it was assumed, would leave in a couple of years to go south again when their husbands were reposted. The younger wives particularly felt the strangeness and isolation of the Townsville environment, which could be exacerbated if they were not entitled to army quarters and had to live among a busy and sometimes unsympathetic civilian community. Jobless, with perhaps no children, and their husbands frequently away on exercises, their days could be very long and lonely.

And from time to time most wives experienced the sombre imaginings that accompanied the preparations for active service. Vietnam was the television war: the battle which raged there in the morning was on everyone's screen that evening in Australia. Everyone had seen the appalling images of Tet which had done so much to polarise public opinion against the war. There was frequent footage of the whirling Dustoff helicopters to remind wives of what might lie ahead. And everyone knew about the army car which might one day draw up at the house, and the padre and another officer, and perhaps another of the Battalion's wives, coming up the path, their faces grim with the news they brought.

All of this was anticipated and understood by the more experienced army wives—they had been through it all before. It was also understood that wives need not suffer this anguish alone. If the preparations for Vietnam affected all wives to a greater or lesser degree, those wives could close ranks and form a support group to confront the difficulties that lay ahead. So most Vietnam-bound units formed wives' clubs or ladies' auxiliaries. There had been such a club during 4RAR's first tour in Vietnam, and it had proved its worth then. Therefore Jan Hughes and Judy Thompson, the CO's and RSM's wives, set about re-establishing it now.

The club's aims were to provide a point of regular contact for the Battalion's wives, mothers and families, regardless of rank, and to arrange and conduct activities which would help them 'To feel relaxed, comfortable and united'.[1] Squash and tennis mornings, buffet lunches, swimming and athletics carnivals, a range of guest speakers and even a hypnotist were some of the activities which provided distractions outside the home. This also ensured that any wife who was not handling the pressure satisfactorily could be quickly identified, and encouraged and helped by her peers. Usually it was a matter of a problem shared being a problem solved, but help was also available for those experiencing more profound emotional or financial difficulties. Trained and qualified counsellors were on hand to all units in 3 Task Force and to the wives as well. And within 4RAR, regimental funds provided limited financial assistance to those few who were having difficulty making both ends meet. Regimental funds also supported major club activities, and WO2 Ploenges and his cooks conjured up morning and afternoon teas and buffet lunches.

Capt Bob Sayce and his wife Margie arrive for the Battalion Ball at the Lavarack Barracks Theatre in 1970. One of his 'extra-regimental' tasks as Intelligence Officer was to find partners for all the unattached Diggers attending the Ball. (Courtesy Col Sayce)

The impetus for all these activities came from the club's elected committee, consisting of a president, a vice-president, a secretary and a treasurer. Other committee members were co-opted as required, most often for major activities like the children's Christmas party. In 4RAR's case it was decided that Jan Hughes and Judith Thompson should head the committee as president and vice-president. This ensured that a wife who needed emotional or financial support could receive it quickly and with a high degree of confidentiality. Christine Upton was secretary, and 'Tini' McKinly was the treasurer.

Committee meetings were held at Jan Hughes' house on a monthly basis, or more often if a major activity was upcoming. Besides planning and organising the various activities and entertainments the committee also produced and hand-delivered a newsletter, and visited the wives of men newly posted into the Battalion.

It's an old military axiom that a happy wife makes for a happy soldier, although 'happy' is probably a relative term when applied to the women who had to endure the lonely months before and during the Vietnam separation. But those pressures were undoubtedly alleviated for many by the friendships and common bonds which grew up within the 4RAR Wives' Club. And the married men serving in Vietnam found comfort in the knowledge that their wives and families were by no means alone in Australia. That sense of comfort was yet another contributing ingredient in the Battalion's success.

The pace was quickening. By August 1970 the Battalion was almost fully manned, though there were still a few establishment positions which had to be filled or refilled because a previous incumbent had been reposted. Capt Keating, the adjutant, left to become an ADC, and his place was taken by Capt Don McKenzie. Capt John McAloney, MC, who had been decorated as the Assault Pioneer Platoon commander in 5RAR, took over Support Company.

But not everyone who was posted in got quite what they expected. The new OC Admin Company recalls that:

> When I got my posting order for 4RAR I made the assumption that I would be a rifle company commander. There was no logical reason why I should have made that assumption, but I did anyway. I wanted a rifle company; I was qualified to have one; I'd spent months preparing myself physically for one; so obviously I was going to get one.
>
> Imagine my horror, then, on reporting myself to Colonel Jim in his office that first morning in August 1970, when he told me I was going to be OC Administration Company. Now even as a nineteen-year-old second lieutenant in the British Army, I had gained the perception that Admin Company was always given to the oldest and most pear-shaped major in the battalion. Now I was going to be one. Me! For the next two years I would spend my days signing requisitions for socks, and worrying because the clerks had run out of paper clips, and trying to pacify the diggers because the cooks had burnt the sausages.
>
> My mind reeling, I lurched out into the morning sunshine, to be met by Captain Chris Babington, who like me, was an ex-Pom, and currently acting-OC Admin Company. I tried to make polite conversation with him, but really all I wanted to do was bang my head on the ground and scream.
>
> I don't remember much about that first month in the Battalion, but at the end of it I went to see the CO. I reminded him that I had been promoted to temporary major for this posting. I told him that I would be happy to revert to captain again if he would let me go as the 2i/c of a rifle company, *any* rifle company.
>
> The CO was damned angry about this suggestion, as well he might have been. His eyes turned to granite, and his authoritative nose lined me up like the barrel of a loaded M60. In fact ever since that day I've known exactly what a mouse must feel like half a second before a large eagle lands on it.

I can't remember what words he used, but whatever they were they left me in no doubt as to where my duty lay. I was to stop whingeing, get off my arse, and start doing the job I was paid for. However towards the end of this uncomfortable interview he said that if ever the command of a rifle company became vacant, he would give it to me.

I left his office feeling very small indeed, not least because he was absolutely right. Anyway, when I realised I couldn't escape, and had thought it through, the only option was to get stuck in, and I decided to make this Admin Company the best in the Regiment. And indeed by the time I left the Company in July 1971, I had completely changed my mind about the job. I can honestly say that my posting to Admin Company 4RAR was among the most challenging and rewarding, and therefore one of the happiest, of my career.

I was extremely fortunate to have WO2 Denny Cook as my CSM. Like me he was a Pom, so we understood each other right from day one. I liked Denny very much as a man, and admired his professionalism and ability as a soldier. He never had any hesitation about coming and telling me if I was getting off track. There would be a tap on my door, and Denny would say, 'Have you got a moment, sir?' very politely but in a way that meant I *did* have a moment. I always emerged from these sessions not much older but a great deal wiser. Much of what was eventually achieved by all of us in Admin Company was directly attributable to WO Cook's wise counsel.[2]

As planned, all individual training within the rifle, and Administration, companies had been completed by the end of June. By the end of August, section, platoon and company training was reaching a satisfactory standard too. The philosophy that all members of Admin Company were infantrymen first, and specialists second, was paying dividends. The Echelon elements of Admin deployed to the field whenever possible, and were now capable of supplying the Battalion and maintaining its own security at the same time. But a good deal of work still needed to be done in polishing the use of the administrative/air net for resupply to the companies.

The platoons of Support Company were also rounding out their specialist skills, and this process gained valuable momentum when the Battalion was ordered to assist 25 Royal Queensland Regiment, a CMF battalion, in the training of its support company in Rockhampton. Also in August, the first of many fire support bases, FSB Flintstone, was constructed by the Battalion and 104 Field Battery.

Each Monday morning B, C and D Company departed for the High Range or Mount Spec training areas, there to continue practising and polishing and testing and perfecting. The advance to contact, searching, navigating, attacking bunkers and camps, defending and withdrawing, contact front, contact left, contact right, contact rear; all the skills and techniques over and over again until the words and the actions became second nature in heat and dust, and rain and mud, by day and night, and always under the infantryman's load of weapons, equipment and fatigue.

Section commanders continued to be demanding of their men, because if they couldn't get it right here in Australia they'd get it wrong in Vietnam, and there was a very high price to pay for mistakes in Vietnam. Platoon commanders and their sergeants were equally demanding, and above them the OC and the CSM watched with critical gaze, assisting and cajoling, admonishing shoddy work and praising good, checking and triple-checking and then checking again. And when at last everyone got it right every time, the CO and the OPSO and the RSM would arrive, and they were not men who were easily satisfied either.

And now, in these last few months, the Battalion had to learn to work with the supporting arms that they would rely on so heavily in Phuoc Tuy Province: artillery, air, APCs and tanks.

The first steps the Battalion took towards working with supporting arms were hesitant and uncertain. But they need not have been, because 4RAR soon experienced the very high level of commitment they were to receive from 104 Battery 12 Field Regiment RAA, from 3 Cavalry Regiment RAAC, from the Engineers, and from the pilots of the Australian Army Aviation Corps. This commitment was as unstinting in training as it was later in Vietnam.

104 Battery 12 Field Regiment RAA had been 4RAR's direct support battery throughout the first tour in Vietnam, and the Battalion was particularly pleased that the association would continue for the second tour. The battery commander was Maj Keith Towning; the battery captain was Capt Neil Graham; and the battery sergeant major was WO2 Max Vandyke.

The battery's six guns were 105mm M2A2 Gun Howitzers; their maximum range was 15 000 metres; and their best fighting range was 9000–10 000 metres. Maj Towning observed: 'The M2A2 was considered to be a very good gun. Its strong points were a good extreme range and from my experience the accuracy did not go off much with longer ranges. The ability to fire in the upper register was also an advantage. I suppose the worst feature was its weight.'[3]

There was an unbending Task Force rule which stipulated that ground troops must conduct their operations within range of the guns, which in the case of the M2A2 obviously meant within 15 000 metres of the gun positions. The principle itself was very sound, because

Australian and New Zealand infantry relied heavily on field artillery. Almost invariably in the ANZAC Battalion, fire was brought down instantly onto contact areas, and the enemy hated it. In 1993, when a D Company reunion group returned to Phuoc Tuy while Gary McKay gathered material for his book *Delta Four*, Mr Tran Tan Huy, the Chairman of the Peoples' Committee of Long Dat District and an ex-CO of D445, said:

> During the war times I served with many units in the Long Dat District especially I took part in many battles against the Australian Forces. Australian soldiers like to fight in the jungle, fight very bravely to fight against us. Hard tactics to fight against. The strengths of the Australians was always to use artillery and planes. They fought as the same as like our guerrillas against our guerrillas, especially the Australian soldiers, they were industrious and hard, fight hard.
>
> And he concluded: Australians are the strongest when we are in contact with you and you fire the guns.[4]

But artillery must be in range if it is to be employed, so a system of fire bases was used to support operations in depth. This meant that after a commander had been assigned his AO, he and his senior artillery adviser selected a location, from the map and by air reconnaissance, from which the guns could cover the AO. The use of the guns from FSBs gave senior commanders great flexibility of operation, and enabled them to penetrate into any part of the province even though the guns themselves were of limited range.

But the deployment of FSBs was not without its risks. An FSB containing a battery of field artillery had to be heavily defended, so that the guns could continue to fire even if they came under ground attack. This meant that the supported unit had to supply troops and often armoured fighting vehicles to defend FSBs. It was a trade-off: you needed the guns to support your infantry. To do this the guns had to be deployed into FSBs, and they in turn had to be defended. Therefore there were fewer troops to search and manoeuvre. But it was undoubtedly a fair swap.

Each of the rifle companies was assigned a permanent forward observer (FO). He was a specially trained artillery lieutenant or captain who, on operations, lived and moved with the company. He was the OC's artillery adviser, and he was also responsible for planning the use of, and calling in, artillery or mortar fire and correcting the fall of shot. He was assisted in these tasks by the FO party, which typically consisted of a bombardier (an artillery corporal) and a signaller. All were trained and capable of calling for fire and correcting the fall of shot.

Company commanders soon learned that they could not use artillery and air support at the same time, because not surprisingly pilots were reluctant to fly through their own artillery fire. Just what the chances were of an aircraft being hit by friendly indirect fire is not known, but it had happened to the Americans. If a company commander did want to use both artillery and air, he would first use artillery while the aircraft were called up and came on station. The guns would then check fire (stop firing) while the aircraft applied their ordnance to the target. When they had done so they went off station, and the guns continued firing. This meant that ground troops in contact had access to almost continuous close support.

Under some circumstances a company commander might have to choose between artillery and air. Most chose artillery. This was because, in contact, the OC usually had his FO lying alongside him and could tell him exactly what effect he wanted the guns to achieve on the target. Usually the time delay between calling for fire until the first rounds were on their way was about two minutes. Thereafter the fall of shot could be moved around as the enemy manoeuvred, or fresh targets could be engaged as they appeared.

104 Battery's response time in Vietnam was always very fast; usually the only factor which might slow that response was the necessity to acquire ground and air clearances from Arty Tac at Nui Dat. These clearances were vital to ensure that the guns did not fire into an area occupied by friendly troops, and that aircraft were clear of the trajectory of the shells.

Calls for fire could be made even if a trained observer was not present. Any hard-pressed platoon or section commander could contact the guns over the radio, tell them his location, tell them the enemy's location, and ask for fire to be brought down. Thereafter he could simply send corrections of 'go left or go right', or 'add or drop', and the plotters in the gun position did the rest. It was infantry/artillery cooperation at its optimum.

Helicopter gunships took much longer to respond, even if they were airborne and in the vicinity of a contact. Fighter ground-attack aircraft (FGA) took even longer. Moreover, the use of fighter aircraft meant that the ground commander had to be content with whatever ordnance the planes were carrying at that moment, which might not be particularly suitable against the target to be engaged. To change a bomb load to suit a target took time, and in battle time is always at a premium. In addition, some aircraft ordnance, such as 500-pound bombs, for safety reasons required ground troops to be 300 metres away from the impact point, which meant that before hard bombs could be used it was necessary to withdraw. Troops in contact were always reluctant to withdraw, because the enemy knew that the best way to avoid casualties from artillery or air-delivered ordinance was to stay close to the opposition. Withdrawal is never an easy manoeuvre, and it becomes even more difficult in close country, particularly when the enemy has a vested interest in staying with you.

The use of gunships or FGA required troops in contact to mark their positions precisely and continuously, and that was most often done with smoke grenades. This could become a nightmare under a thick canopy, because the smoke might not get up through the foliage, might disperse widely, or might drift back over the friendly position. However once the airborne forward air controller (FAC) had clearly identified the friendly position, he would mark the enemy location by firing white phosphorus marker rockets at it. He would then talk the fighters or gunships onto the target and give the pilots corrections for their point of aim. But it all took time.

So there were considerable advantages in selecting guns over air. These advantages were: the guns' rapid initial response to calls for fire; the speed and accuracy with which the fall of shot could be adjusted; the fact that supported troops did not have to move before fire could be brought down; the fact that fire could be 'walked in' to within 50 metres of supported troops without causing own casualties; and the fact that artillery shell fuses could be altered in a few seconds to get the best effects from the rounds on specific targets. These advantages, for most commanders at company level, tended to make guns the weapon of choice in most contacts.

Air support for the ANZAC Battalion in Vietnam would be of several different kinds. 161 Independent Recce Flight, Australian Army Aviation, flew both light observation helicopters and fixed wing aircraft. Initially the helicopter was the Bell Sioux, which was replaced in 1971 by the Bell 206B Kiowa. The fixed wing aircraft was the Pilatus PC-6 Turbo Porter.

The helicopter was obviously the more versatile of the two because it could take off and land wherever there was a small cleared space. The CO would be allotted a Kiowa as his direct support aircraft on a continuous basis. It would be used extensively for command and control, reconnaissance, as a rebroadcast station if radio communications became uncertain, and for various liaison tasks. It also enabled the CO to visit his commanders in the field when the tactical situation permitted, or to give them moral support and assistance from the air during a contact. All Aviation Corps pilots were trained to correct artillery fire while flying their aircraft.

The pilots were remarkable young men. There was always a swashbuckling aspect about them, heightened by their sky blue berets, the Aviation Corps wings surmounted by the crowned lion on their breast, and the inevitable 9mm pistol, worn, for convenience sake, in a shoulder holster. They were invariably cheerful, and no task was ever too difficult or too much trouble. And they were, besides, immensely courageous.

American air support would also be available to the ANZAC Battalion in Phuoc Tuy, usually in the form of helicopter gunships, fighter ground-attack aircraft and Dustoff casualty evacuation helicopters.

In 1971 the Americans used the Cobra helicopter gunship. It had a crew of two, and the gunner sat behind and slightly above the pilot. Its principal weapons were rockets and miniguns, the latter having a cyclic rate of fire of 6000 rounds a minute.

Cobras worked in fire teams. A light fire team was two aircraft; a heavy fire team, three. Sometimes they deployed a Pink Team, which normally consisted of a light fire team accompanied by a Cayuse light observation helicopter (LOH). While the Cobras cruised 'high and dry' at 3000 feet, the LOH meandered slowly at treetop level. It was not unusual to see the observer in the LOH with his legs dangling out of the door, and an M60 laid across his knees, perhaps nonchalantly smoking a large cigar. This studied insolence was a challenge, and when it was taken up by the enemy, which it usually was, the Cobras would pinpoint the incoming fire and descend with shattering effect onto their position. The ANZAC Battalion loved Pink Teams.

The United States Air Force provided fighter ground-attack aircraft, usually Broncos, Phantoms or Super Sabres. Their armament was miniguns, rockets, hard bombs and napalm. FGA response time varied, but once they were on station, pilots went to remarkable lengths to give good service, just as the gunship teams did.

FACs could be air force or navy pilots who had flown fighters themselves. In the FAC role they flew the light, slow, high-winged Cessna 01 Bird Dog observation plane, and they were not only totally dedicated men but also extremely skilful flyers. And because the enemy understood very well what the arrival of a Bird Dog overhead implied, FACs were almost always subjected to fierce ground fire.

American Dustoff crews frequently flew on behalf of the Task Force throughout its tenure in Phuoc Tuy, and the ANZAC Battalion, too, would benefit from their dedication and courage. Their level of commitment was outstanding, and they took enormous risks to pluck wounded men from a contact area and get them to hospital. Indeed it was not unheard of for a wounded man to be on the operating table at 8 Field Ambulance in Vung Tau, or at some other specialist hospital, within 30 minutes of being hit.

9 Squadron RAAF, flying UH-1H Iroquois helicopters, would provide the Battalion with a troop-lift and cargo capability and gunships, armed with miniguns, rockets and pintle-mounted M60s operated by door-gunners. The squadron also flew Dustoff helicopters.

In Vietnam, 1 Field Squadron RAE allotted two-man splinter teams, consisting of a corporal and a sapper, to each company on a permanent basis. These men were highly trained and skilful combat engineers, and their tasks included the disarming of booby traps, the lifting and neutralising of anti-personnel and anti-tank mines, and demolitions of all kinds, including enemy bunkers and installations, stores and equipment, and unexploded ordnance. The corporal was the OC's adviser on all technical engineer matters.

It was the role of engineers 'to fight as infantry when required', and the splinter teams took to their task of accompanying their assigned rifle companies into battle with great enthusiasm. In fact on one occasion, Cpl Len Smith, D Company's splinter team leader, was heard to remark that if he'd known that being an infantryman was so much fun, he'd have been one years ago. Like their comrades in the other Arms, the men of the splinter teams always served the ANZAC Battalion with loyalty and dedication.

Armoured personnel carriers (APCs) were used extensively in Phuoc Tuy Province, and they proved time and again how versatile a fighting vehicle they could be, even in country that many considered unsuitable for armour.

The work-horse was the M113A1 APC, which could carry a section of fully equipped infantrymen and provide them with some degree of protection against small arms fire and shell fragments. The ANZAC Battalion would use them frequently for such tasks as troop lift, convoy escort, resupply and casualty evacuation, as well as for defence tasks in and around FSBs and the Battalion CP on Courtenay Hill. The 'tracks', as the vehicles and their crews were affectionately known, also turned their hands to ambushing, and they achieved some remarkable results. They could also form part of a cordon for village search, or part of a blocking force round suspected enemy bunkers or camps. Whenever circumstances permitted they supported attacking troops and tanks with fire and manoeuvre.

APCs were normally armed with 30-calibre or 50-calibre machine-guns. The Fire Support Vehicle mounted a 76mm gun in a Saladin turret on the standard chassis. Armoured Command Vehicles were used

A Fire Support Vehicle similar to those used by A Squadron 3 Cavalry Regiment. The 76mm gun and coaxial machine-gun were mounted in a Saladin turret.

as mobile command posts; specially equipped mortar-carrying M113s gave the Mortar Platoon both mobility and protection, and enabled the mortars to be fired from inside the vehicles when halted.

The worth of the tracks had been demonstrated early in Phuoc Tuy Province at the battle of Long Tan, when their timely intervention, dash and courage had played a significant part in assisting the beleaguered D Company 6RAR, and their supporting artillery, to inflict a crushing defeat on the enemy. The part played by the APCs at Long Tan was in the best traditions of the RAAC, and it set the standard for all the armoured crews thereafter.

Perhaps one of the few criticisms that could be levelled at the preparations for Vietnam is that there was no opportunity for 4RAR to train in Australia with tanks. Only very few members of the Battalion had ever worked with them, a deficiency which may in part have stemmed from suggestions that tanks were unsuited to the Vietnam battlefield, and that infantry and tanks were unlikely to work together in Phuoc Tuy. In addition, 1 Armoured Regiment's home was at Puckapunyal in southern Victoria, and was therefore too far away for accessible tank/infantry cooperation training. It was a shortfall, but not a disastrous one, and when the time came for the Battalion to work with the Centurions of

A Centurion tank. Used by C Squadron 1 Armoured Regiment in South Vietnam, they were the decisive weapon in bunker battles.

C Squadron 1 Armoured Regiment in battle, the crews always went to considerable lengths to 'make it work'.

The tank in service in 1971 was the British designed and built Centurion Mk V/1. It weighed 54 tonnes and had a top speed of 35kmh in open country. The armour around the hull was 125mm thick, while that around the turret was 154mm. The tank's armament included a 20-pounder gun mounted in the fully rotating turret; one 50-calibre and two 30-calibre machineguns; and six smoke dischargers in two sets of three on either side of the turret. The Centurion had a four-man crew: commander, driver, gunner and radio operator/gun loader. It was a fine old warrior, versatile and resilient, and it could negotiate most of the country to be found in Phuoc Tuy, even if it meant doing so at snail's pace. In thick country tanks needed close infantry support to protect them from enemy tank-hunting parties. Care had to be taken to ensure that the infantrymen were close enough to the vehicles to provide this protection, but not so close that they might be injured or killed by falling trees and timber. But it was in bunker assaults that the Centurions really earned their laurels, and how they did so for the ANZAC Battalion is described in a later chapter.

The bond of professional respect and affection which grew up in 1971 between the Battalion and 104 Battery, A Squadron, C Squadron, the splinter teams of 1 Field Squadron, the pilots of 161 Recce Flight and their American comrades, would become one of the enduring high points of the Battalion's second tour in Vietnam. And the commitment and cooperation between the men of these fighting Arms in Vietnam may well have provided the Australian Army with one of its finest hours.

It was October 1970, and looming on the horizon was the Sub-Unit Course at Canungra. This would be the first big test of the Battalion's professionalism, when everyone, from the CO to the youngest private soldier, would be put under the microscope. There would be some uncomfortable interviews after Canungra, because whatever deficiencies were identified by the JTC staff, who applied their own exacting standards, would have only four months more to be rectified.

As one company commander recalls:

> We went to Canungra towards the end of training for Vietnam, and it provided a very useful tool in the preparation cycle. It allowed battalion and company commanders to step back and assess not only the standard of training they had achieved, but also the quality of their junior leaders. I'm sure a study of the records would show that several commanders, at all levels, were correctly revealed as being unsuitable for active service by their performance at Canungra. It's also human nature for commanders to take their own pace when training their soldiers. Canungra therefore provided an opportunity to judge their sub-units against outside, and sometimes more critical, standards.
>
> My understanding was that Canungra also carried out constant combat analysis on after action reports from Vietnam. These lessons learned were incorporated into the training programme, so that new operational trends could be prepared for in Australia.
>
> However when I went through Canungra before my first tour, we were still feeling our way into properly preparing units for Vietnam. At that stage JTC was a nightmare to go through. My recollection is that Battle Ridge was run like a penal camp for the Hitler Youth. Many instructors of all ranks strutted about hurling unrelieved abuse, but otherwise making little real contribution to the preparation of units for war. I'm sure that many people gave up trying after a while because no matter what they did they'd always be wrong. Maybe the management saw that as a toughening experience before battle. In my view, though, the management was wildly off track.
>
> But by 1970, when I went through again with 4RAR, an entirely different atmosphere pervaded JTC. If anything the Sub-Unit Course was physically more demanding. The standards to be achieved were certainly much higher. But the instructors left no doubt in anyone's mind that they

> were there to help, and that we would be given every possible assistance to sharpen our fighting edge.
>
> Each company and platoon were allotted officer, warrant officer, sergeant and corporal instructors/assessors. They were very demanding of us, as they should have been. But they were also very helpful and constructive, and they played a much-appreciated role in our final preparations.
>
> The last assessment exercise took place in the Wiangaree State Forest, just over the border in NSW. During the retreat in Burma, General Slim had once tried to cheer his staff up by saying that 'Things could be worse: it could be raining'. Well at Wiangaree things could never be worse, because it was always raining. In 1967 when I went through with B Company 2RAR it was raining. In 1970, when I went through with Admin Company it was *still* raining. Even with a fridge full of beer and a dozen Swedish nymphets, Wiangaree would have to be the most horrible place on earth.[5]

So in October and November all 4RAR's companies passed beneath Battle Wing's critical gaze. And Admin Company was permitted to set aside its specialist role of maintaining the Battalion, and passed in its own right through the crucible of JTC, becoming the only administration company to have done so in the Vietnam years.

It was a gruellingly thorough course, but at the end of it almost every individual, and all sub-units of the Battalion, came through and was well reported on. Afterwards a copy of the battle wing aide-memoire was sent to the CO. He had it reproduced and issued in quantity to the companies with his own foreword, which said:

> The JTC period of training has been invaluable in that an unbiased group of DS have patiently examined our individual and collective skills and provided constructive criticism. The need for battle discipline, and therefore self-discipline, cannot be debated. To avoid any regression in training, this Aide-Memoire is issued to all officers and NCOs.[6]

It was a painstakingly detailed document running to 38 closely typed pages, and it specified every individual and collective immediate action drill, system and procedure that one man or sections, platoons and companies would need to live, fight and survive in Vietnam. In short, it reinforced and rounded out everything the Battalion had learned and practised over the last ten grinding months. And it restated the standards yet to be achieved in the last test exercises before the Battalion left for Vietnam.

But by now it was the end of the first week in December, and the Battalion went on annual leave.

By January 1971 there was a new sense of excitement throughout 4RAR, and perhaps, too, just a slight tightening of the stomach. Vietnam was no longer 'next year'—Vietnam was four months away.

The last of the new postings-in had occurred. Maj Ted Stevenson had arrived from RAAF Staff College to replace the newly promoted LtCol Reg Pollard as OPSO. And Maj Don McIver had arrived from New Zealand to take up his duties as Battalion second-in-command. He remembers that:

> I was accepted in a very positive way by 4RAR and I felt I fitted into the team quickly. After the final training and exercises with the Battalion in Townsville I was quite comfortable with the role. I took over all the duties of an operational 2i/c. For example I deployed as 2i/c on all exercises after my arrival and my predecessor (Maj Keith Houley) stayed in base. I did not become involved in the detailed planning for the deployment to SVN on HMAS *Sydney* even though I eventually became CO Troops on board. Nor did I assume responsibility for formal disciplinary procedures or home base administration.[7]

The final exercises began, and everyone discovered that the first challenge was to regain the physical condition lost during Christmas leave. But Exercise Granite Vale quickly saw to that. It also revealed another significant deficiency: the Battalion still needed to smarten up its use of the administrative/air net. The first attempts to have the Battalion resupply requirements sent over the 'admin/air' net, as they would be in Vietnam, brought the AQ cell, the company 2i/cs and the Regimental Signals Officer to the brink of nervous breakdown. The net was clogged for hours with maintenance demands being read back and re-read, only to be amended again at the last moment, while CQMSs fumed and sweated getting everything prepared and packed for delivery.

The method of combat resupply to sub-units of the ANZAC Battalion was one of those systems which had evolved over time in Vietnam to meet the necessities of jungle warfare and its constant tempo of operations. It was a procedure that, once understood and perfected, was simple, efficient and responsive. It was also pivotal to keeping the companies in the field and operating efficiently for 30 days out of 35.

Companies were normally informed by radio, about 48 hours in advance, of the date and time of their next resupply. The company commander would then select a suitable resupply location within his AO, either from the map or from local knowledge. If this location was in the general direction of the company's advance, so much the better. If not, the OC adjusted his search pattern so that the company arrived at the resupply location an hour or so before delivery time.

If the resupply was to be by helicopter, the resup point would be a clearing large enough to allow the aircraft to land and discharge their cargo. If it was to be delivered by APC, almost any area would do, although one where the going was not too thick was preferable. In either case, the company was required to secure the area so that it did not come under attack during the procedure.

As soon as the platoons were notified of resup day, the section 2i/cs asked each man what items of clothing or equipment he needed. For example, a dented SLR magazine might have to be exchanged, or a new pair of bootlaces acquired. When the section 2i/c was certain that his list was complete, he handed it to the platoon sergeant, who would then consolidate all the section lists and add platoon HQ's requirements as well. He would also carefully check the platoon's strength state to ensure it was exact. It was from that figure that the CQMS in Nui Dat made all his calculations for rations, water and other necessaries.

The platoon sergeants then passed on their consolidated lists and strength states to the company 2i/c, often by radio. He in turn added the CHQ requirements and strength state, and then sat down to prepare a consolidated 'maintdem'.

There were three categories of resupply in Vietnam. A scheduled resupply was known as a maintenance demand or maintdem, and they occurred as a matter of routine, usually every five days. However, if between maintdems the sole of a man's boot came away from its upper, or a platoon sergeant found that his entire stock of Paludrine anti-malarial tablets was water-damaged, those or similar items could be replaced by submitting a priority maintenance demand, or primaintdem. The overall number of primaintdems was small, and because they concerned only individual items were fairly easy to satisfy. The CO's Possum would fly over the company or platoon location and the new boots or Paludrine tablets, packed in a sandbag, could be conveniently dropped from treetop height.

The third and most immediate category of resupply was the operational demand, or opdem, whose purpose was to replenish those items without which a sub-unit could not fight. So immediately after a contact it was vital to replenish ammunition stocks and replace any damaged weapon or part. Therefore whenever an opdem was submitted it was instantly actioned. It must be emphasised, however, that there were occasions when it was essential for ammunition to be replenished during a battle, and this was achieved by the quickest expedient means. 1ATF's history is replete with instances in which helicopter pilots and APC crews put themselves in positions of considerable danger to bring more ammunition to hard-pressed infantryman.

When preparing the maintdem, the company 2i/c used a commodity code. This was not a security code, as its purpose was not to conceal activities or intentions from the enemy. It was a kind of shorthand, which both minimised the likelihood of error in transmitting the maintdem over the radio net, and also the time taken on air to do so. Company, platoon and section commanders and their 2i/cs all carried copies of these commodity codes. Every item of clothing and equipment available in the Battalion was assigned a letter or series of letters and/or numbers. For example, a pair of GP boots size 6 medium might be 'A', while size 7 medium might be 'AA', and so on. This saved a good deal of writing, and obviously considerable transmission time on the net.

When the company 2i/c was certain that his maintdem was ready to go, he sent it by radio to the AQ cell, where it was processed and then passed to the relevant CQMS in the company lines at Nui Dat. The CQ and his storeman and assistants then gathered the requested items into platoon lots, packed them usually into sandbags, and labelled them with the platoon's number. The CQ would also centralise the combat rations needed by the company for five days. If the total company strength was 100, he needed 500 ration packs. If US C rations were available, and usually they were, the CQ allotted each man two days' C rations and three days' Australian CRPs, or vice versa, making sure as far as possible that the five days' types were all different. The rations were also packed into sandbags, labelled, and placed into platoon lots.

Water normally went out in jerrycans, but if the tactical situation was uncertain, it might be delivered in pre-filled waterbottles. Jerrycans were preferable, because it meant that everyone could fill their waterbottles, have a much-needed guzzle and refill them before the jerrycans were back-loaded. Any remaining items, such as radio batteries, were added to the platoon lots. Finally, wrapped in plastic bags, came the most eagerly awaited commodity of all: mail from home.

On resupply day the CQ and his assistants, using the company Landrover and trailer, took everything down to Eagle Farm, the Battalion's helicopter landing area. Here, still in platoon lots, it was pre-positioned under the watchful eye of Capt Mike Wadsworth, Admin Company's New Zealand 2i/c. He was assisted by Sgt Ian Fryer, who controlled the pad and ensured that each helicopter set down in the right place and in the right order.

Meanwhile, in the area of operations, the company would be tactically disposed around the landing place so that neither the aircraft nor those on the ground could be attacked. When the helicopter flight leader reported that he was inbound, a fluorescent marker panel was placed out in the landing area and securely pegged down to provide the pilot with a visual reference which stood out among the sea of olive-green foliage. When he spotted the marker panel, the flight leader reported that he had the landing pad 'visual' and he would ask for smoke to be thrown. A smoke grenade was immediately tossed onto the landing place, positioned so that the smoke was visible to the pilot without obscuring his vision. The smoke also confirmed the wind direction. When the volume of smoke had built up sufficiently, the pilot reported the colour he saw, and ground control would confirm that colour back to him. This tactic minimised the chances of the enemy luring a helicopter down by also throwing smoke. Exactly the same procedure for receiving helicopters was adopted, regardless of whether the resupply was delivered to a concentrated company or to individual platoons.

OCs always had the nagging feeling that the arrival of helicopters or APCs might reveal the company's location to the enemy. In fact this was not as likely as it might seem. Helicopter pilots tended to fly at treetop height, which made their heading difficult to estimate, and their exact landing point almost impossible to judge. Moreover the acoustics of the jungle were such that the sound of approaching or departing armoured vehicles or helicopters could appear to come from many directions at once, and was in any case quickly absorbed by the foliage.

Notwithstanding the need for security and tactical good sense, there was always something of a holiday atmosphere about resupply day. For the company commander it meant that his callsign was fully 'bombed up' and ready to begin seeking out the enemy again. It might also give him an opportunity to see his platoon commanders face-to-face, often for the first time in days. This meant that he could confirm orders which might previously have been transmitted in code; discuss future intentions; and canvass ideas on how best to discomfit the enemy for the next five days.

It also gave the company 2i/cs a chance to speak with platoon sergeants on minor administrative or personnel matters, and allowed the CSM to get around the section commanders and soldiers to find out how things were going. The company's medical corporal also used the time to move between platoons and dispense treatment or assess any ailments which might need the RMO's intervention.

For tactical security reasons there was little chance of diggers from different platoons mingling, but at least there was a break in the normal day-to-day routine of bush bashing. And it was pleasant to be able to untie the boots, relax against a tree, and read a book or a letter from home.

As often as circumstances permitted, the CO and RSM would also arrive during the resupply. As RSM Thompson rightly pointed out, it was most important on operations for the diggers to see their CO and RSM as often as possible. Being out in the scrub for a month at a time meant that the soldiers often felt somewhat isolated from the comforting presence of the rest of the Battalion family. The CO and the RSM symbolised that presence, and their arrival reassured the diggers that they had not been forgotten, and that their efforts were, in fact, very much appreciated. So it was not at all unusual to find the CO contentedly puffing at his pipe while sharing a mug of coffee with a young soldier who was vigorously expounding his ideas on how 274 Regiment should be dealt with. Elsewhere within the perimeter the RSM could be found surrounded by junior NCOs and giving fatherly advice which often started, 'Well, when I was a section commander . . .'

As soon as platoons received their bulk issues, the men opened their ration packs and traded the items they disliked for those they preferred, placing discarded items like sachets of sugar, tubes of jam or condensed milk and oatmeal blocks onto a 'gash' pile in the centre of the section or platoon area. Individuals were then at liberty to take any of those items, and almost nothing was wasted. Once the horse-trading was finished, each man secured his rations in his large pack. Any unwanted items were put back into sandbags, along with cardboard packing from radio batteries, plastic wrappers from CRPs, and any other rubbish. All these, together with empty jerrycans, were taken back to the landing area, and at a predetermined time, one or two helicopters returned to back-load them. The company's outgoing mail was also handed to a door-gunner or the pilot for safekeeping and despatch by the CQMS.

That done, the company saddled up and moved out of the resupply area to begin again looking for the enemy. Apart from trampled grass there would be no sign that anyone had been there, and the next shower of rain obliterated even those signs.

And showers of rain were something the Battalion grew used to on the second major training exercise. During Exercise Third Stab, the Mount Spec training area obligingly dumped 91.5 centimetres on to the Battalion in ten days. The indefatigable 104 Field Battery in FSB Sapphire only just managed to cling precariously to the high ground, while FSB Saffron wallowed ankle-deep in mud on the plain below. Those who had been to Vietnam before nodded wisely and told those who had not that this was very realistic training.

CSM Denny Cook and the CQs of B Company and Admin Company, S/Sgts 'Toad' Fletcher and Digby Lawrence, suggested tactfully to OC Admin Company that the bed of a dry creek might perhaps not be the most suitable place to put the Echelon CP. But officers always know best, and so the 2.5 metre hole was prepared and occupied. Two nights later the Echelon was hit by the edge of a cyclone, and by morning the CP had filled to within 20 centimetres of its roof.

And during the cordon and search of 'Hoa Long', GOC Northern Command, the fiery and meticulous MajGen A.L. McDonald, arrived

The officers of the 4th Battalion pictured in April 1971, one month before leaving for South Vietnam. *Back Row* (L to R): Lt M.D. O'Neill, 2Lt D.N. McDaniel, Lt R.J. Martin, 2Lt G.J. McKay, 2Lt R.J. Swarbrick, Lt A.C. Grecian, 2Lt G.D. Spinkston, Lt G.D. Bryant, 2Lt M.F. Murphy, 2Lt K.M. Byrne, Lt S.V.L. Willis, Lt P. S. Andrews. *Middle Row* (L to R): 2Lt P.F. Darby, Lt J.S. Callon, Capt J. Sullivan, Capt G.R. Shannon, Capt H.C. Babington, Capt R.L. Sayce, Capt P.R. Trevillian, Capt T.W. Roderick, Capt P.[illegible] Schuman MC, Lt J. Ballantyne, Lt P.A. O'Brien. *Front Row* (L to R): Capt D.D. McKenzie, Capt J.D. McAloney MC, Maj J.H. Taylor, Maj K.F. Houley, Lt Col J.C. Hughes MC, Maj D.S. McIver, Maj E.H. Stevenson, Maj F.R. Hogarth, Maj R.E. Boxall, Maj F.M. Kudnig. (Beverley Studio Townsville)

to see for himself. When he had done so, he departed, having pronounced himself well satisfied. The Battalion heaved a sigh of relief.

The final exercise was Monaro Mall, but it was still the cyclone season in North Queensland, and so the exercise was relocated from Shoalwater Bay, to High Range, to Mount Spec and, finally, to the Mount Stewart training area overlooking Townsville. It provided a novel if somewhat unrealistic exercise setting. The Battalion CP was co-located with FSB Murphy along the Ross River road; the Echelon dug itself in at the Mount Stewart re-entrant; and the companies manoeuvred throughout the close training area.

And then suddenly it was all over. There were no more exercises, and the realisation came home to everyone that the next time the Battalion deployed it would be in Phuoc Tuy Province.

Pre-embarkation leave was taken from 2–8 April 1971. At 2330hr on 1 May the Battalion advance party left Townsville by air, arriving in Vung Tau and then Nui Dat the next day. They began at once taking over from 2RAR.

On 13 May, after a march through Townsville watched by families and friends, the main body went aboard HMAS *Sydney*. Disembarking at Vung Tau on 23 May 1971, they went straight to Nui Dat.

PART 2

The sharp edge of battle

There are usually three courses open to the enemy,
and of these he will adopt the fourth.

Field Marshal von Moltke

8

The enemy

The Vietnamese have always been a fiercely independent people, and have always been prepared to fight for that independence.

In 111 BC the Chinese began their expansion south along the Red River Delta into what used to be North Vietnam, building roads to the coast and harbours for their ships which were beginning to trade with India and the Middle East. China's aim was not only expansion for economic reasons, but also to impose their civilisation—technical, cultural, administrative and political—onto the peoples of Indochina.

The victorious Chinese divided Vietnam into military districts, each under a military governor, but at first they allowed the Vietnamese to maintain their own administration. But this benign military government began to change when the Chinese came to understand that Sinocisation could not go forward while the feudal Vietnamese aristocracy organised resistance to it. Gradually the military governors became less lenient; civil officials from China arrived to replace Vietnamese administrators, and they were more energetic, more effective, harsher.

Even so, the Chinese colonisation of North Vietnam brought benefits with it. New and improved methods of irrigation were introduced, as was the metal plough and the use of water buffalo as draft animals, and these innovations increased agricultural output. Pottery-making methods were improved, the arts flourished, and Buddhism was introduced, so that in the thousand years of Chinese rule the Vietnamese people became the most sophisticated on the Indochina peninsula.

Nevertheless the Chinese had come as conquerors, and they were exploiting the natural resources of Vietnam: precious metals, the forests of teak and sandalwood, ivory from the herds of elephant which roamed them, and the pearls which thrived in the warm offshore waters. Then too, there were taxes to be squeezed out of the people, and these same people could be used as forced labour.

The first rebellion against the Chinese came in 39 AD, and was led by the Trung sisters, whose followers overran the Chinese troops in their strongholds and established an independent Vietnamese kingdom. But within three years another Chinese army put down the rebellion and imposed an even more repressive central administration.

A second rebellion in 248 AD fared no better, and it was not until the fall of the ailing T'ang dynasty in China that a series of rebellions in Vietnam resulted in the crushing defeat of a Chinese army in 939 AD, and independence for Vietnam until 1407.

But now Chinese domination was replaced by fierce power struggles between local Vietnamese landowners and feudal lords, and only when the first of the three great Vietnamese dynasties began, the Ly (1009–1225), did tranquillity and some limited economic progress come to the country. The Chinese trade roads were extended, and the network expanded, so that major cities were now connected. A postal service was set up, dykes and waterways were constructed, and agricultural output improved once more. The national capital was moved back to Hanoi, and in 1076 a trained and competent civil service was established. But there was almost no international trade, and precious little national trade either, and only the aristocratic elite cared much about literature and the arts. Even so, the Vietnamese were their own masters again, and that was what mattered.

Yet always independence came at a cost. In 1057 the Chinese advanced south again towards Hanoi, and between 1128 and 1216 the Cambodians and the Chams waged a series of campaigns against Vietnam. Under this pressure the Ly dynasty foundered and was replaced by the Tran dynasty (1225–1400).

And now, undoubtedly, came a foretaste of what was to come seven centuries later. Kublai Khan's Mongol armies invaded Vietnam in 1257, 1284 and 1287, but these armies, estimated to be between 300 000 and 500 000 strong, were first absorbed by Vietnamese resistance, then swamped by it, and finally defeated by Tran Hung Dao, who is still venerated today as a national hero.

But by 1400 the Tran dynasty had also lost both its vigour and its grip on political power. Tran made an appeal for assistance to China, and this provided the excuse the Chinese needed to renew their imperial expansion into Indochina generally and Vietnam in particular. They invaded Vietnam again in 1407, and so profound was the political division within the country that the Chinese invasion could not be resisted.

Now the third and most influential dynasty, the Le (1418–1600), emerged under the aristocratic and powerful landowner Le Loi. He organised and led a national resistance against the Chinese in 1418, and by 1428 they were finally driven out of Vietnam. Next the Chams were expelled from their lands, which extended from Da Nang in the north to Cape Varella in the south, and by 1471 their territory had been absorbed into Vietnam and their lands given to peasant farmers.

The Vietnamese continued their push south. The rich Mekong Delta, which the declining Khmer rulers were unable to defend, was seized. Saigon was taken, and by 1757 Vietnam, except for the southernmost province of Soc Trang, which was added in 1840, took on its modern size and shape. Yet the Vietnamese remained fiercely hostile to change. There was almost no technical, social or cultural innovation, and still virtually no national or international trade. The economy remained based on agriculture, which in the main meant the growing of rice, with subsistence fishing on the coast. Portuguese, Dutch and English trading companies were always rejected, and their fleets seldom even revictualled in Vietnam's ports.

But the French were more persistent. They began arriving on the Indochina peninsula in 1858, and their attempts to first trade, then colonise, continued until 1883, when they withdrew because of the lack of a coherent French foreign policy. They renewed their efforts in 1897, and this time they were more aggressive and more successful. By 1900 Vietnam was administered entirely by French public servants, and the country's natural resources were being unscrupulously exploited and exported for the benefit of French investors seeking quick returns. Only a small wealthy class of Vietnamese prospered under the French colonial occupation, while the great majority of the people were much worse off. Between 1880 and 1930 the area of land under rice cultivation quadrupled, but the consumption of rice by peasant families decreased. New agricultural lands, opened up by improved irrigation methods, were not given to the landless but were sold or given to those who collaborated with the French. About 50 per cent of the population owned no land at all, and loan repayments for those with land were crippling. Projects which benefited only the French and their investors were built with forced labour. And the worst of all the taxes, that on salt, which had become a state monopoly, reached a level 3000 per cent greater than it had been in pre-French days. This economic exploitation continued until 1954, with only a three-year pause when the Japanese invaded the peninsula in 1942.

When the war in the Pacific ended, the Vietnamese nationalist, Ho Chi Minh, demanded independence from France, and his struggle continued for nine years from August 1945 until the Viet Minh victory at Dien Bien Phu on 7 May 1954. In July that year an agreement was signed at Geneva between communist-dominated North Vietnam and

American-backed South Vietnam, and the country was partitioned at the 17th parallel of latitude.

Much of Vietnam's early history mirrors that of other Asian, Middle Eastern and European countries over the same period of time. But for the Vietnamese, these centuries of resistance to colonial domination helped to forge a robust individual and national character: independent, patient, hardworking, charming, gentle, stubborn, aggressive, relentless, cunning and courageous.

From these ancestors, who had defeated the Chinese, the Mongols and the French, came the soldiers that 4RAR/NZ (ANZAC) Battalion would encounter in Phuoc Tuy Province in 1971.

Perhaps one of the few criticisms of the training and preparation of Australian units for Vietnam concerns the lack of depth in understanding the enemy.

Over the years of 1ATF's operations in Phuoc Tuy Province, a wealth of very accurate information on all aspects of the enemy had been obtained. Maybe that was the problem: there was so much information, in so many different places, and in so many different documents, that it became overwhelming. In addition, enemy units were often known by several different titles. For example, D445 Provincial Mobile Battalion was also known as D445 VC Local Main Force Battalion. All enemy units had cover names and unit designator numbers which further added to the confusion, as they were undoubtedly meant to do. But even though units preparing for Vietnam gave instruction on various aspects of the enemy, it seldom seemed sharply enough focused. It's probably true to say that although Australian soldiers knew *about* the enemy, few really *understood* them.

And yet an intimate understanding was very necessary. Commanders at all levels, when planning their operations, and the soldiers who would carry out those plans, needed to know how the enemy thought, what motivated them, how they would react in any given tactical situation. Where would they most likely site their base camps? What sort of security and early warning would there be around them? What did a bunker system really look like from ground level? And would the enemy defend their bases fiercely, or just withdraw without a fight?

Then, too, war stories told by soldiers returning from Vietnam, often by those who had never encountered the enemy, tended to either over-exaggerate or disparage the abilities of the VC and NVA units. The result was that many who served in Vietnam went there believing that the enemy were either inept bandits or super-warriors. The truth was that Vietnamese communist soldiers were neither of these extremes. But they all shared common characteristics—they were courageous, relentless, cunning, committed, tough and well-motivated. They were, in short, an enemy worthy of their Australian and New Zealand opponents.

The enemy which 4RAR would encounter in Phuoc Tuy Province were of four distinct kinds and organised into well-established units: the Chau Duc District Committee, with its own organic rifle company, C41, and its network of communist party chapters and village guerrillas; D445 Provincial Mobile Battalion; 274 Viet Cong Main Force Regiment; and 33 North Vietnamese Army Regiment. The men of the ANZAC Battalion came to refer to these units simply as Chau Duc, D445, 274 and 33rd.

It needs to be understood from the outset that enemy regiments, battalions, companies, platoons and squads were much smaller numerically than their Australian counterparts. While an Australian battalion had a strength of about 850 all ranks, even at the best of times, say in 1965, a communist battalion might number only 400, and by the end of 1971 in Phuoc Tuy Province, that figure could be halved, and sometimes even halved again. Similarly, an Australian rifle company, with its attachments for Vietnam, numbered about 135 all ranks, its platoons 35 each, and its sections ten men. But a communist company in Phuoc Tuy probably had a strength of no more than 50, with platoons of fifteen and squads of four men each. Village guerrilla 'units' might total only one or two individuals.

There was also a high disparity between the figures quoted for enemy dead and enemy wounded. It's usual after a conventional battle to find that there are more wounded than there are killed, say in a ratio of 5:1. However the enemy in Vietnam went to extraordinary lengths to take their dead and wounded with them when they withdrew from the battlefield, and the ANZAC Battalion seldom encountered enemy wounded for this reason. How many of the wounded survived their injuries will, of course, never be known. They faced surgical operations under very harsh conditions, often without proper anaesthetics and instruments. Post-operative care and drugs would have been similarly meagre. This is not to suggest that the enemy's medical personnel were indifferent to the suffering of their comrades. On the contrary, they were known always to have done the best they could with their limited resources, and ex-Viet Cong soldiers speak highly of their dedication and compassion.

Chau Duc District Committee 1954–71

The relatively high population density of Phuoc Tuy Province, with its well-established network of good roads, thickly forested areas and its proximity to the sea, had made the province important to the communists since the days of the war against the French. Therefore the Chau

Fishing coracles at Lang Phuoc Hai village on the south coast of Phuoc Tuy Province.

Duc District Committee was formed in Phuoc Tuy to provide a link in the communist chain of command; as an interface between political activity and military operations; and to organise and control the activities of its subordinate village party chapters and guerrilla units.

Chau Duc's area of responsibility included the important population centres of Binh Ba, Ngai Giao, Suoi Nghe, Binh Gia and Hoa Long, and the major province highways of Route 2 and Route 15, but not the provincal capital of Baria, which had its own special organisation. HQ Chau Duc was usually located, with its administrative elements, in a network of caves in the Nui Dinh hills about eight kilometres north-west of Baria. Its only rifle company, C41, was generally based in the Suoi Chau Pha valley, adjacent to the north-east slopes of the Nui Dinhs.

In June 1968, after the Americans redefined their corps areas of responsibility, the VC Command also reorganised and consolidated its own area of operations, boundaries and chains of command. As part of this reorganisation the provinces of Long Khanh and Phuoc Tuy were merged to become what the VC referred to as Ba Long Province. The chain of command was, therefore, from Military Region 7 to HQ Ba Long Province to HQ Chau Duc District Committee to its village party chapters and guerrilla units.

HQ Ba Long also controlled D445 Provincial Mobile Battalion, which could be deployed anywhere in the Province with other local guerrilla units placed under the battalion's command. Conversely, D445 could be placed under the command of HQ Chau Duc if the situation demanded it. Units organic to HQ Ba Long, such as its Engineer and Sapper Reconnaissance companies, could also be deployed in support and under command of Chau Duc or D445 if worthwhile targets presented themselves.

Within this somewhat flexible command arrangement was the provision by MR7 of sapper units for operations in Chau Duc's AO, even though there was unlikely to be any liaison between Chau Duc and those units. Superimposed on all this was the fact that 274 VC and 33 NVA Regiments might also be conducting operations in the same area at the same time, often without inter-unit liaison.

Like all other communist units, HQ Chau Duc and C41 had always experienced difficulty with resupply, but with the start of the Pacification Programme in 1969 that problem became even more pronounced. This was because Chau Duc had traditionally used villages like Binh Ba, Hoa Long, Suoi Nghe and others for resupply, and one of the principal aims of Pacification was to deny access to those population centres. This was achieved by aggressive and persistent ambushing by both day and night, which not only denied the enemy resupply, but also caused them numerous casualties and cut them off from their source of recruits.

So while in August 1970 HQ Chau Duc, C41 and village party chapters and guerrilla units were known to total 180 all ranks, by May 1971 that figure had dwindled to about 86. Of those, HQ Chau Duc had 39, village chapters and guerrilla units had 35, and C41 totalled twelve. As a consequence of ongoing casualties in general and the loss of senior party officials and military officers in particular, and through surrenders, artillery and air attacks, ambushes, and the lack of food and medical supplies, the morale of Chau Duc was poor. In addition, its influence over village party chapters and guerrilla units was also waning. And communication between HQ Chau Duc and HQ Ba Long Province, which had previously been on a regular weekly basis, was now intermittent and fraught with danger.

Nevertheless in May 1971, Chau Duc struggled on with its task of conducting its political work through its village party chapters, farmers', women's and youth associations, and proselytising section; and with very limited military operations by C41 and the village guerrillas.

HQ Chau Duc and its various units were armed with a wide array of small arms, but no heavy weapons. Among them were Colt, P38 and Browning automatic pistols, a Thompson SMG, and Garand, SKS, M16, K54 and AK47 rifles. C41 had a similar collection of small arms, and also boasted a Browning automatic rifle and an RPD LMG. Ammunition for these small arms was reasonably plentiful, but on 24 October 1970 there were only three rounds each for C41's only RPG2 and 60mm mortar, and the chances of obtaining more were remote.

Chau Duc were invariably dressed, like the bulk of the working peasant population, in 'black pyjamas' and Ho Chi Minh sandals. It was a uniform easy to replace, and made its wearer less obtrusive. They also wore whatever equipment came to hand from their own sources, or could be captured from ARVN, RF or PF personnel. Some webbing was bought through the black market, and much of it was homemade.

Now, also, they vigorously avoided any contact with the Allies, and if they did make contact by chance, their tactic in all circumstances was to 'shoot and scoot'.

But the influence and effectiveness of Chau Duc should not be measured by their dwindling numbers, meagre resources, or reluctance to stand and fight. The fact that they existed at all meant that Allied troops were tied down in countering their activities. The units of Chau Duc could still gather information, act as couriers, set mines and booby traps, carry out small-scale sabotage missions, undermine the Pacification Programme, intimidate and murder civilian officials and village headmen, and squeeze money and supplies from the population at large. And they could, if necessary, assist in the activities of their more potent local, main force and NVA comrades.

And that made them dangerous.

D445 Provincial Mobile Battalion 1957–71

On 6 May 1971 the Battle Intelligence Section of HQ 1ATF issued an order of battle paper on D445, the first paragraph of which said this:

> Throughout the period of deployment of 1ATF in Phuoc Tuy Province, one of the most formidable forces with which the Task Force has regularly had to contend is D445 VC Local Main Force Battalion of enemy Ba Long Province. D445 is not a main force battalion but it has repeatedly exhibited characteristics which cause it to be ranked at least equal in capability to the main force units which now operate in or near Ba Long Province, such as the battalions of 33NVA Regiment, or D2 Battalion of SR4. Indeed D445 in early 1971 is superior to the battalions of 274 Regiment, which suffer from morale problems.[1]

D445 had its beginnings in 1957 when two companies under the command of a pro-French political party deserted and moved into the Thi Vai hills north-west of Baria. There they amalgamated into one company, came under VC control, and were retitled C40. Not much is known about the activities of C40 between 1959 and 1963, but sometime in that period another company, C45, was raised from ARVN draft dodgers. In 1963 the two companies, C40 and C45, took part in a number of minor operations alongside other local guerrilla groups. These were probably shakedown operations designed to provide realistic training, and if possible to obtain more weapons and equipment.

In December 1963, C40 and C45 were combined, and now with a strength of 100 personnel were retitled C445. More recruits followed, were trained and partially equipped, and formed another company of 100 all ranks which became C445/40. In September 1964, the two companies joined with the Long Dat District Company for an attack on the fishing village of Lang Phuoc Hai on the coast south-east of Dat Do. It is not known how many casualties the unit took, but there were enough to cause a lowering of morale. In November, the companies ambushed ARVN troops on the road between Dat Do and Long Phuoc Hai, and suffered five killed and five wounded. Again in November they combined with 1 Battalion 274 VC Regiment for an attack on Binh Gia, 11 kilometres north of Nui Dat, suffering close to two platoons worth of personnel killed or wounded and a large number of weapons lost.

In February 1965, C445 and C445/40 formed the basis of D445 Provincial Organic Mobile Battalion. Recruits were obtained and trained, and as a result D445 now had four rifle companies: C1, C2, C3 and C4. The battalion's bases were established in the Tan Rhu–Song Rai area west of Xuyen Moc, and the rest of the year was spent in training and political indoctrination, the acquisition of food, equipment, weapons and ammunition, and the development of the base areas. Another company, C5 Sapper Reconnaissance, with a strength of 30 personnel, was added, bringing the battalion's strength up to 400.

Now D445 began to flex their muscles in earnest. In February 1966, they attacked The Horseshoe, barely a kilometre north of Dat Do, killing ten ARVN Rangers and capturing their weapons. But while withdrawing from this engagement, they came under heavy air attack, losing 25 killed and five wounded. Even so, a month later, the battalion attacked a civic action team and its escort, again just north of Dat Do, killing 40 and wounding eighteen, and seizing 40 weapons for the cost to the battalion of nine killed.

In June 1966, D445 had its first contact with 1ATF, being caught in a search and destroy operation round Long Tan, and suffering 50 killed and 20 wounded, and losing ten weapons. It was an ominous portent.

Two months later, during the small hours of 17 August 1966, 1ATF base at Nui Dat was heavily mortared as a preliminary to a ground attack. The next day D445, attacking alongside 275 VC Regiment, were met by units of 1ATF in an encounter battle. The climax of the battle of Long Tan came in the early evening and in deluging rain, when the two enemy units faced D Company 6RAR, assisted by A Squadron 3 Cavalry Regiment and the guns of 1 Field Regiment RAA. By late that night both D445 and 275 Regiment had ceased to exist as effective operational units. It will never be known exactly how many enemy soldiers, fighting like their Australian opponents with great courage, were killed at Long Tan. Surrendered enemy personnel said later that D445's casualties had been 70 killed and 100 wounded: almost 50 per cent of their total strength.

But it was close. In his follow-up report to the battle, Brig David Jackson said of D445 and 275 Regiment:

> The enemy force was well organised and equipped and showed great determination and skilful battle procedures at company level with control by visual signals and bugles. He used massive quantities of ammunition. Fortunately some of his shooting, particularly with automatic weapons, was a little too high for maximum effect. However, there is no doubt whatsoever that the Long Tan battle was a very close run thing indeed. Had the enemy been allowed another fifteen minutes, it is likely that D Coy 6RAR would have been completely overrun.[2]

Somehow D445 found the will to continue. Throughout the rest of 1966 they took part in four small actions, losing another five killed and four wounded. During one of these, they captured 184 ARVN recruits who were practising on the rifle range at Long Huong two kilometres west of Baria. Some 60 of these recruits remained permanently with D445, while the others either escaped or were released as being unsuitable.

At the start of 1967 D445 began operating in the Long Green. This was a forested area extending along the southern side of Route 23, and coming to a narrow finger about 500 metres east of Phuoc Loi on the outskirts of Dat Do. It was an important area to the battalion for two principal reasons. First, its close proximity to heavily populated areas made it an abundant resupply and recruiting source; second, it was relatively easy to harass the military posts in the area, particularly with attacks by fire, and then withdraw quickly into the security of the Long Green.

Although ARVN units were unwilling to carry the fight to D445 in the Long Green, 1ATF in the first months of 1967 showed no such reluctance. In February the battalion was again mauled by 6RAR, losing an estimated 50 to 75 personnel killed. And it was during this operation that it became apparent for the first time that North Vietnamese regulars were serving in the ranks of D445.

Throughout May, July and August 1967, D445 kept up the pressure, always achieving limited successes, but always, too, at a cost. Then, during the Tet Offensive, they took part in an attack on Baria and the Van Kiep Training Centre in which their losses were put at 40 per cent of the battalion's strength.

It is difficult to comprehend at this distance in time how a unit such as D445 Provincial Mobile Battalion could sustain such a large and prolonged series of losses and still, with relentless courage and tenacity, keep coming back. It might be understandable if they were operating in an environment where recruits and resupply, weapons, ammunition and medical facilities were plentiful and efficient. But they were not. Even before 1ATF arrived in Phuoc Tuy Province, D445 faced difficult conditions. The ARVN may not have been particularly vigorous in their ground operations against the VC, but they had generous air support, and they had artillery, and those were not difficult to direct, and they inflicted heavy, and seemingly crippling casualties. Nor did the situation become any better for the VC after the arrival of 1ATF in Phuoc Tuy in May 1966: indeed it became a good deal worse.

And yet on 6 May 1968, this time fighting alongside D440, D445 attacked Cam My in the north of Phuoc Tuy, and lost 57 killed by artillery and 36 by ground fire. On 6 June, when they attacked 43

Padi fields and the Nui Dinh foothills just west of Baria.

ARVN Regiment along the Suoi Luc just over the northern border of Phuoc Tuy, another 58 were killed. On 22 August, nineteen died in an assault on Long Dien.

On 23 February 1969, during Second Tet, D445 attacked Baria. C1's objective was the ARVN artillery FSB; C2's the logistic compound; C3's the waterworks; and C4 provided covering fire for these assaults. When 1ATF Ready Reaction Force arrived, the battalion withdrew, leaving behind ten personnel killed and twelve wounded.

On 15 May 1969 the battalion attacked Dat Do again. Then Hoi My. Then on 4–5 September Dat Do yet again. Then the RF compound at Phuoc Loi on 7–9 November, and the Horse Shoe on 31 December. Always with courage. Always with casualties.

And it would continue like this. From 1 January to 31 December 1970, D445 took part in 23 missions. From 4 January to 22 April 1971, another 21 missions. Always with courage. Always with casualties.

With the exception of Chau Duc and its units, who were local guerrillas and therefore received only rudimentary training, the tactics of D445, 274 and 33rd were very similar. If they varied at all it was only in minor detail, although 33rd, being regular soldiers of a sovereign country, were by far the most polished performers.

Most VC and NVA units learned early that the only sure way to avoid casualties from air attacks and artillery was to dig bunkers, and D445 was no exception. All their permanent camps had them, and they were laid out in a wide triangular formation with the apex facing the most likely enemy approach. HQ elements were positioned in the centre for easier control, and depth sub-units secured the base of the triangle, which was also the rear approach.

Bunkers were always well constructed, being about three metres square, with sawn timber as the basis for overhead protection (OHP). Layers of soil, each tamped firmly down, were placed over these timbers, and subsequent rain and general weathering rendered the OHP almost as hard as concrete, guaranteeing protection from all but direct hits. OHP was kept as low to the ground as possible, and was camouflaged to blend in with the surroundings.

One-man fighting pits, 0.8 metre deep, that could be reached from both inside and outside the bunker, were dug at the two corners facing the most likely enemy approach. Bunkers were mutually supporting, which meant that each one could cover at least two others with observation and direct fire. They were also sited in depth, so that Allied troops attacking the system from any direction would have to fight their way through numerous defended points. Bunkers were sometimes linked by fire-lanes, so that the defenders could see and have a clear shot at the attackers.

Mines and booby traps were sited around the camp, and sentries were positioned about 70 metres outside it. Squad-sized clearing patrols went out three times a day to make a complete circuit of the camp about 300 metres out. Up to three watch-towers, often positioned in convenient trees, were also sited and manned to give early warning of Allied approach. Standing patrols and sometimes ambushes were deployed at suitable points round the system.

Non-permanent structures were built above ground and carefully camouflaged to prevent detection from the air. These structures, which were only woven palm roofs on supporting uprights, were used for messing, briefings, group activities, training and political indoctrination.

When a bunker system came under assault, the point of attack was defended by small arms, automatic and often RPG fire while the commander made an assessment of the situation. If he judged that the attacking force could be driven off, he would give orders for the system to be defended. Those not under direct attack would then encircle the attackers from one or two flanks simultaneously. But if the attacking force was of overwhelming strength, the commander would order those

The enemy. Tran Tan Huy, a former commander of D445 Provincial Mobile Battalion during the war, and Chairman of the District Peoples' Committee of Long Dat in 1993, believed that 'Australian soldiers like to fight in the jungle, fight very hard and very bravely to fight against us'.

The enemy. A maimed ex-Viet Cong soldier begs in Ho Chi Minh City (Saigon) in 1993.

under direct attack to cover the withdrawal of the remainder of the unit. The unit would then move out of the system on the side furthest from the attack, and either wait there until the attackers withdrew, quit the area altogether for an alternative base, or march for three to five hours and construct a new system.

D445 moved either as a battalion or as individual companies, depending on the tactical situation. Sub-units usually travelled with a 30-minute separation. Single file was the formation most often used, with 7 metres between individuals. Scouts moved about 500 metres ahead of each company. Existing tracks were seldom used because of the danger of ambush. But if they were ambushed while on the move, those not in contact would withdraw, encircle the ambushers, and assault.

It was known in May 1971 that D445 had six ANPRC-25 radio sets, but these would only have been used sparingly because of the difficulty of acquiring batteries. Converted transistor radios were thought to be used for monitoring Allied nets. The battalion also had nine telephones, which would have been deployed in defended locations. Bugles were used for communication, especially during an attack, and troops in contact always used hand signals or voice. D445 also relied heavily on runners for the carriage of messages between battalion HQ, companies and platoons in all phases of war. Individual shots were sometimes used to keep contact with other sub-units when on the move.

The members of D445, like most enemy units, wore black pyjamas and whatever webbing equipment could be obtained or manufactured locally. The battalion was armed much like 274 Regiment, the personal weapon for most being the AK47, with RPG2s and RPDs at squad level, and some 60mm mortars. C4 also had three RPG7s; but by May 1971 the battalion had lost its 82mm mortars, and its mortar platoon had been disbanded.

Also in May 1971, surrendered personnel were reporting that 1ATF operations had at last taken a toll of the strength of D445 Provincial Mobile Battalion. C1 numbered 24 all ranks, C2 had 22, C3 27, and C4 a mere eighteen. Battalion HQ and C5 Sapper Reconnaissance Company could muster between them only 68, making the total battalion strength 159 all ranks.

But morale was still high, and D445 was still active and aggressive.

274 Viet Cong Regiment 1964–71

274 Regiment was almost exactly the same age as 4RAR, having been raised at the beginning of 1964. The nucleus of the regiment had come originally from 308 NVA Division, while the bulk of recruits arrived from VC guerrilla D800 Dong Nai Battalion. Similar main force regiments were being raised in the South in readiness for the drive by North Vietnamese troops into the central provinces of Vietnam. The aim of the offensive was to cut the country in half, and it was scheduled to begin in 1965, with the ultimate objective being the downfall of the corrupt and chaotic South Vietnamese government. Raising, equipping and training took just over a year, and it was therefore not until March 1965 that the Dong Nai Battalion was ready for operations under its new title of 1/274 VC Regiment.

Meanwhile 3 Battalion was forming from C202 Local Force Company from Song Be. Last to join the regiment was 2 Battalion, which had originally been formed in Bien Hoa Province where it was known as 265 Battalion.

Although placed nominally under command of 5 VC Division in August 1965, 274 nevertheless operated under the direct control of the Central Office for South Vietnam (COSVN). And throughout 1965 the regiment used as its base the Hat Dich area, from which it carried out harassing operations into Long Khanh and Bien Hoa provinces.

In 1966, probably to counter the arrival of 1ATF at Nui Dat, 274 Regiment began operating almost exclusively in northern Phuoc Tuy Province; and on 9 December 1966, for the loss of only two men killed, 2 Battalion overran the ARVN Training Centre at Van Kiep, causing heavy loss of life.

Little was heard of the regiment after this considerable success, but in November 1967 they were back in the Hat Dich once more. Here they received a strength increase from 320 NVA Regiment, and began training and preparation for the first Tet Offensive, which was to commence at the end of January 1968. Their objective, which they would attack together with 275 VC Regiment, was the large and important airbase and logistic complex around Bien Hoa and Long Binh.

On 31 January 1968 the two regiments began their attacks, and were bloodily repulsed by American units and 1ATF, comprising 2RAR/NZ (ANZAC) Battalion and 7RAR, 4 Field Regiment, A Squadron 3 Cavalry Regiment, 1 Field Squadron, and elements of 161 Recce Flight, all of who had been redeployed from Nui Dat.

In a signal to the Commander 1ATF, Brig Ron Hughes, the brother of LtCol Jim Hughes, after the operation had concluded, Gen Weyand, commanding III Corps, said:

> Upon the termination of Operation COBURG, please accept my highest commendation and appreciation for the exceptional performance of the 1st ATF in defeating the enemy's TET Offensive attacks against the critically important Bien Hoa—Long Binh complex. The action in discovering the movement of the 274 and 275 Regiments into their attack positions, the subsequent disruption of their attacks and the way-laying of the enemy forces as they withdrew were key factors in their defeat and reflect great credit upon the officers and men of your fine command; well done.[3]

Whether 274 and 275 Regiments knew they had suffered these losses at the hands of Australians and New Zealanders is not known. But whatever the case, 274 Regiment withdrew back to the Hat Dich, remaining there until May 1968 to reinforce, retrain and build up supplies. Then, in June and August, 274 carried out a series of battalion ambushes along Highway 1 leading to Saigon. Throughout December 1968 all three battalions conducted operations along the Phuoc Tuy–Long Khanh border areas, suffering the combined losses of 121 killed. As a result, the regiment again returned to its Hat Dich base to refit.

On 3 February 1969, during Second Tet, while again attacking Long Binh, 3/274 suffered 194 killed. The same night 2/274 mounted a ground assault against the US Bear Cat base in Long Khanh Province, and also took heavy casualties. As a consequence of these losses, 274 was uncommitted to battle for the rest of 1969, while 2/274 returned to the vicinity of Long Binh to obtain supplies for the regiment.

Throughout January and February 1970, 1 and 3 Battalions had only infrequent and light contact along the Phuoc Tuy–Long Khanh borders, and now showed a marked inclination to withdraw immediately when contacted, even from defended locations and bunkers. So with the return of 2/274 to the Hat Dich, the regiment set itself once more to replenishment and retraining.

A document captured on 28 January 1971 indicated that the regiment was probably reorganising into company-sized sub-units for smaller scale operations. This interpretation was borne out when, on 15 May, 2/274 launched an attack by fire followed by a ground assault onto an RF post just south of Xuan Loc. Six RF personnel were killed and eleven wounded, for a cost to the battalion of eight killed. And, on 17 May, an RAAF convoy was ambushed eleven kilometres south of Long Binh on Route 15. The ambush, which was poorly planned and executed and which caused no casualties, was thought to have been carried out by 3/274.

By late May 1971, 274 Regiment was reported to be detaching platoon-sized groups with the mission of reinforcing, training, and therefore upgrading, the effectiveness of local guerrillas, among them the Xuan Loc and the Cao Su–Cam My units.

In late May 1971, as the ANZAC Battalion began its second tour in Phuoc Tuy, 274 Regiment was assessed as having a total strength of 610 all ranks. As was usual with VC and NVA regiments, RHQ consisted of B1 (Military Staff) with personal weapons and four RPG2s; B2 (Political Staff); and B3 (Rear Services Staff); with personal weapons and one RPG2.

1 Battalion's strength was 100 all ranks, and had on its establishment ten RPG2s, two RPG7s, two RPDs, one 12.7mm HMG, 60mm mortars, and one 82mm mortar.

2 Battalion's strength was 80 all ranks, and the establishment included six RPG2s, 2 RPDs, one HMG, two 60mm mortars, and one M79.

3 Battalion was 70 strong, had eight RPG2s, one RPG7, one RPD, two 60mm mortars, and one M79.

The other sub-units of 274 were C16 Mortar Company, armed with four 82mm mortars; C17 Recoilless Rifle Company with two 75mm RRs; C19 Engineer Company with three RPG2s and one RPG7, C20 Signal Company with one RPG2, C21A Reconnaissance Company with one RPG2, C21B Sapper Reconnaissance Company with three RPG2s, C22 Transport Company, C23 Surgical Team, and K24 Convalescent Company.

Individual soldiers were usually armed with AK47s, but there was also a mix of captured Allied personal weapons, including Colt automatic pistols and M16s. Uniform and webbing was similar to that of D445, being black pyjamas, Ho Chi Minh sandals, and whatever webbing could be obtained or manufactured.

Like other VC and NVA units, directives for an attack were received by RHQ 274 Regiment from the superior headquarters about one week in advance of the operation. The regimental staff, using elements of Reconnaissance Company, then carefully reconnoitred the objectives, after which detailed and meticulous plans would be made. Battalions would normally receive their orders about two days in advance, at which time sub-units began thorough rehearsals both on models and on ground resembling the objectives. With particularly sensitive targets, orders were only given just before the attack to ensure security. In these cases, once orders had been given, personnel were confined to the base or camp area.

Detailed orders and exhaustive rehearsals were necessary when communications equipment was damaged or in short supply. It also meant that once launched, an attack plan could not be quickly or conveniently modified as the battle unfolded.

Objectives were first prepared by mortar and recoilless rifle fire, and then taken under ground attack on several converging axes. The attacking rifle companies were often accompanied to and through their objectives by sappers whose task it was to clear obstacles and neutralise strong points. One company was always held in reserve. Before First Tet, 1/274 particularly favoured 'human wave' attacks, but discontinued them because of the very heavy casualties which resulted.

Large- and small-scale ambushes were favoured by VC and NVA units, and if well planned and executed they could yield quick results at little cost. 274 Regiment tended to mount vehicle ambushes in company or reinforced company sized groups along one side of a road or track. Having chosen the decisive moment to spring the ambush, companies often used mortars and recoilless rifles to thicken up the volume of fire, and to slow down any pursuit as they withdrew from the ambush site. 3/274 had the reputation as experts at ambushing armoured columns.

Resupply

As with all VC and NVA units operating in South Vietnam, resupply could often be both tenuous and unsatisfactory. Shortages of supplies, particularly food and ammunition, either through failure of the supply system or losses to Allied action, frequently caused the postponement of operations.

274 Regiment was nominally supplied by the J85 Rear Services Group of MR7, but the regiment was also expected to take vigorous steps to acquire supplies for itself. This often meant liaising with local village guerrilla units and enlisting the help of communist sympathisers in order to procure food and money. Supplies of all kinds could also be obtained from sympathisers and agents through black market sources. Less frequently, villagers could be cajoled or intimidated into supplying food, money, and other necessaries.

Although the staple food of all communist troops was rice, considerable use was also made of wheat and grains of all kinds. In May 1971 the ration scale was 250 grams of flour per man per day, and the scale of rice issue was 700 grams per man per day. However that did not necessarily mean that each soldier received those daily quantities.

Concealment and storage of flour and rice was always a problem for enemy supply services. Even if safely concealed, grains and flour were subject to temperature and humidity which could not be controlled and which therefore shortened their usable state. Other factors affecting

An old lady street-seller at Vung Tau.

condition were the amount and type of protective wrapping, whether stored above or below ground, and whether the bags were stacked singly or multi-layered. As a rule of thumb, flour and grains stored below ground in plastic wrapping would remain in a satisfactory condition for about a year. Stored above ground, flour maintained a satisfactory condition for up to six months. Polished rice and corn had a life of one month when stored above ground, and six months below. Rear services personnel also endeavoured to rotate stores and caches so that perishable items were used before they deteriorated too far.

It was known that NVA units consumed more flour than VC, who preferred rice. Flour was used as the basis for soups of all kinds, and was first mixed with water and salt and then fashioned into noodles or dumplings. Alternatively, it would be mixed with water and salt, rolled into balls and steamed to form biscuits or damper.

Rice, both polished and unpolished, was eaten with whatever vegetables, meat, poultry or fish came to hand, supplemented by any edible plants and animals which might be found in the forest. And *nuc mam*, a sauce made from dried fish, with a pungent smell which Europeans tended to find unpleasant, was also used extensively with rice.

Flour and rice were never eaten on the same day. Captured documents and personnel stated that menus were fairly random with not much attention to good nutrition. But this was hardly surprising, and reinforces the fact that food supplies were tenuous and hard won, rice was often glutinous and rancid, the flour weevilly, and accompanying foodstuffs frequently in an unpalatable condition. Nevertheless it was a choice between eating whatever was available or starving.

Cooking was usually done at squad or patrol level. For daily carriage, rice and/or flour was rolled into balls, one for each day, and placed into a cloth tube carried around the neck, over the shoulder, or in the pack, by each soldier. The task of cooking was allotted to a different soldier each day, and he carried a small set of boilers for the purpose. Breakfast preparation began at 4 am, and the meal was eaten before first light. The evening meal was often cooked and eaten after last light, fires being concealed below ground level and covered with branches. Darkness helped to hide whatever smoke might escape.

33 North Vietnamese Army Regiment 1965–71

33NVA Regiment was exactly one year younger than 4RAR, having been raised in February 1965 in North Vietnam's Quang Binh Province. At that time it had been designated 101B NVA Regiment, and was the replacement for 101 NVA Regiment which, as part of 325 NVA Division, had moved into South Vietnam in December 1964. This was part of the buildup by the North Vietnamese which led to the raising of VC main force regiments and divisions for the offensive in the South.

But the regiment's history had not been a happy one. In September 1965, after moving for two months through Laos and Cambodia, the regiment entered South Vietnam at Pleiku Province. Now titled 33 NVA Regiment, it was assigned to 1 NVA Division, and in the months ahead was to lose nearly a third of its personnel in a series of battles with 1 (US) Airmobile Cavalry Division. This caused 33rd to withdraw back into Cambodia to refit and retrain.

Returning to Pleiku Province in February 1966, the regiment was again mauled by the Americans in a series of battles, the most expensive being in October that year when they lost another 332 personnel.

In 1967 the regiment, less 2 Battalion, first moved to Dar Lac Province, and then in December moved further south again into the Nam Lyr base area. Here they reorganised, reinforced and refitted before being positioned to take part in the First Tet Offensive in January 1968.

In the opening five days of Tet, 33rd lost nearly 700 personnel killed in action. In early August a further 300 were killed; and at the end of the month, while attacking FSB Schofield in Binh Duong Province, another 103 died.

Withdrawing a third time to Cambodia, the regiment was again reinforced, and then sent to Phuoc Long Province in support of 5 VC Division, which now moved to War Zone C. In January 1969 it moved again, this time into War Zone D, adjacent to the large air and logistic bases of Bien Hoa and Long Binh.

In February 1969 a prisoner from 33rd, captured in Long Khanh Province, stated that the regiment was now ordered to combine with 274 VC Regiment in an attack on HQ 18 ARVN Division at Xuan Loc.

33rd remained in the Black Horse–Xuan Loc area until December 1969, endeavouring to set up lines of supply and reinforcement from War Zone D. Throughout this period they were constantly in contact with 2 Brigade of 25 (US) Infantry Division, at whose hands they suffered further casualties.

In January 1970, as 4RAR began training for the second tour, 33rd was identified in Bin Tuy Province, obviously trying to avoid battle in order once again to reinforce and refit. Throughout 1970, RHQ and 1 Battalion remained co-located around Nui Ong, while 2 Battalion was engaged on resupply duties, and 3 Battalion refitted in what was known as the Rice Bowl area of southern Long Khanh Province.

Like 274, RHQ 33rd was organised into three sections: Military Staff (B1); Political Staff (B2); and Rear Services Staff (B3).

B1 had command and control responsibility over the regiment for all tactical operations. These operations were based on directives originated by COSVN. Detailed plans and orders for operations were issued through the NVA formation to which the regiment was assigned, which meant 5 NVA Division in 33rd's case.

B2's task was the political indoctrination of the regiment. This was conducted on a carefully structured schedule, weekly classes being taken by platoon commanders, and monthly classes by political officers attached to each company. A good deal of significance was placed on this political indoctrination by all communist units and formations in Vietnam, and it is believed to have had a significant effect in raising and maintaining the soldiers' morale.

B3 staff responsibility was for resupply to the regiment of weapons, ammunition, equipment, food and medical supplies. To achieve this it was necessary to coordinate with the supply services of MR7, in which 33rd was now operating. One battalion at a time was rotated through the task of collecting supplies and positioning them in caches throughout the area of operations for pickup by sub-units of the regiment.

33rd's three battalions were similar in organisation. 1 Battalion consisted of a headquarters, three rifle companies, and a heavy weapons company.

Headquarters Company had a military, political and rear services staff; and four sections, those being medical, communications, mail runner and reconnaissance-security.

The rifle companies were designated C1, C2 and C3; were armed with AK47s, RPGs, and one 60mm mortar each. Heavy Weapons Company was C4, and was equipped with two 82mm mortars and one 12.7mm HMG. In January 1970 the battalion's strength was about 250 personnel.

The rifle companies of 2 Battalion were designated C5, C6 and C7, Heavy Weapons Company was C8, and the battalion numbered about 270 personnel.

3 Battalion's rifle companies were C9, C10 and C11; C12 was Heavy Weapons Company, which besides the two 82mm mortars had two 12.7mm HMGs. The battalion's strength was about 300 all ranks.

33rd's other companies were Mortar (C16), with two 82mm mortars and 25 personnel; Recoilless Rifle Company (C17), with up to three 75mm RR and 20 personnel; and Anti-Aircraft Company (C18) usually having four 12.7mm HMGs and ten personnel. Engineer Company (C19), with fifteen personnel, was armed with AK47s and RPG2s, and equipped with picks, shovels, saws and machetes. C20 was Signals Company, with fifteen personnel; C21 was Reconnaissance Company, had 25 personnel, and was armed like the rifle companies.

C22 was Transportation Company. It had 50 personnel, and its task was to transport weapons, ammunition and supplies from caches and deliver them to the regimental rear-services staff. They were also responsible for evacuating dead and wounded, and own or captured weapons, from the battlefield. These tasks usually required man-packs and litters, because there was seldom, if at all, access to wheeled vehicles, although bicycles could be heavily laden and pushed along even in forested areas. Local guerrilla units and sympathisers were also pressed into service for these tasks if they were available and the security situation permitted.

Medical Company (C23) had a strength of about fifteen personnel, and was responsible for treating minor sick and wounded. Critically wounded patients, if it was thought they could survive the journey, were passed on to hospitals throughout MR7.

Sapper Company (C24) was equipped with AK47s, bangalore torpedoes, satchel charges and mines. Their tasks included probes into Allied positions, the destruction of key installations and strong points, and mining and booby trapping. The company had about 30 personnel. Convalescence Company (C25) had 25 personnel, and cared for and sustained the sick and wounded until they were fit to return to duty.

The tactics employed by 33rd, like most communist units, were to some extent guided by the endemic lack of radio sets, making speedy communication between RHQ, battalions and sub-units difficult, and operational plans hard to modify once launched. Therefore, as in 274 Regiment, an attack would be extensively reconnoitred and meticulously planned before very detailed orders were issued.

The objective would be prepared by mortar, recoilless rifle and HMG fire prior to H Hour, and when the infantry launched their attack it would be along several axes simultaneously. Sappers usually accompanied the infantry in order to breach wire obstacles and minefields with bangalore torpedoes, and to neutralise strong points using satchel charges.

When in an unprepared defensive position or encounter battle, 33rd's immediate action was first to put down a heavy volume of fire and then withdraw, leaving stay-behind parties to cover the rearward manoeuvre before themselves withdrawing.

However when in a well-prepared defensive position, which usually meant a bunker system, the element in contact would normally stay and fight, while the commander assessed whether he could defeat the attackers. This could include sending uncommitted troops around to probe the attackers' flanks. If the attackers showed signs of wavering, pressure would be increased until the attack was broken off. However if the attacking force showed a determination to maintain their assault, the commander would usually give the order to withdraw. In this case the headquarters element would withdraw first, followed by the next least committed elements. When the unit was clear, those covering the withdrawal would then break contact and retire.

33rd favoured the use of major ambushes. These were normally sited along *both* sides of a road or track, and might extend for up to two kilometres in length. The convoy or column to be attacked was allowed to move into the ambush which, at a predetermined moment, would be sprung by engaging the head and tail of the column. Small arms, automatic, RPG and 60mm mortars would open fire first, and under suitable circumstances 82mm mortars, recoilless rifles and HMGs would also be used to thicken up the fire. These last would also cover the unit's withdrawal from the ambush position.

33rd was very cautious when on the move. In open areas or when crossing obstacles, sub-units would disperse and move quickly until cover was regained. In close country a system of shots was used for signalling and keeping in touch. Night defensive positions were always carefully selected, and were normally at least 500 metres from roads and 300 metres from rivers or streams. NDPs were triangular, with the apex pointing towards the most likely Allied approach.

Because Chau Duc and D445 were recruited and trained in Phuoc Tuy, and 274 Regiment had operated extensively there since 1966, they knew the province well, and were able to navigate accurately without maps or compasses even through thick forest. However 33rd, not being locals, were unable to do this, and they carried both maps and compasses and used them regularly.

33rd were also dressed and equipped differently to D445 and 274 Regiment. They wore olive-green uniforms, with pith helmets and sometimes chest webbing. However they, too, favoured Ho Chi Minh sandals, and would pick up and use any Allied weapons and equipment they came across.

These, then, were the principal units that 4RAR/NZ (ANZAC) Battalion could expect to meet in Phuoc Tuy Province. There were others as well; the Cau Su and Cam My guerrillas were similar to Chau Duc's guerrilla units, and faced the same morale and supply problems. They were a nuisance factor, and a dangerous one at that.

But it was the main force units, and 33rd in particular, that posed the principal threat to the ANZAC Battalion.

9

Good morning, Vietnam

4RAR's area of operations throughout the second tour was Phuoc Tuy Province in the 3 Corps area of South Vietnam.

The province measured about 60 kilometres east to west and 40 kilometres north to south. It was neatly bisected by Route 2, an unsealed road which ran north from the provincial capital of Baria. Continuing on, Route 2 crossed the Phuoc Tuy–Long Khanh province border in the vicinity of Courtenay Hill adjacent to Cam My village; at Xuan Loc, 25 kilometres further north, it turned due west, became Route 1, and eventually came to Saigon.

There were two other principal roads in Phuoc Tuy. Route 15, sealed, started at Vung Tau, where the 1st Australian Logistic Support Group was located. Turning west at Baria, it followed the coast and continued on to Saigon. Route 23, unsealed, started at Baria and went east. Just short of Xuyen Moc, a track referred to as Route 328 led through the destroyed and abandoned township of Thua Tich with its derelict ARVN outpost. From there it became a foot-track which finally crossed into Binh Tuy Province. At Xuyen Moc itself, Route 2 became Route 329. Both 328 and 329 were little better than muddy tracks over which bullock carts might be coaxed. But by 1971 Thua Tich and Xuyen Moc had been deserted for years; none but the soldiers of both sides ever went there; and the whole area was shadowed, threatening and always gloomy.

Apart from the larger coastal hills—the Nui Dinhs and Nui Thi Vais west of Baria, and the Long Hais south-west of Dat Do—the land was almost flat. Here and there small knolls rose out of the plain. Some were almost conical with hollowed centres, indicating that once there had been volcanic activity in the area—like The Horseshoe, immediately north of Dat Do. But mostly there were only small hillocks, seldom more than a kilometre long and half that wide, rising sharply, then subsiding back into the plain.

Inland for a kilometre or two the influence of the sea could be felt: the breeze was salt and cooling. But soon that influence dulled and the air turned sullen and humid.

The southern third of the province was mainly open rice paddies dotted with villages. In the wet season, from mid-May to early October, when humidity was very high, the winds blew always from the south-west and brought tumbling purple clouds from which came heavy rain, drenching and often ice-cold. Then, when the paddies had flooded, the men and bullocks struggled in preparation, and the women placed out the rice. Later, when the crop was gathered in, it was threshed and bagged and stored carefully away, for this was the staple food.

November to February was the cool dry season—but everything is relative, and in Vietnam it was never really cool and seldom completely dry. March and April were the hottest and driest months.

Most of the inhabitants of the province lived lives of unrelieved poverty. A large proportion dwelt in the towns of Baria and Dat Do and in the fishing villages at Long Hai and Lang Phuoc Hai on the south coast. The rest of the population lived in the villages and hamlets that clustered along Route 2. Many of the smaller hamlets, and all individual houses further out in the countryside or in the forest, had been destroyed by government decree, and their inhabitants moved to larger settlements. These, surrounded by wire fences and high bunds, could to some extent be protected and controlled by RF or PF units. This centralisation, though restrictive, was designed to cut off a valuable source of resupply to VC and NVA units. Several of the new settlements had been built by the Royal Australian Engineers; they were considered lavish, because they had proper road systems, electric light, reticulated water, schools and clinics.

The people had freedom of movement throughout the day in the towns, the villages, the fields, and along the roads. Civilians were not permitted in the proclaimed Free Fire Zones, and anyone found there was assumed to be VC or NVA. Nevertheless, rules of engagement applied both in the zones and the province as a whole. Under the terms of a long-standing curfew, those working outside the settlements in the paddies, gardens and rubber plantations had to be back in their villages by 6 pm and were forbidden to leave again until 6 am. In major towns, curfew started at 10 pm and was rigorously enforced by the civilian police, whose white shirts and caps had earned them the nickname White Mice. They were much to be feared by day or night because they frequently shot first and asked questions afterwards.

The curfews had been in place for years, and the people knew that only the VC, the NVA and the Allies moved by night; and that all, in the dark, were equally lethal.

It was the forests that covered the greater part of Phuoc Tuy Province. Sometimes the trees were only saplings among undergrowth so tangled and dense that two men might pass within a few metres of one another and not be aware of it. Elsewhere the trees were much taller and had thick trunks that rose heavily up, and between which visibility could be 50 metres or more.

The forests must once have been places of great beauty. In the mornings, before it became too fierce, the sun sent bright shafts through the canopy, and these were reflected and intensified by the dew on twig and leaf. In the late afternoons, when the sun pressed more gently down, a man might be lulled to drowsiness by the endless piping of insects and the warmth of the earth. But that was before. Now, in 1971, the forest was made sombre by the presence of enemies.

One man, or several hundred, could be concealed indefinitely beneath the tree canopy, and if those men also dug themselves bunkers they would be almost impossible to find. Those searching would be unlikely to locate them by flying over in aircraft, nor could wheeled vehicles penetrate. It was an environment most suited to men on foot: infantrymen. Even then, movement was slow and the searching long, tedious and most often fruitless.

For those reasons the VC and NVA had chosen the forests for their bases. From the forests they could come out to attack the villages, ambush the roads, confiscate the rice or demand taxes and recruits, before disappearing back into the safety of their gloomy lairs. While the VC and NVA were loose in the forests they posed a threat to the rest of the province. Therefore it would be in the forests that 4RAR/NZ (ANZAC) Battalion would operate continuously from May until November 1971.

And the Battalion would need support. They would need guns, and men to serve them; and others, moving with the infantry, to correct the fall of shot. And there must be tanks, because they could be used to advantage in the cleared areas and, with determined leadership, in the forests as well. Armoured personnel carriers were required to lift the weary infantrymen when circumstances permitted, and to position them rapidly or keep pace with the tanks. And the careful expertise of combat engineers was essential for clearing mines and booby traps and to destroy enemy installations; and helicopters were needed to take the troops into the clearings, or for command and control tasks, for resupply or casualty evacuation. Signallers were essential to provide that vital web of communication without which little could be achieved. And behind them were the men who supplied the equipment and transported it, and others who repaired and maintained it, and accounted for it.

All this great effort had only one objective: to bring the infantrymen up with their elusive enemy so that they could destroy him. 'Ground'—the villages, the paddies, the hills, the forests—had no tactical significance of itself. It provided only a place where two enemies might stand, ultimately, toe to toe.

The tempo of operations had varied since 1966. The first two battalions to operate under 1ATF control, 5RAR and 6RAR during the period June 1966 to May 1967, had done so exclusively within the province. Their initial task was to ensure the safety of the Nui Dat base while it was being developed so for the first few months operations concentrated on clearing the enemy from the area immediately surrounding Nui Dat. This was achieved by cordoning and searching the villages to the north and south along Route 2 in order to damage the communist infrastructure; and patrolling in considerable force, particularly to the east of the base. And it was there, in late July 1966, that 6RAR made first contact with D445 Provincial Mobile Battalion, killing thirteen of them, and wounding nineteen others. This was the first of many encounters that units of the Task Force would have with D445.

But it was the battle at Long Tan in August 1966 that did most to establish in the minds of the Viet Cong and their sympathisers that they could never dominate the province while Australians, and a little later the New Zealanders, were there.

When 5RAR and 6RAR were relieved in April and May 1967 by 7RAR and 2RAR, the same type of operations continued. But they tended, of necessity, to be reactive. The enemy would spring an ambush, attack a village or mortar an ARVN post, and an RAR battalion, or elements of it, would be reacted into the area by APC or helicopter. Most often the enemy would be gone by the time they arrived, and they were then committed to following up. It was also not unusual for a battalion to mount an operation which was scheduled to last only a few days, and then find that it developed rapidly and yielded good results, so that it could eventually last for anything up to six weeks. Major operations were frequently mounted into enemy known or suspected supply areas like the Rung Sat, the Hat Dich and the Long Green, or onto major enemy positions. Sometimes contact was made, sometimes not. The object of all these operations was to keep the enemy off balance and on the move, and they achieved that.

But the tempo of operations changed markedly for 1ATF at the end of January 1968, when the First Tet Offensive began. Thirty-six of the 44 provincial capitals throughout South Vietnam were attacked by VC and NVA forces, with a major effort being directed towards the capture of Saigon. Therefore, on 24 January 1968, HQ 1ATF, 2RAR, 7RAR and other supporting elements were flown into AO Columbus on the border between Bien Hoa and Long Khanh provinces. It was there that Operation Coburg, mentioned in the previous chapter, took place. The task was to deny enemy access to the major logistic and air bases at Long Binh and Bien Hoa, and to prevent them from using rockets and other heavy weapons against those vital installations. Meanwhile 3RAR, who had arrived in Vietnam the previous December, remained at Nui Dat to secure the Task Force area and the approaches to it, and to protect the civilian population centres.

Operation Coburg heralded the start of main force operations for 1ATF, both inside and beyond Phuoc Tuy. The aggressive stance taken by successive Task Force commanders, together with the inclusion on the order of battle of a third battalion and New Zealand troops in 1967, the Centurion tanks of 1 Armoured Regiment in February–March 1968, and other additions in strength, enabled the Task Force, under Brig Ron Hughes, to increase both the tempo and the weight of operations against the enemy. These main force operations continued until April 1969, when they were augmented by the start of the Pacification Programme.

Pacification was defined by the US Military Assistance Command as:

> The military, political, economic, and social process of establishing or re-establishing the local government responsive to and involving the participation of the people. It includes the provision of sustained, credible territorial security, the destruction of the enemy's underground government, the assertion or reassertion of political control and involvement of the people in government, and the initiation of economic and social activity capable of self-sustenance and expansion. The economic element of pacification includes the opening of roads and waterways, and the maintenance of lines of communication important to economic and military activity.[1]

This lofty and ultimately unattainable design translated for 1ATF and its current Commander, Brig Sandy Pearson, into a sustained effort to keep the enemy well away from the population centres which were their traditional sources of food, money, materials and recruits. At the same time, aggressive operations continued into the known and suspected enemy base areas east and west of Route 2. Pacification in Phuoc Tuy, with its concomitant activities of retraining and improving the AVRN,

RF and PF, began in April 1969, and was focused mainly on the population centres in the southern third of the province.

But in 1970 the tempo of operations in 1ATF changed again. Pacification continued, but on 22 April that year Prime Minister John Gorton announced that 8RAR would not be replaced when they went home that November. Thereafter there would be only two battalions on the orbat (order of battle), which, Mr Gorton confidently predicted, would only require some small modification to the role of the Task Force. But the new Commander 1ATF, Brig Bill Henderson was not so sure. 'Withdrawal,' he said succinctly, 'will merely mean that we will have to work very much harder than at the moment, which is already pretty hard. The problem is that we still have the same area to cover . . .'

So when 4RAR/NZ (ANZAC) Battalion arrived in Phuoc Tuy to begin operations in May 1971, 3RAR was the only other battalion on the Task Force orbat. Pacification was progressing, principally in the south of the province; as were continuous operations to keep 33 NVA Regiment out of the province; to keep 274 VC Regiment and D445 constantly on the run within it; and to make life for the Chau Duc District Committee and its sympathisers as hazardous as possible.

The 1st Australian Task Force operational base was located at Nui Dat, ten kilometres north of Baria. When it was first established, in June 1966, the base sat astride Route 2. But in 1967, for security reasons, a bypass road was constructed 1.5 kilometres to the west of Nui Dat, its purpose being to keep civilian traffic and prying eyes well away from the base.

The base was named after the prominent Nui Dat feature, a hill which stood 103 metres above sea level and dominated the surrounding area. There were in fact two Nui Dats in close proximity. The second was situated five kilometres to the east; it overlooked the site of the battle of Long Tan, and was sometimes referred to as Nui Dat Two. But whenever people mentioned Nui Dat, it was the one in the 1ATF area they were talking about. And, by common usage, the Task Force base became known as 'The Dat', and for most Australians and New Zealanders who served in Vietnam, The Dat became their home, and the focus of their lives for twelve months.

The base was about six square kilometres in area, roughly three kilometres north–south and two kilometres east–west. Nui Dat Hill had been assigned permanently to whichever SAS squadron was currently on the orbat. Their helicopter pad, Nadzab, was situated at the foot of the hill at its northern end, with two other pads, Hornbill and Pelican Heights, in close proximity. The SAS position overlooked and defended the western and north-western approaches to the Task Force position.

North of the hill, and running east–west, was Luscombe Field, the 1ATF short takeoff and landing strip. It was used principally by the Caribous of 35 Squadron RAAF, the Iroquois of 9 Squadron RAAF, and rotary and fixed wing aircraft of 161 Recce Flight AAAvn. It was from Luscombe Field that all operations requiring heliborne insertion began. At the eastern end of the airstrip was a specially constructed amphitheatre in which, from time to time, various concert party performers entertained the troops. This was Luscombe Bowl.

Canberra Avenue bounded the north side of Luscombe, and marked the southern boundary of the battalion lines there. In May 1971 3RAR was in residence. Their task was to defend the north-western, northern, and north-eastern approaches to the base.

The ANZAC Battalion's lines, alternately occupied by 2RAR, 4RAR and 6RAR, were sited along the eastern side of the base, and it was their task to defend the eastern approaches to it. On the south-eastern corner of the Task Force position was the third battalion area, occupied until recently by 8RAR but now being used by the Australian Reinforcement Unit and by AATTV as a training centre for the ARVN. These positions defended the eastern, south-eastern, and southern approaches.

Brig Bruce McDonald, OBE, MC commanded 1ATF during 4RAR/NZ (ANZAC) Battalion's second tour in Phuoc Tuy Province. Throughout 21 September 1971 he 'provided cool, calm, helpful support to the CO and the Battalion'. (*The Fighting Fourth*)

At the extreme south-west corner of The Dat were the artillery lines, occupied now by 12 Field Regiment RAA. They had the responsibility for defending the approaches from the west, south and southwest, and their guns glared defiantly over the bunds to emphasise this fact.

Between the artillery lines and the SAS on Nui Dat Hill was HQ 1ATF, the epicentre of which was the Task Force CP. It was from here that Brig Bruce McDonald, OBE, MC, commanded, controlled and monitored all operations.

Beyond the eastern end of HQ 1ATF were the lines belonging to 1 Field Squadron RAE and 22 Construction Squadron RAE. Among other vital services, including the supply of water, the engineers operated and maintained a very efficient electrical power grid to all units 24 hours a day.

Besides Canberra Avenue, which ran round and through the whole area, there were numerous other roads bearing well-known and nostalgic names: Ingleburn Avenue, Tianjara Road, Chatham Avenue, Malacca Road, Scheyville Loop, Moorebank Road and Liverpool Road.

Most units had a helicopter pad in or close to their location that sometimes bore names which were significant to those who had originally constructed them. The northernmost was LP Porky, after 7RAR's regimental mascot; the easternmost was Eagle Farm, named for Brisbane's principal airport; and among the others were Kiwi, Kapyong, Koala and Kings Cross. The engineers' LP was Wombat because, so it was widely believed, they were never happier than when digging.

In 1966 the battalion's positions on the north and east of the area had been sited in a rubber plantation. Since then the rubber had been unworked, and now most of the trees were rotten, and had the disconcerting habit of collapsing onto the tents beneath. And despite the shade afforded by the trees, much of the Task Force area was in the open, so that it was invariably very hot, and in the dry season dusty as well. But the Construction Squadron's all-weather roads minimised that problem, as did the periodic spraying of road surfaces with diesel oil.

The whole 1ATF position was surrounded by thick barbed wire entanglements. These, too, were sprayed regularly with diesel to prevent the growth of weeds and foliage. Claymore mines were fixed in banks in the wire, and well-constructed and sandbagged bunkers were sited at regular intervals along the perimeter. Machineguns, manned day and night, were sited to sweep the open ground beyond with interlocking arcs of fire. There were gaps in the wire which could be opened when patrols and ambushes went out; and several gates allowed exit and entry for armoured vehicles. The main gate, located on the old Route 2 south of the base, was controlled by the Military Police.

Mortar and artillery DFs thickened up the defences along all the approaches to Nui Dat, and 161 Recce Flight conducted visual reconnaissances over the area at dusk and dawn every day. At all times the 1ATF Ready Reaction Force, consisting of a rifle company mounted in APCs, could instantly be dispatched to any point from which the enemy might be threatening; and the 1ATF Defence and Employment Platoon provided a backup counter-penetration force.

But in 1971, while a ground attack on the Task Force position could never be discounted, it was unlikely. The enemy had a great respect for the aggressive inhabitants of the Nui Dat base, and the memory of Long Tan was still fresh in everyone's minds.

Within the ANZAC Battalion's area, Infantry Crescent, running north–south, divided the BHQ, Support and Administration Company lines from those of the rifle companies, which were on the extreme outer perimeter. Victor Company lines were the most northerly.

Turning in from Canberra Avenue, the main entrance to BHQ was Ruapeha Road, named in honour of the New Zealanders of the ANZAC affiliation. It was a wide and neatly maintained avenue, and its centrepiece was the Battalion flagpole and the Memorial Cairn, bearing on brass plates the names of the members of 2RAR, 4RAR, 6RAR and their New Zealand comrades who had lost their lives while serving in Vietnam. It was at this place, when circumstances allowed, that Anzac Day dawn services were held.

The main BHQ buildings, including the Intelligence Section, the RAP and the Officers' and Sergeants' Messes, were Lysaght huts with concrete floors, louvred windows and, in some cases, ceiling fans. Huts of varying materials, but usually weatherboard walls and corrugated iron roofs, provided office and stores accommodation, kitchens, shower and toilet blocks. Water was contained in numerous large tanks which stood atop robust timber towers about three metres high. These were replenished by tankers which made their ceaseless rounds every day throughout the Task Force area.

Tents 16 feet by 16 feet, with sandbagged blast-walls to just above waist level, provided sleeping accommodation. The only exception was the CO's house, built in 1967 by 2RAR's Pioneer Platoon for their CO, LtCol Chick Charlesworth. It was a well constructed timber-frame cottage complete with plumbing and air conditioning. But nobody begrudged successive ANZAC COs this comparative luxury. Each bore on his shoulders the ultimate responsibility for the lives and well-being of every man under his command, and if this task was made easier by a good night's sleep, then everyone benefited. Besides, LtCol Hughes was always out at Courtenay Hill, and so used the cottage hardly at all.

It's said that necessity is the mother of invention, and there were all sorts of novelties to be found in the ANZAC lines. Perhaps one of the most inventive was the Nui Dat Urinal, which proliferated particularly outside messes and canteens. These urinals worked on a siphon system, and were comprised of 44-gallon drums with the tops cut out, sunk to ground level, and filled with a mixture of oil and water. The oil naturally floated on the water, so that hygiene and cleanliness was maintained while odour was minimised. However, it was not unknown for those who lost their footing through carelessness or over-indulgence to fall into these useful facilities in the dark, and sometimes in daylight as well. Such occurrences always provoked considerable hilarity in those who witnessed them, though the victims received no sympathy whatsoever.

The rifle companies' lines were almost identical in layout, and the entrances into them came off Infantry Way. Company kitchens were situated near these entrances in order to facilitate the delivery of rations and the removal of garbage. Close to the kitchen stood the diggers' dining room, with their canteen, known always as 'The Boozer', next to it. Then came the CQMS's store and office, the company office and the company CP, which was well dug in, had overhead protection, and would withstand all but the heaviest attacks by indirect fire. The OC's tent, and that of the 2i/c, CSM and CQMS were all close to the CP, as was the combined officers' and sergeants' mess. There was nothing haphazard about the layout. It was functional as well as having an eye for smartness, so that tents were all in neat lines, guy ropes were braced tightly to their steel pickets, and the area was emu-bobbed daily. This avoided any untidiness which would displease platoon sergeants and the CSM on their rounds.

The three platoons' lines ran from CHQ towards the perimeter. Each platoon was tasked with the defence of a portion of the wire and the manning of bunkers and weapon pits which overlooked it. When the companies were out on operations, which they were for 30 days out of 35, the task fell to the company rear details and left-out-of-battle personnel, augmented by those members of BHQ, Support and Administration companies who were not otherwise employed in CPs or other locations. The responsibility for base defence belonged to OC Administration Company, who was assisted in this task by the TAOR patrol master, WO2 Wilmen.

Within the platoons it was usual for the platoon commander and his sergeant to share a 16 foot by 16 foot tent. All the other tents accommodated four men, with a steel locker and a standard metal bed for each. Beds were placed in the corners of the tents to give their occupants maximum protection from the mandatory sandbagged blast-walls. Individual metal trunks went under the beds, and contained whatever could not be fitted into the steel lockers. Mildew grew on everything. A table and four chairs occupied the central position, used for writing letters, playing cards or similar activities.

Each tent had a flysheet over it, and usually its canvas walls were rolled up so that air circulated while the interior remained dry even under the onslaught of frequent tropical storms. Before the tents were erected, empty artillery shellcases had been driven into the dirt to create supports for a timber floor. At the entrance to each tent there was usually some form of bootscraper to assist in the removal of the red clay that stuck like glue to any footwear. All tents had electric light, and most of the occupants chipped in to buy electric fans.

At night 'mosi' nets were rigged over each bed, to afford protection not only from malarial mosquitos, but also from a range of aggressive local fauna. These included small spiders with bright red eyes that lived in the crevices between the sandbags, rats and possums fossicking for spilt food, and poisonous millipedes and scorpions. Rumours of five-metre cobras ensured that nets were always rigged and firmly tucked in round the mattresses, even though they only gave psychological protection against the larger predators.

While mosquito nets kept out all but the most determined nocturnal visitors, they also restricted air circulation. It was always very hot and humid at night, and this was not helped by the plastic-covered mattresses and pillows which were issued in the interests of hygiene. But infantrymen are nothing if not philosophical about their discomforts. They are also extremely adaptable, and few lost much sleep just because it was hot or things went bump in the night.

And in fact a good deal did go bump in the night. Occasionally a sound like heavy furniture being dragged over wooden floorboards indicated that B52s were flying an Arclight mission. Usually the guns and mortars fired nightly harassing and interdiction missions (H & Is) at various times between dusk and dawn. In most cases these H & Is were chosen at random from the map, and impacted on points which might just possibly be used by enemy soldiers travelling in the dark: track or creek junctions, for example, or a point at which the forest met a plantation. Whether or not these missions ever hit anything will probably never be known, but they had a psychological value. They told the enemy that even at night, even in the most inaccessible terrain, the Task Force was awake and searching for them. And it told them that tomorrow, and the day after, and for all the other days while Australians and New Zealanders were in Phuoc Tuy Province, they could never be certain of their safety.

Although the rifle companies, the Battalion CP and Support Company spent little time in Nui Dat, most of Admin Company spent most of their time there. Apart from them, each company invariably had some members who were not out on operations. The CQMSs and their assistants worked from Nui Dat, although the CQs often accompanied the regular resupply whenever it was tactically feasible. But there were always personnel who needed a few days off. Forward scouts, as we have seen, were under constant pressure in front of their sections and platoons. Therefore, from time to time, platoon commanders might decide to rest a scout or anyone else who had been particularly hard worked. Other men might have minor injuries or ailments which would not heal under the constant daily grind of searching out the enemy. So they remained in their company lines and, unless excused all duties by the RMO, were employed under the supervision of the company 2i/c, the CQ or the company clerk. Later, when the company took R & C, or individuals became entitled to R & R, they staged in and out through their company lines as well.

And there was always plenty to do. By day, apart from assisting in the preparation of the 5-day resupply, there was maintenance to be done around the lines. Fallen rubber trees and branches needed to be cleared, tents re-sandbagged, laundry sorted, stocks checked in the company ammunition bunker, damaged stores returned and new items collected, the officers' and sergeants' mess and The Boozer had to be regularly stock-taken. And there was, for minor wrongdoers, the digging of new latrines. By night there were invariably gun pickets or radio watches to be done, or listening posts or ambushes to be deployed into the TAOR. All this was the routine and accepted part of life in Nui Dat.

But Nui Dat was not without its excitements. On one occasion an enterprising NCO came up with a simple plan to rid his tent of the depredations of a pack of rats. One evening he opened a tin of pecan cake, which most ANZAC members considered to be a particularly horrible American confection. This he placed on the floor of his tent after inserting the detonator from a Claymore into it. He then trailed out the electrical initiator cord and carefully concealed himself outside the tent in such a way as to be able to observe the cake.

After a while several large rats entered the tent, and as soon as they got busy he pressed the clacker and the issue was instantly resolved. But every solution produces its own problems: there were now so many bits of rat stuck to the inside of the tent that it had to be taken down and replaced with another.

And OC Admin recalls:

I was in the Battalion Rear CP one morning with Don McIver and Ted Stevenson, when we received a message to say that Victor Company's ammunition bunker was on fire. Cpl Jock McFallan was duty driver, and he took the three of us to within a couple of hundred metres of the fire, at which point he was told to stop and wait for us there. We then walked towards the billowing black smoke. I'm not sure that we really knew what we were going to do when we got there, but I can remember being a bit sceptical about trying to drag smouldering boxes of grenades and M72s out of a blazing inferno. However the problem solved itself when we were still a hundred metres away, and the bunker blew up with an earth-shattering roar. Jock McFallan said later that the three of us just disappeared in a massive fireball, and he thought we'd been taken out. But we'd thrown ourselves instantly to the ground, and apart from being a bit hard of hearing we seemed OK. But then all the things that had gone up in the air with the explosion started coming down again: it was very uncomfortable for a while there. But at the end of it we were alive, and there were no serious casualties elsewhere either.

A few days later I was called from the CP Rear to D Company's lines, where a soldier who'd been getting depressing letters from home had decided to demolish the inside of his tent with an automatic SLR. This he kept pointed at me throughout the uncomfortable half hour or so that I chatted to him. But eventually he applied the safety catch and put the SLR down.

They say that bad things happen in threes, and within a few more days this proved to be so. I was down at Eagle Farm one afternoon when one of the Admin Company boys, while clearing his M16 prior to cleaning, loosed off a five-round burst into the trees just above my head, but did no other damage.

So I was quite pleased when the CO told me, a few days after all this, that I was to take over D Company. All things considered, it seemed to me that I would probably be much safer out there with 274 Regiment and 33rd than being back here in The Dat. But as it turned out I was wrong about that.[2]

The CO exercised command and control through the Battalion CP. For almost all of the second tour, the CP was located on top of Courtenay Hill, about 600 metres west of Route 2 and two kilometres south-west of Cam My village.

In the autumn of 1970, B Company 2RAR/NZ (ANZAC) Battalion and 1 Field Squadron had established an NDP adjacent to two hills in the Phuoc Tuy–Long Khanh border area. These hills became known as Big and Little Dien Bien Phu, and the sappers quarried them to obtain fill for the reconstruction and subsequent maintenance of Route 2. In June 1971 the forward Task Force CP occupied the larger of the two hills, and remained there throughout Operation Overlord, after which the CP returned to Nui Dat.

After Overlord, 4RAR's CP moved onto the larger feature, which had now acquired the somewhat less pessimistic name of Courtenay Hill, after the French de Courtenay rubber plantation which was situated just across Route 2. The Battalion CP was to remain there for the next 114 days and nights until the withdrawal to Nui Dat in October that year.

The great advantage of Courtenay Hill was that it had excellent observation over a large part of the area in which the Battalion would be operating. Because the radio sets in use were VHF, and therefore required line of sight for best results, good observation also meant good communication. Moreover the sappers' quarrying operations had created steep sides to the hill, so when all the foliage had been removed it became the basis of a formidable defensive position. Even so, there was always a chance that it might receive a ground attack, and certainly attacks by fire. Therefore Support Company, led by the indefatigable Assault Pioneer Platoon, set about constructing bunkers and strong points, and various other structures as well. Over time, 100 000 sandbags were filled and expertly laid, and wire obstacles were constructed with Claymores and trip flares deployed in banks. Two helicopter pads, water and refuelling points were built, and the Hill put into a strong state of defence.

From the CP, the CO and his operations staff were able to communicate by radio with those elements of the Battalion manoeuvring in their assigned AOs, and also with any supporting arms assisting them. This was achieved over the Battalion command net, the Battalion administrative/air net, and various other radio nets that were established for the purpose. In addition, the CP was a callsign on the Task Force command net, which meant that the Task Force Commander and his staff had direct radio access to the CO, and vice versa. All these nets remained open and manned 24 hours a day, as did those in the companies and platoons, which meant that commanders at all levels were able to communicate direct with their units and sub-units in a matter of moments at any time of the day or night.

Maj Stevenson, as the CO's principal operations staff officer, directed and controlled the day-to-day running of the CP, and was responsible to the CO for its efficient functioning. The OPSO also understudied the CO in all operational matters during his absence.

Co-located with the CP was the Fire Support Control Centre, presided over by the BC, 104 Field Battery, Maj Keith Towning. 104 Battery was 4RAR's direct support battery, as it had been on the Battalion's first tour. This was a happy association, and the work done for the Battalion by the battery was of faultless and untiring high quality. Indeed there are many members of the Battalion who owe their lives to 104 Field Battery, as is recounted later.

10

The quantum leap

Victor Company arrived at Nui Dat from Singapore on 7 May 1971, and was immediately placed under operational command of LtCol John Church, CO 2RAR/NZ (ANZAC) Battalion. From 8 to 14 May the company had settled into Nui Dat and completed in-country orientation, and were now out on Operation Iron Maiden, which for them had started at 0400hr on 15 May.

The operation commenced with a cordon and search of the Viet Cuong and Ngu Yen Hiep rubber plantations north and east of Cam My village. This was a known VC supply area, and because civilians would be detained within the cordon the Task Force was assisted by RF units, National Police and South Vietnamese officials from Duc Thanh District.

The troops taking part were inserted into the area by A Squadron 3 Cavalry Regiment, and Victor Company provided the eastern side of the cordon which was designed to keep civilians, VC and any of their sympathisers confined within it. In fact the initial sealing-off of the search area went well, and 46 civilians who were unable to explain their presence were detained. Many of these were carrying unaccountably, and therefore suspiciously, large amounts of food and currency, and as a consequence they, and sixteen VC suspects, were taken away to District Headquarters for questioning. As it turned out, nothing could be decisively proved against most of them, and almost all were released and allowed to return to the area where they had been detained.

When the cordon withdrew, Victor Company continued to search the Courtenay rubber plantation and the forested areas adjacent to it; and 1 Troop A Squadron, who were in support of the New Zealanders, were tasked by Maj Monks with reconnaissance, ambush, reaction, redeployment and resupply tasks. But it was frustrating work. The company frequently encountered small groups of civilians who declared themselves to be rubber tappers. They came, they said, from Cam My village, where they lived, and the food they had with them, they insisted, was for their own use. The VC were 'number 10'; the Uc Dai Loi—they made the assumption that the New Zealanders were Australian—were 'number 1'. And there was not much that Maj Monks and his men could do about it.

On 17 May, Lt Fry's 1 Platoon saw six armed men about 200 metres away in the rubber. A check was made by radio to ensure that these were not members of the Cam My PF platoon. They were not, and 1 Platoon moved in to attack them while an APC section put in a blocking position with PF troops in support. But the enemy soldiers were alerted when rubber tappers began hastily leaving the area. Gathering these workers into a group, the enemy used them as a screen against the New Zealanders, and despite the best efforts of 1 Troop, the PF and 1 Platoon, the six enemy made good their escape. Shortly afterwards 1 Platoon surprised another suspect, but he jumped onto a bicycle and pedalled rapidly away.

But in late May an SAS patrol operating to the west of Route 2 found evidence of what looked like VC main force activity. This was in an area that had been used frequently by 274 Regiment, and new foot tracks and felled trees suggested that they might be back there again and re-establishing their camps and bunkers. On withdrawal of the SAS, Victor Company deployed into the same area at 1700hr on 30 May, and began searching and ambushing anything that looked promising. And at 1300hr on 2 June, Cpl Rata's section of 2 Platoon sprang an ambush on three enemy using a track and killed one of them. A search of his clothing and equipment revealed him to be a member of the Finance Section of HQ 274 Regiment.

The Battalion had drawn first blood, and Victor Company was understandably elated.

4RAR officially took over its ANZAC title and the responsibility for the conduct of operations from 2RAR at midnight on 23–24 May, the day the main body landed from HMAS *Sydney* and arrived in Nui Dat. They immediately began in-country training. This always ran to a pattern. The Battalion first settled into their accommodation, got to know the layout of the Task Force area generally, and the Battalion area particularly; went through the various daily routines, including stand-to at night and in the mornings; re-zeroed and test fired their weapons on the ranges outside each company's lines, watched a firepower demonstration which included the use of artillery, APCs, tanks and air support; and carried out close patrols in the immediate TAOR. Along the way they also acclimatised to the humidity.

It was a sensible week's transition which took each battalion from a training environment to an active service one, and gave them an opportunity to experience the real thing while not dropping them totally in the deep end.

But that interim week was now over, and while Victor Company remained west of Route 2 and continued to seek out 274 Regiment, B, C and D Company, on 3 June 1971, were deployed into AO Erica to begin Operation Bhowani Junction. This was a two-day shakedown operation, and its purpose was first to give the companies an opportunity to use, under active service conditions, all the routine systems they'd learned in training, and second to position them into the AO as a preliminary move before the start of the next operation, Overlord, which would begin on 5 June.

As 8RAR had not been replaced when they went home to Australia the previous November, there were now only two battalions available to Commander 1ATF, 3RAR and 4RAR, even though the size of the area of operations was the same. This meant that from now until the withdrawal of the Task Force from Phuoc Tuy on 7 November 1971, operations would be continuous. The pressure on the enemy and the Battalion alike would be unyielding, and the four rifle companies and Support Company would be out here in the forests of Phuoc Tuy, 30 days on, five days off, for the next five months. The Battalion CP and the Rear CP would operate 24 hours a day until 7 November, and Admin Company would be toiling in Nui Dat to support this substantial effort against the relentless enemy.

And indeed the enemy situation along the northern border of Phuoc Tuy was currently extremely threatening. Throughout May, 1ATF intelligence staff had been receiving reliable information that VC and NVA units were building up along the central southern border between Phuoc Tuy and Long Khanh provinces. The main area of concentration appeared to be Suoi Nhac, about ten kilometres southeast of Black Horse.

It was also known that in mid-May 3 Battalion 33 NVA Regiment had carried out a reconnaissance around Nui Le in northern Phuoc Tuy, though its purpose was not immediately known. After the reconnaissance the battalion had slipped back over the border, and was now establishing bases in the Suoi Nhac area. D445, who had withdrawn from Phuoc Tuy in late April, and now numbered only 100 all ranks, were with them, assisting with local knowledge and resupply. One company from D65 NVA Engineer Battalion, and K8 Support Company of

HQ Ba Long Province, with elements of Chau Duc and the Cau Su guerrillas, were also in the Suoi Nhac area. And RHQ and 1/274 were thought to be just south-west of Black Horse.

The intelligence assessment of all this activity was that Suoi Nhac had been selected by the enemy as an area for retraining, resupply and refitting. It was particularly suitable as a site for enemy base locations because of the very thick vegetation which provided good concealment from the air. The area also provided plentiful water, and was close to the population centres along Route 2 with their resupply potential. The enemy were also well aware of the difficulties the Allies encountered in obtaining clearances to operate along, or over, provincial borders, a factor giving them an added level of security.

Clearance difficulties for cross-border operations could be profound. If it had only been a matter of arranging clearances between 1ATF and the Americans it would not have been so difficult, because liaison and cooperation between the two had always been very good. But the involvement of the South Vietnamese military and civil authorities raised the degree of difficulty to nightmare proportions. Language was one problem; civilian bureaucratic fussiness was another; poor communication and passage of information between ARVN, RF and PF units yet others. Moreover, the South Vietnamese military and civil authorities had certainly been penetrated by communist sympathisers who would also make the getting of clearances as troublesome as possible. Eventually semi-permanent boundary clearances were arranged for 1ATF, which gave Brig McDonald the opportunity to operate against the enemy there and deprive them of their sanctuaries.

But the presence in close proximity of 3/33rd, 1/274, D445, elements of HQ Ba Long, Chau Duc and others along the northern province border was of considerable concern. And those dispositions were assessed as being the most serious and threatening for many months.

While the rifle companies positioned themselves in AO Erica, a reconnaissance was carried out for the siting of FSB Trish. For Operation Overlord, the FSB would be occupied by the Battalion CP, Support Company and 104 Battery, and was sited in a clearing adjacent to the south-east corner of the Courtenay rubber plantation.

Overlord would be a Task Force-controlled search and destroy operation. Brig McDonald's aim was to disrupt the enemy's activities in the Suoi Nhac area, to destroy as many of them as possible, and to keep them on the move and preferably out of Phuoc Tuy. To control the operation, the Task Force CP would be on Courtenay Hill and co-located with FSB Cherie.

CSM Support Company, WO2 Gary Holmes (left), with the BC, Maj Keith Towning, and the OPSO, Maj Ted Stevenson (right), at the Battalion CP position on Courtenay Hill. (*The Fighting Fourth*)

The ANZAC Battalion, with A Squadron operating on its west flank, was ordered into blocking positions along the line of the Suoi Ran, which flowed roughly parallel to the Phuoc Tuy–Long Khanh border, in AO Juno. 2/8 Battalion 3 Cavalry Brigade (US) from Black Horse would occupy blocking positions to the north-east in AO Omaha. As soon as these blocks were in place, 3RAR, supported by the tanks of C Squadron 1 Armoured Regiment, would begin driving the enemy onto them from the north-west in AO Gold. It was a classic hammer and anvil operation.

Although 4RAR'S role was to block enemy escape routes from the north, they would not do that from solely static positions. A gap of up to 500 metres separated each company from its neighbour, but these gaps had to be covered, and that meant patrolling and ambushing them. It also meant very careful coordination by the Battalion CP in order to prevent friendly clashes. Therefore all four companies patrolled their areas by day, and put ambushes in by day and night. And when they put in their NDPs, the company commanders did so in the expectation that they might be confronted by large groups of enemy seeking to escape 3RAR's advance.

When the Battalion CP opened at FSB Trish at 0749hr on 5 June, information and enemy sightings began to come in at once. At 0835hr 2/Lt McDaniel's 6 Platoon reported finding the week-old tracks of four people heading east to west. The track would be ambushed. At 0910hr Lt Mullane's 3 Platoon found a booby trap with a four-kilogram charge which had failed to explode. They destroyed it. And that night, at 1920hr, an enemy soldier walked into a trip flare set by 1 Section 1 Troop A Squadron, but he lived to tell the tale.

Next day, 6 June, at 1440hr, a CHQ C Company sentry fired a Claymore and then a burst of M60 at a lone VC, but he too escaped with his life. At 1600hr Lt Willis' 5 Platoon saw one enemy soldier moving close to their location, but although he was carrying a weapon, fire was not opened on him, and he got away.

Throughout 6 June 3RAR found plentiful signs of the enemy, and next day they and the tanks of C Squadron encountered elements of 3/33rd in a bunker system. The enemy fought fiercely with heavy machineguns, RPGs and small arms. Three Australians, including two RAAF crewmen, were killed and twelve others were wounded. Captured documents identified the enemy as C10 Company 3/33rd. Later in the day A Squadron, under the operational command of C Squadron, killed a member of 33rd's C12 Heavy Weapons Company. But apart from him, 33rd's casualties were unknown, and 3RAR continued to push south.

On the same day in 4RAR's AO, a sentry from 2/Lt Murphy's Tracker Platoon on the perimeter of FSB Trish reported movement to his front, but a patrol sent out to investigate could find no evidence of the enemy. Later that afternoon a CHQ C Company sentry failed to see an enemy soldier passing to his front but when a second enemy appeared he opened fire. The enemy immediately returned fire, hitting the sentry in the leg, and then withdrew. Later still, at 1535hr, CHQ C Company reported hearing movement between their location and that of their 7 Platoon; and then 7 Platoon heard groaning between their location and CHQ, although a search of the area found nothing.

There was a pattern in all of this, and it was a pattern that would continue throughout the Battalion's first operation: a curious and unsettling ineptitude, or a reluctance to commit, that was difficult to interpret. It could not have been inadequate training, because training had been unrelentingly thorough, and the Battalion had come through it all with flying colours. Nor was there anything wrong with the quality of the soldiers or their leaders, because all the weak links, at every level, had been removed and replaced. The enemy was certainly there; they could be heard and seen moving about. And yet 4RAR's sentries and patrols were not taking positive and aggressive action. And if they *did* open fire, they were not only not hitting the opposition, they were themselves becoming casualties to returns of fire.

Probably it was inexperience. Maybe results would have been better if the enemy had been allowed to get a little closer before fire was opened on them. Or maybe it was over-eagerness. The dark figures moving through the shadowed forest were balanced correctly enough on the rifle foresight, but the thumping pulse and the sweating palm and the uncareful jerk of trigger always seemed to send the shot wide.

Or maybe it was an unwillingness to fire the shot at all. Maybe, now that this was reality, there were some young men who could not summon up the particular courage that it took to extinguish a human life. Or at least not *this* time. Maybe next time, when the footage had been replayed in the mind's eye, and the man inside had come to terms with the soldier outside. Maybe next time he would make that quantum leap.

On Day 4 of Operation Overlord, 8 June, V Company at 1600hr, and Maj Hogarth's B Company at 1615hr, redeployed to positions which brought them onto the Suoi Ran itself. The block and search boundaries between the two companies were adjusted to ensure that a friendly clash was not possible. At 1655hr Maj Kudnig's D Company, the easternmost of the four, advised the CO that D Company 2/8 Cavalry (US) were also adjusting their block positions. The two sub-units, Australian and American, were using 4RAR's marrying-up procedures to ensure there would be no clash between them.

That evening B Company heard the sound of machinegun fire coming from the general area of an artillery defensive fire task they had just brought down, and C Company confirmed the report. Then 2/Lt McKay's 11 Platoon heard movement to their right and a clanking of metal over towards 12 Platoon. Twenty minutes later 161 Recce Flight sent a Pilatus Porter flareship to investigate, but it revealed nothing and the rest of the night was quiet.

It remained quiet next day, although at 1307hr 6 Platoon found an old and dilapidated bunker, and something that looked like a mine marker. At 1809hr a soldier from D Company had to be evacuated after touching a poisonous bush and then rubbing his eyes.

All companies were informed that next day 3RAR and the tanks would change the direction of their advance, and instead of pushing the enemy from north to south would advance from west to east. Their right flank would now be bounded by the Suoi Ran; and 4RAR's rifle companies were therefore required to withdraw 500 metres in order to provide 3RAR with room to manoeuvre.

At 0940hr on 10 June, Day 6, 3RAR were informed by 4RAR that they were now clear to begin their advance. But it was an uneventful day in AO Juno, and similarly quiet for 3RAR in AO Gold. The enemy were either lying very low or most of them had already slipped away.

On Day 7, the Tracker Platoon found what they at first thought was an enemy camp, but more careful investigation showed that it was more likely to be an old Allied platoon NDP. Then a Support Company patrol out of FSB TRISH found an enemy rest area which had been used twelve hours previously. And just after midday 6 Platoon found a camp with eight bunkers that had been used in the last two days. With it was a quantity of equipment and documents, but no enemy soldiers. A short time later Lt Grecian's 9 Platoon found 300 rounds of AK47 ammunition and a pair of rubber sandals. But still no enemy soldiers. In the late afternoon a patrol from D Company saw one enemy dressed in black pyjamas, but he got away.

Then at 1045hr on 12 June, Day 8, an APC carrying a section of 1ATF's Defence and Employment Platoon was ambushed four kilometres west of Route 2 on the province border. Two cavalrymen and five D & E members were killed instantly when Claymores being carried aboard the APC detonated, and B Company and Lt Swarbrick's Pioneer Platoon were redeployed to assist. But the enemy had withdrawn immediately after springing the ambush, and nothing came of B Company's follow-up.

Also on 12 June, the Tracker Platoon, patrolling on the eastern side of Nui Le in the area of 33rd's May reconnaissance, located 30 kilograms of rice, six Australian sandbags and an old hoochy. But no enemy. And at stand-to that night, a clearing patrol from FSB Trish contacted two enemy near the perimeter. They were engaged, but without results.

As 3RAR and the Centurions were no longer making any contact whatsoever with the enemy, the operation concluded at midnight on 13–14 June.

From 1ATF's point of view Overlord had been a success. 3/33rd and the other enemy units with them had been forced to withdraw from their bases in the Suoi Nhac area, and their training and resupply activities had been disrupted. Even so, an unidentified enemy force had still had enough resilience, aggression and presence of mind to ambush the D & E Platoon before finally withdrawing. It was a defiant counter-challenge.

From 4RAR's perspective Overlord had been a fairly lacklustre affair, and the Battalion's results were indicative of its inexperience. But much had been learned, and there was plenty to reflect on. Those in FSBs and on Courtenay Hill, for example, would have to be aware of the very real possibility of enemy action against them: anything from reconnaissance by one or two individuals to a ground attack and attacks by fire. Drills for these situations would have to be worked out and observed by everyone. It also needed to be emphasised that while aircraft, artillery and mortar flares provided excellent illumination at night, the flickering shadows they set up while descending could give the illusion that the jungle had come alive with charging enemy.

The rifle companies had learned that, for coordination and safety purposes, at least one radio would have to be switched to any neighbouring sub-unit's frequency. And marry-up procedures would have to be strictly observed to avoid any chance of friendly clashes.

The range at which fire should be opened on the enemy, particularly when using small arms and Claymores together, needed to be clearly defined. And great care would have to be taken when siting sentries so that arcs of fire from the remainder of the section and platoon were not masked by their presence. The benefits of a single well-aimed shot, as opposed to exploratory bursts of fire, were again stressed. Most of this was only fine-tuning, but it was important fine-tuning. Company commanders fixed platoon commanders with a steely gaze and made terse comment.

But the principal lesson learned by the Battalion was the relative ease with which 3/33rd and its supporting units had slipped through the blocking forces deployed to confine them. It was a salutary lesson for a newly operational battalion.

At 2015hr on 12 June, the CO issued orders for FSB Trish to be dismantled. The Battalion CP and Support Company would take over Courtenay Hill permanently when the Task Force CP departed for Nui Dat on the morning of 15 June. The four rifle companies were also given new orders and fresh tasks. They would be positioned into their new AOs by A Squadron throughout 13 June, and after a resupply would begin their next operation, Hermit Park, on 14 June.

But then on 13 June there was an encouraging little footnote to be added to the Battalion's part in Overlord. At 1730hr in its new AO, Cpl Brown's section of 9 Platoon sighted an enemy soldier at a range of 50 metres approaching the NDP. When he was 20 metres away the section opened fire and killed him. He was carrying an AK47 with three magazines, 91 rounds and an American compass. Subsequent examination of captured documents revealed him to be a recently promoted squad 2i/c from C24 Convalescent Company 274 Regiment.

Before we follow the ANZAC Battalion into Operation Hermit Park, it's worth pausing for a moment to examine the functioning of the Battalion CP, because its role was pivotal. Without the CP the rest of the Battalion, and its supporting arms and services, could not operate effectively.

On operations, all military formations and units require an organisation which will enable their commanders to exercise control over their subordinates. At Task Force level it was the Task Force CP, which usually operated from Nui Dat and was well equipped and housed in relative comfort. The ANZAC Battalion's CP, from 15 June 1971 onwards, operated from a bunker on top of Courtenay Hill and was proportionally less elaborate. Each rifle company had a CP of sorts: mostly it was just a shellscrape into which the radios were placed to give them protection from direct fire. At night, light-proof sheeting was thrown over the hole so that those crouched inside could operate using penlight torches. At platoon level the CP was not really a CP at all, and anyone needing to use the radio or refer to a map at night just pulled a poncho over his head. But the point was that no matter how crude it might be, there was always somewhere that provided a commander with a place where he could see a map, use a radio and codes, receive and issue orders, and send information.

There was no standard layout or manning for a battalion CP in Vietnam. This was because the personality and leadership style of each CO varied, and therefore the method and style of command each exercised from his CP also varied. Some COs maintained tight control over their operational staffs and insisted on approving every order that originated from the CP. Others, who had particularly effective OPSOs, preferred to spend as much time as possible away from their CPs visiting their own and supporting troops whenever circumstances allowed. Even so, most battalion CPs were similar, and varied only in minor matters of layout and scales of manning.

In the early days of 1ATF's operations in Phuoc Tuy, and during the fierce and bloody battles of First and Second Tet, battalion CPs were almost always dug into the ground and had substantial overhead protection in place. However, in June 1971 4RAR's CP on Courtenay Hill, because of solid rock just below the surface, could not be completely dug in. Nevertheless it consisted of a stout timber framework with well sandbagged blast-walls. A sandbagged corrugated iron roof provided protection from the weather and from indirect enemy fire. The fact that Courtenay Hill was long and narrow gave the CP additional security, because such targets are notoriously difficult to hit with indirect fire.

Inside 4RAR's CP were two tables, the larger of the two being the Battalion operations table. Seats were allocated to the operators of the Battalion command net, the admin/air net, and the TF rear link; to the OPSO, the duty officer and the duty operations clerk.

The smaller table was provided for the FSCC, manned by the BC, Maj Towning, and his BC's party, Sgt Mottershead, Bdr Sullivan and Gnr Connors; and for the Mortar Platoon commander, Capt Sullivan, and his assistant fire controllers.

Between the Ops and FSCC tables was the CO's chair, so that during a battle he could see and hear everything that was going on; analyse the information coming in; ask for additional information if necessary; make decisions after consultation with the OPSO, the BC and the IO; and then issue the relevant orders to the right people over the appropriate net.

Round the walls of the CP were map displays, which were covered with thick clear plastic sheeting. Information relating to the current operation was placed on these maps in coloured chinagraph pencils (red for enemy, blue for own troops) and kept constantly updated. Separate maps showed details of artillery and mortar fire plans, patrol and enemy information. There were also boards displaying general data, strength states, copies of written messages in and out, and duplicates of the duty officer's log.

The CP was manned 24 hours a day. If the situation in the AOs was quiet, the Ops table would be manned by a duty officer and a radio operator, and the FSCC table by a single artillery or mortar fire controller. But during a contact or battle the full CP staff would instantly assemble, and they would be joined by the adjutant and by the commanders or liaison officers from any supporting units. The CO would be called to the CP, or if he was away from the Hill would be alerted by radio. Depending on the situation, he might go straight to the contact area or return at once to the CP. As he travelled everywhere in his direct support helicopter, he was never more than a few minutes' flying time from the CP anyway, and always reachable by radio.

Communications was the vital web. All sub-units were connected by the umbilicus of radio to their next higher headquarters, and so on up. Individual APCs, tanks, forward observers, FACs and aircraft all had their own nets, or were a callsign on the net of the unit they were supporting. In most cases there was radio compatibility between different Arms, which meant that a platoon or company commander could switch frequency and speak, for example, directly to a tank or APC troop commander, FAC, MFC or artillery forward observer. Each sub-unit or individual had a callsign for instant identification and unambiguous recognition on the net. There were also generic titles: infantry were Foxhounds, armoured fighting vehicles were Ironsides, artillery were Shelldrake, engineers were Holdfast and so on. To differentiate between tanks and APCs, the callsigns of tanks were prefixed with the word 'Tango', and APCs with 'Tango Alpha'.

For normal routine running of the CP the duty officers were the adjutant, Capt McKenzie; the IO, Capt Sayce; the RSO, Capt Shannon; and the RSM. Other Support Company and BHQ officers and warrant officers were co-opted as necessary. Besides their other duties, each worked a rostered shift in the CP so that the whole 24 hours was covered.

Duty officers deputised for the CO and OPSO during periods of low activity and made routine decisions for them. They also ensured that information going out to the sub-units in the field, and information being received from them, was accurately recorded in the duty officer's log. On-coming duty officers were always carefully briefed by their predecessor on the current situation, and on any incomplete action that needed to be followed through.

Radio operators were provided, obviously, by 4RAR'S Signal Platoon and by a detachment from 104 Signal Squadron RASigs, who maintained the rear link communications between the Battalion and the Task Force CP. Operations clerks, who kept the various maps up to date, assisted in the compilation of the duty officer's log, and answered telephones and routine radio calls, were provided from Capt Sayce's Intelligence Section.

A heavy responsibility fell on the shoulders of the IO and his men because it was they who obtained, collated, assessed and issued both past and current information about the enemy, including their strengths, weapons and tactics, and, as far as possible, their locations and likely intentions as well. Without this information the Battalion would be fumbling in the dark. As has been seen, Operation Overlord was mounted in response to reliable intelligence about enemy intentions and locations in the Suoi Nhac area. All operations were mounted for similar specific reasons, and were not just random affairs that sent battalions to potter about in the hope they might eventually fall over the enemy.

Information that was gathered, sifted, analysed and then turned into intelligence, came from numerous sources. Civilians, agents, informers, PWs, surrendered enemy personnel, SAS patrols, captured documents, radio intercepts, and air reconnaissance were some of the sources available. Information on enemy locations and movements could also be gathered electronically by sensors which picked up motion vibrations. Unfortunately these sensors were not always able to distinguish between human and animal movement, and there were apocryphal stories of fierce bombardments being brought down on herds of pigs and troops of monkeys. Airborne radar, and 'people-sniffer' missions flown by aircraft that detected concentrations of body heat or chemicals in human sweat, were also frequently used. Whatever the source, information and intelligence eventually found its way down the organisational chain to battalion level. There it was resifted and put into a form that would have practical use for the planning and conduct of operations.

COs chose their intelligence officers with considerable care, because they needed to be men who were methodical, meticulous and capable of working without close direction and, to some degree, in the rarefied atmosphere of solid fact, not so solid fact and pure guesswork. In turn, IOs chose subordinates who would work well in a small group, often unsupervised and frequently under the pressure of deadlines and fatigue. A sense of humour was considered indispensable. In 4RAR's case these requirements had been met in abundance, and the Battalion was very well served by Capt Sayce, his deputy Sgt Farrell, by Sgt Sievers, the New Zealand intelligence representative, and the other members of the section.

A particularly innovative item introduced by Capt Sayce was the 4RAR/NZ (ANZAC) Battalion Weekly Intelligence Review. This was a digest of strategic and tactical intelligence, starting with the general situation in North Vietnam, Laos and Cambodia. More specific information covering the 1, 2 and 4 Corps areas came next, then an assessment of 3 Corps and the 1ATF TAOR; and finally, detailed information on enemy activity in Phuoc Tuy Province and the adjacent border areas. Meteorological data for the following week was included, and the whole package provided the CO and the company commanders with a wealth of useful information for planning and executing day-to-day operations.

During preparation in Australia several of the section had undertaken Vietnamese language training at the RAAF School of Languages. Principal among them was Cpl McGurk, who had served in Vietnam during 2RAR's first tour, and was now a qualified and accomplished linguist. Capt Sayce recounted:

> In addition to soldiers who had attended language training in Australia, there were a small number of ARVN interpreters attached to the Battalion who worked under my direction. They were attached to companies on operations, but were only marginally effective. Strangers among us, facing an uncertain future, they were not comfortable or completely trusted. The exception was Sgt Hai. He worked and cooperated well with us and had a happy disposition, despite an astute understanding of what the withdrawal of the TF from the Province would mean in the long term.
>
> When a PW was taken by one of our sub-units, every attempt would be made to insert Cpl McGurk and Sgt Hai into the location to carry out a battlefield interrogation. First, because he might have information of an urgent local tactical significance. Second, he would most likely still be in a state of shock after being captured, and would therefore talk more freely, particularly when treated decently by our soldiers. But by the time TF took him into custody he had started to come out of shock, and was more guarded in his responses. Mac understood all this, and that was why he was such an asset to the Section and Battalion.[1]

But now it was 14 June, and H Hour for Operation Hermit Park was 0600hr.

Although it was gratifying to know that the intelligence which had led to the mounting of Overlord had been correct, it was also very worrying. It will be recalled that in mid-May, 3/33rd, a battalion of the most potent of all the enemy units facing 1ATF, had conducted a reconnaissance into northern Phuoc Tuy in the general area of Nui Le. Having done that, they had moved back into Long Khanh Province to begin resupply, refitting and retraining. But what was the purpose of the reconnaissance? Intelligence assessments from 1ATF suggested that 3/33rd and their supporting units were planning sapper attacks and attacks by fire on the villages, hamlets and military posts along Route 2. These operations aimed at disrupting the Pacification Programme and to apply pressure on the Allies for more troop withdrawals from Vietnam. But what if the Nui Le reconnaissance was a precursor to an operation aimed specifically at 1ATF? By now, mid-June, the enemy would have known that 8RAR had not been replaced the previous November. There had certainly been plenty of comment about it in the Australian newspapers at the time, together with speculation about further troop withdrawals, and it would be naive to think that such information would not get back to COSVN and eventually to 33rd, 274 and the others. A reduction in strength of one battalion from the Task Force orbat meant a reduction in infantry strength of 30 per cent, and infantry was the primary Arm in Phuoc Tuy Province. And there had been other concomitant reductions in strength as well. That could suggest to astute enemy commanders that there might now be insufficient troops to maintain the tempo of operations in depth throughout the province and guarantee the security of the Nui Dat base at the same time. Not only is revenge sweet, but the enemy might reason that with the Australian and New Zealand commitment to the war already being wound back, increased casualties would cause uproar in Canberra and Wellington, and might very well hasten more withdrawals.

Or could the Task Force be brought to battle somewhere else; in the forested areas east or west of Route 2 perhaps? 1/274 Regiment was very familiar with the Suoi Ca area to the west, and already had bunker systems there. And 3/33rd, the ambush experts, had reconnoitred the Nui Le area to the east. Not only that, but three weeks ago, on 17 May, 3/274 had mounted an abortive ambush on an RAAF supply column south of Long Binh on Route 15. Could that possibly have been a rehearsal for something bigger? Nor would it take long for the enemy to realise that Courtenay Hill, with its bunkers and aerials and battery of guns, was a significant permanent installation, and therefore also a potential target.

But for now all this was speculation, and the best way to keep the enemy from concentrating and preparing a major attack was to seek him out, inflict casualties and keep him on the move.

The ANZAC Battalion's main targets during Hermit Park would be 1/274 Regiment and Chau Duc's C41 Company. RHQ 274 and their 2 and 3 Battalions were out of Phuoc Tuy, in the southern part of Long Khanh, reinforcing and resupplying. 1/274 were reported to be in their traditional bases along the Suoi Ca west of Route 2 and close to the tri-border area. They numbered approximately 100 all ranks.

Chau Duc District HQ, with the Ngai Gaio village guerrillas, were thought to be near the Cu Bi rubber plantation five kilometres south-west of Xa Bang: C41, numbering no more than 20, were known to be in the Suoi Chau Pha valley north-east of the Nui Dinhs. The combined Binh Ba and Duc My guerrillas, numbering in total thirteen, were

The CO visiting Capt Rod Earle and members of 1 Troop A Squadron in the Courtenay rubber plantation during Operation Hermit Park. It was during this operation that the Troop carried out one of its most successful night ambushes. (*The Fighting Fourth*)

assessed to be four kilometres west of Binh Ba and trying to obtain supplies from that village.

All these units were known to have received reinforcements in May and June, and would continue operating against the hamlets and military posts along Route 2. So Hermit Park would be a battalion search and destroy operation, and it would be mounted astride Route 2 to counter the enemy's activities in the area. The operation was scheduled to last from 14 June to 27 July, and would be controlled by the Battalion CP on Courtenay Hill, where the guns of 104 Battery would also be located in FSB Cherie. Throughout the operation the ANZAC Battalion would be supported by sub-units of A Squadron and C Squadron. The 155mm self-propelled guns of C Battery 5/42 Artillery Battalion (US) would be in general support for the period 18–27 July from Courtenay Hill.

The CO's concept of operations was that from 14–20 June the Battalion would maintain continuous patrols and ambushes to the west of Route 2, the aim being to interdict 1/274's supply routes from the south-west and north-west of Courtenay rubber.

Then, from 21 June, C and D Company would search and ambush to locate Chau Duc's C41 Company along the Chau Pha valley in the south of the AO. V and B Company would do the same in the north. These operations would continue for as long as useful results were being achieved. At that stage the CO would reassess progress, and might redeploy the Battalion into any location which seemed to offer further gains.

For the first three days there was not much to report. B and D Company found a few old bunkers and destroyed them; CHQ C Company contacted a party of three or four enemy without result; and D Company redeployed from the eastern end of Courtenay rubber to the west of Route 2. Meanwhile the Tracker Platoon concentrated at Courtenay Hill after dismantling FSB Trish.

But at 0845hr on Day 4, 17 June, Cpl Pollard's section of 8 Platoon contacted six enemy soldiers dressed in greens three kilometres west of Xa Bang. Members of the section were outside the platoon ambush point checking the Claymores when they saw six enemy soldiers moving from east to west. The Claymore party were seen as they withdrew into the ambush position and although they killed one enemy with small arms fire, the rest withdrew. On the same day, at 0950hr and at almost the same place, Cpl McKinley's section made contact with an unknown number of enemy, but without discernible results.

Also on the 17 June, at 1855hr, CHQ B Company were in an NDP on the provincial border five kilometres west of Route 2. One of the

CHQ sentries, Pte Marum, heard noises in the high grass to his front. Standing up to get a better view, he saw two enemy, fired two aimed shots and then the rest of his magazine into the place where the second VC had dived for cover. Cpl Crapp then fired into the same area, and a short burst of AK47 fire was returned, but it went wide and high. A search revealed the body of one enemy with his AK47 and a pack. He was later identified as belonging to 1/274.

Four minutes later, at 1859hr, 2/Lt McDaniel's platoon contacted a squad of enemy moving east to west in front of the platoon's perimeter. They killed one man and captured his AK47, personal equipment and the food he was carrying. A sweep was carried out under artillery illumination, but no other enemy were located.

During the morning of 18 June Lt Grecian's 9 Platoon, four kilometres south-west of Xa Bang, contacted four enemy, but after a brief fire-fight the enemy withdrew north and appeared to have suffered no casualties. Then at 1140hr Cpl Templeman's section of 8 Platoon found three enemy in a small camp. Lt O'Brien later reported: 'Platoon heard chopping sounds and crept to within 20 metres of the enemy camp. While moving the M60 into position enemy heard [8 Platoon's] movement and withdrew behind a large tree which could not be penetrated by M60 or SLR'.[2]

Nevertheless the platoon assaulted into the position and located a blood trail. Searching the camp, which they estimated to have been in use for about three days, they found a quantity of documents and personal equipment.

Maj Boxall commented, 'The platoon initially had considerable difficulty in getting close enough to correctly apply rules of engagement. In so doing they were detected, and the enemy opened fire and fled.[3] The Battalion comment in the after action report stated somewhat gloomily that, 'Rules of engagement, although necessary, are difficult to apply in thick jungle'.

Two days later, at 1715hr, Cpl Pollard's section again found one enemy in almost the same place as his previous contact, but the man escaped to the west. And again, on 21 June, at 1835hr in the same area, Cpl Templeman's section contacted three enemy soldiers armed with AK47s and an RPG. Frustratingly they also escaped, this time to the south.

But later that night Capt Earle's 1 Troop A Squadron, which had come under operational control of the Battalion earlier that day, achieved a significant success just north of the province border. The troop was deployed in a series of APC ambushes, sited in sections on the edge of a rubber plantation. It was very dark, raining heavily, and visibility was negligible, when 1 Section heard voices which they estimated to be no more than three metres away. They instantly fired a bank of Claymores and trip flares, and opened fire with 50- and 30-calibre machineguns, M16s and M79s. Capt Earle's narrative continues:

> Troop HQ and 2 Section reacted into the contact area to clear it and relieve the pressure on 1 Section. Contact continued spasmodically until 0300hrs. After clearing the area we occupied an NDP to protect the bodies [from being dragged away], having recovered twelve of them to the one location. At 220800hr approximately, an infantry element [the Tracker Platoon] cleared the area, which was again searched by the vehicles, resulting in a further one wounded enemy located and captured.[4]

The ambush had been very carefully planned, and the killing ground was sited along an old APC track on the edge of the rubber. As ill-luck would have it for the enemy, it also appeared to be their rendezvous point for whatever task they were carrying out that night. The ambush was classically well sprung at very close range, with a very heavy weight of fire deluging the killing ground. This was followed at once by the artillery DF, which included HE and illumination rounds. The aggressive follow-up by troop HQ and 2 Section resulted in additional VC being killed and wounded, and completed the rout of the enemy. The final total was thirteen VC killed by body count, with two more wounded and captured. An assortment of weapons and 22 packs were also recovered, and throughout the rest of the operation, wounded enemy were captured and new graves containing more enemy bodies from the ambush were uncovered. There were no casualties in 1 Troop. It was a very fine piece of work indeed, and it started a trend.

During the afternoon of 24 June, Day 11, in an area covered in thick bamboo and scattered heavy scrub, CHQ V Company put in a quick ambush along an east–west track that was showing signs of recent use. Maj Monks ordered Cpl Lee's Support Section to move a little further west to check the immediate approaches to the ambush and confirm that the footmarks were in fact recent. Cpl Lee reported that he was:

> . . . moving south-west along a track, possibly used by VC, when we came upon a well used VC track running north–south. On investigating, it was found to have been recently used, as sign [footprints] showed movement was north to south. On further investigation it was found that the track then swung west. At this point it was noted that logs were across the track and light trees were bent over the track and tied down; to the left of this track were two diversion tracks which ran parallel for 15–20 metres then

> swung out. The two scouts were checking the north track when I noticed movement to my front about 30 metres away. I identified it as VC and fired. I then saw two other VC who fired at the scouts, hitting the lead man [Pte K.H. Harding]. Contact drills were carried out. During the contact drill one RPG was fired but was non-effective.[5]

Having fired the RPG the enemy withdrew, leaving behind one of their number dead. But Maj Monk's immediate priority now was to get Pte Harding to a point where he could be extracted by helicopter as quickly as possible. While L/Cpl Carter, V Company's medical assistant, worked skilfully over the wounded scout, a circling light observation helicopter confirmed that there were several clearings just to the north, and a Dustoff helicopter was ordered up. However the clearing was too small for the aircraft to land and a Stokes litter was therefore winched down. But as it was retrieved it kept snagging the trees, and could not be recovered into the aircraft. The pilot identified a larger clearing 50 metres further on where he could land, and it was from there that Pte Harding was eventually evacuated.

Cpl Lee's reaction in opening fire on the enemy had been swift and decisive. The contact and subsequent fire-fight had lasted for fifteen minutes, and in that time his men had fired 140 rounds of M16, 120 rounds of SLR and 400 rounds of M60, which indicated good fire discipline within the section. One enemy body was recovered and later identified as being from C2 1/274.

But the Battalion was saddened to learn that Private Ken Harding had subsequently died of his wounds at 2100hr that night.

Next day, 25 June, at 1117hr, Lt Campbell's 2 Platoon found signs indicating bunkers about 400 metres from where Cpl Lee's contact had taken place. He established a pack base, then began carefully probing forward. He related that:

> After deployment to the edge of the suspected area one VC wandered towards the Platoon, and we dropped him at 15 metres range. Our machineguns then opened up at the sound of 6–10 enemy voices. The Platoon immediately drew heavy RPG, MG, rifle and claymore fire from a frontage of 50 metres. We withdrew under cover of Bushranger to the pack base to evacuate our two WIA. The enemy followed us and continued heavy harassing fire, causing one additional WIA. Bushranger was used to clear the perimeter and provide suppressive fire during Dustoff. After Dustoff the Platoon withdrew further west to allow an assault from the east.[6]

Lt Campbell's narrative is brief and concise, but the events he describes actually took three hours to unfold. And as testament to the tenacity of the enemy and the ferocity of the battle, his platoon expended 3500 rounds of M60, SLR and M16, and to that must be added the supporting fires of artillery and Bushrangers.

While Lt Campbell and his platoon were so engaged, Capt Earle's 1 Troop, and the Centurions of Maj Bourke's C Squadron, with Lt Fry's 1 Platoon under operational control, were preparing to attack the bunkers. Quick orders were given at 1435hr, and at 1445hr the squadron group, 'Crossed the start line on a bearing of 5100 mils' (approximately north-west).

Maj Bourke recounted:

> The group continued on the same bearing for 50 metres when first contact was made. Enemy fired two RPG rounds in quick succession at tank c/s 3B whilst it was endeavouring to smash down a bamboo clump. One of these rounds struck the crew commander's MG, destroying the MG and wounding the crew commander and [radio] operator. The radio set was penetrated by a small piece of shrapnel. C/s 5 [commander 5 Troop] discovered the firelane used by the enemy and immediately returned fire. C/s 3 [commander 3 Troop] moved to the left of c/s 3B and suppressed the area with fire. The position was consolidated and the wounded immediately evacuated by an element of 1Tp A Sqn 3 Cav Regt. C/s 3 was regrouped under command of c/s 5.
>
> The assault was recommenced and a second adjustment of the axis was made. Immediately following the change of axis c/s 5 was engaged by RPG fire. The round struck the gun barrel and the driver received head wounds from the splash. The area was saturated with fire and then enemy returned small arms fire over a frontage of 150 metres. The whole [C Squadron] group returned heavy fire. The small arms fire ceased. C/s 5C was fired on by three RPGs, two of which hit the tank. The first struck the [20-pounder gun] muzzle, damaging it. The second struck low down on the running gear. C/s 5C destroyed the source of the fire with an APCBC round [armour-piercing capped ballistic capped] that removed 8.5 inches [21 centimetres] of the damaged muzzle. He followed this with five canister rounds and MG fire. The position was consolidated and the casualty evacuated by an element of 1Tp A Sqn 3 Cav Regt.[7]

Lt Fry said:

> After the tanks reorganised themselves again they pushed on. We followed as before. We had only moved another 20 metres and again an RPG opened fire. This time we saw the RPG firer and a few others. Then

> almost simultaneously to my forward section opening fire at the seen enemy, we received heavy automatic and some RPG fire from the south. The enemy was moving from east to west, and then they seemed to turn and move away from the bunker area in an easterly direction. The whole c/s 11 [1 Platoon] was laid out along the left hand tank's tracks, and they fired into the area where the enemy had been seen. There was a break of a few seconds and then the enemy returned a great amount of automatic and RPG fire. This lasted about fifteen minutes. The tanks and APCs then swung into line with us and fired canister, 50 and 30 calibre into the area.[8]

Capt Earle's troop, supporting C Squadron in the attack on the bunker system, had:

> . . . secured the start line; protected the flanks and rear; evacuated casualties; and resupplied the tanks in contact with ammo. In addition at approximately 1700hr we engaged the enemy withdrawal to the east along the south side of the lane cut by the tanks. Nil result. The enemy engaged us with AK47. One RPG was seen but not used, probably due to thick scrub.[9]

By last light the area was secure. The battle had lasted from 1117hr, when 2 Platoon had begun pushing into the bunker system, until about 1700hr, when the tanks, APCs and V Company had secured the complex and resistance ceased. But tank main armament, 50 and 30 machinegun and infantry small arms had to be replenished, and it was decided to consolidate the force for the night. The assault into the complex would continue next morning, and H Hour was set at 1000hr.

Before the advance began again, the damaged tanks were taken to Route 2, where they were made serviceable by a forward repair team from 106 Field Workshop RAEME and sent back to Nui Dat. By 1255hr the force had reached the extremities of the complex without any further resistance. Numerous additional bunkers were located, but the system was deserted. The enemy had used three tracks to withdraw during the night and, heading north, had taken most of their equipment with them. Drag marks and grazes on trees and saplings showed where litters had passed. Only five VC bodies were counted and an RPG recovered. It was the usual main force tactic: defend the position fiercely until dark, then withdraw.

Maj Bourke summarised the principal lessons learned from the battle:

> It would appear that enemy when in contact with tanks will withdraw by moving to the flanks and then dashing past the tanks firing small arms in a

sporadic fashion hoping to inflict casualties on the turret crews. This is the second contact in which this has occurred. In both contacts artillery has been employed to cut off very close to the enemy's rear.

The enemy will fight tanks from inside his bunkers if he is forced to do so. It must be assumed that he accepts the backblast from the RPG into his bunker. This has also occurred in the last two contacts.

When engaged by heavy tank fire the enemy has fired RPGs into the trees above the tank, no doubt hoping to inflict casualties on the turret crews with the splash of the round.

Infantry platoon commanders when operating under command of armour must ensure their [radio] operators maintain continuous radio watch and that the operator stays very close by them at all times.

The positioning of blocks close to the contact area must be weighed very carefully against the obvious advantages of giving the tanks complete freedom of fire with all types of ammunition.[10]

Lt Campbell, whose platoon had found the bunkers on the morning of 25 June, also had comment to add after the battle:

Enemy very aggressive in both defence and counter. Enemy came well forward of bunkers and attempted a flanking movement. Considered that enemy was forewarned by contact the day before. M60s drew considerably more fire than other weapons. Had to stop using them.

Although artillery laid on and platoon commander requested fire, there was unacceptable delay before fire started. Bushranger seemed to be best neutralising weapon but one must repeatedly insist that they bring their suppressive fire closer to friendlies in order to get the best effect.[11]

In fact artillery fire had been brought down very quickly, but its effectiveness was reduced because of numerous calls to check fire. These were probably due to the proximity of Bushrangers, and the difficulty in distinguishing live from dead shrapnel in close country. Maj Towning, the BC, was well aware of this problem, and had already gone to considerable lengths, at some risk to his career, to put it right. He recalls:

During our training in Australia I had become concerned that the current Artillery doctrine on close target procedure appeared to be inappropriate for SVN, as it had been devised by the British for south-west Europe and limited ammunition.

This doctrine required each gun to be ranged one at a time. Each gun would be fired at a safe distance and walked into the required position. As you can imagine this takes a long time and is hardly suitable when you are in close contact. So, given that ammunition was not a problem in SVN (the

> Yanks were providing it free of charge) I decided that I would train my FOs to range with all guns at the same time and walk them back together. However the biggest problem was the TF Standing Orders on Artillery Support. These orders required that the first round fired during an engagement was to be directed 1000 metres from own troops' location.
>
> As you can see this posed enormous problems for us. Fortunately during our first deployment into a FSB in Courtenay rubber, the TF Commander queried the positioning of the DFs. I told him it was because of his standing orders. After a discussion with Jim Hughes and myself it was decided that as a trial 104 Battery could drop the first round as close to own troops as required by the supported commander. The modified close target procedure used by 104 Battery had been trialled on High Range. The method of trialling was quite illegal, but I wanted the FOs to have some experience in rounds falling quite close to them and it was impossible to do this without breaching safety regulations.[12]

Moreover Maj Towning did not believe that air-delivered ordnance provided troops in contact with anything like the same degree of close support that field artillery did. And for the reasons already outlined in Chapter 7, many experienced commanders at all levels in Vietnam would agree with him.

There were another 21 contacts of varying significance before Operation Hermit Park concluded on 26 July. Nine of those contacts resulted in tangible results or, in the vernacular of the Vietnam war, 'something you could put your foot on'. At 1900hr on 1 July (Day 18), four kilometres north-west of Xa Bang, the indefatigable and aggressive 1 Troop killed two more VC, wounded another, and recovered an AK47 and a K54.

On 2 July (Day 19), Cpl Menner's section of 10 Platoon attacked four enemy soldiers in a partly constructed camp and killed one of them. 2 Platoon ambushed two enemy soldiers on a track three kilometres north-west of Xa Bang on 9 July (Day 26), killing one of them and recovering his AK47. And Pte Brown, a CHQ B Company sentry in an NDP, engaged three enemy at 1650hr on 13 July (Day 30), killing one and wounding another and recovering an AK47.

The same day at 1843hr 6 Platoon, carrying out a track squat (a quick ambush), engaged four enemy, killed one, wounded another and captured an AK47. On 20 July (Day 37), 1 Platoon engaged an enemy squad, later identified as being from C23 1/274. They killed one of the enemy and two others, who were fired on at a range of three metres, were known to have been hit. Their bodies, however, were dragged away.

Pte Kirke of 6 Platoon, at 1420hr on 21 July (Day 38), initiated a contact rear by calmly firing two aimed shots at a following enemy. He killed one man, and the platoon subsequently located two heavy blood trails.

Then at 1615hr on 22 July, Lt Andrews' 7 Platoon carried out a textbook ambush on three enemy soldiers who 'Appeared to be alert and watching their arcs. They were moving quickly and did not see any sign of the ambush killing group'. Firing two Claymores and 100 rounds of M16, the platoon killed all three, recovered three AK47s, eight magazines, three packs, a quantity of documents, three torches, three mosquito nets, and a quantity of fresh fruit and rice. Maj Boxall later commented: 'This ambush was particularly commendable because only the required amount of firepower was used to kill the enemy and support the search. The ambush commander was certain that there were only three enemy present and exercised good fire control.'[13]

Also on 22 July, at 1624hr, the tail-end-Charlie of 2/Lt McDaniel's centre section and the platoon stretcher bearer saw an enemy soldier moving level with them on a parallel track. They alerted the rest of the section, then immediately opened fire and killed the man.

In total there were 30 contacts of varying size and intensity during Hermit Park. Seventeen of those contacts resulted in countable enemy casualties. A total of 35 VC were killed, five prisoners taken, and one enemy soldier surrendered. Fourteen AK47s, five K54s, one RPG2 and one M79 were recovered, as was a quantity of documents, equipment, stores, clothing and food. Many bunkers and camps were located and destroyed. Undoubtedly the enemy had suffered other dead and wounded as well, but they had been dragged away and then evacuated on litters. It will never be known exactly how many enemy fell to the ANZAC Battalion, to the guns of 104 Battery, to the tanks of C Squadron, the APCs of 1 Troop A Squadron and to the Bushrangers, but the losses in men and material were certainly substantial.

It must be emphasised, too, that a wounded man was a considerable liability to the enemy medical system. It takes four men to carry a litter any distance, and it's exhausting labour. The wounded man would then need medical attention and perhaps surgery and if he survived his injuries, the surgery and the gangrene, he would require additional nursing and convalescence. For those reasons, though it sounds brutal, it may well have been more effective to wound an enemy soldier in Vietnam than to kill him.

The cost of Operation Hermit Park to the ANZAC Battalion and to C Squadron was one man killed, Pte Ken Harding of Victor Company; four Australian crewmen from C Squadron and four New Zealanders wounded.

There had been two additional losses to 4RAR during the operation, both of them non-battle casualties. One was Cpl 'Tassie' Wilkinson, an experienced and fatherly section commander in 2/Lt Spinkston's 12 Platoon. During Hermit Park he had suddenly become ill with a fever, and arrangements were made for his evacuation by helicopter. Unfortunately this entailed a prolonged approach march to a suitable LP, and although Cpl Wilkinson's equipment was distributed among the platoon, the effort of getting to the LP taxed him severely. He was eventually evacuated by the CO's DS Possum, but to the great sadness of everyone, he died a few days later in hospital.

The second non-battle casualty was OC D Company, Maj Franz Kudnig. Over the months of training in Australia he had concealed the fact that he was suffering from a stomach ulcer. Now, under the extreme physical and emotional pressures of active service in Vietnam, he became unable to continue and had to be evacuated, first to hospital in Vung Tau and then to Australia.

Maj Kudnig had done an outstanding job in preparing D Company for active service. He had been meticulous in even the most minute detail of infantry training, and the company was superbly fit and tough as well. But he was by nature rather a forbidding man, and at the time some of the younger and less experienced members of the company tended to fix on his unbending exterior and overlook the considerable contribution he had made in readying the company for battle. Indeed it is tempting to wonder whether the company would have come so well through the next operation, Iron Fox, and later in September during Operation Ivanhoe, had it not been for Maj Kudnig's unrelenting persistence as a trainer of men.

He was succeeded in D Company by OC Admin Company, and in turn Admin Company was taken over by a new arrival in the Battalion, Maj John Robbins.

11

Ironsides and foxhounds

Throughout July the ANZAC Battalion had repeatedly encountered 1/274 VC Regiment in their traditional base areas in the north of the province west of Route 2 but, despite almost continuous Task Force pressure, 274 seemed determined to cling to those bases. Even as Operation Hermit Park came to an end, reports persisted that 1/274 were still in bunkers in the vicinity of the Suoi Ca. So Brig McDonald decided to follow Hermit Park immediately with Iron Fox, which would be another hammer and anvil operation.

The operation was mounted on very specific information as to the location of 1/274, gained partly from the previous operations in the area, partly from agent reports, and partly from SAS patrols. As VC and NVA units tended to site their bunkers on rising ground within 300 metres of a water source, and as the Suoi Ca contained plentiful water year round, and thick undergrowth gave good cover from air observation, it was no longer a matter of *if* the ANZAC Battalion found 1/274, but *when* they found them.

Phase 1 of Iron Fox would be an almost conventional advance to contact by 4RAR along the Suoi Ca, while 3RAR and A Squadron held blocking positions on three sides of the search area. Phase 2, which would begin as soon as the attacks on the bunker positions had been completed, would consist of follow-up search and block operations by both 3RAR and 4RAR. Both phases would be supported by 12 Field Regiment from FSBs Cherie, Debbie and Kate.

The Task Force CP would control the operation from Nui Dat, and the ANZAC Battalion, with its supporting units, would be commanded from the CP on Courtenay Hill. But the Battalion would have only three of its four rifle companies available in Phase 1: B, C and D, because

V Company had been detached to operational control of 1ATF as Ready Reaction Force. And besides its usual supporting elements, the Battalion would have the Centurion tanks of Maj Bourke's C Squadron under operational control throughout Phase 1.

The CO's plan was this: B Company would advance along the south bank of the Suoi Ca, with C Company moving roughly parallel on the north bank. Meanwhile D Company would shadow the advance at a depth of one kilometre north of C Company. Then, when either B or C Company made contact, D Company and the tanks would marry-up, swing south and take the enemy in flank. FSVs from A Squadron would be positioned with the eastern blocking force so that they could get forward to provide shock action and fire support to any attack B Company might make south of the creek. Like all good plans, it was simple, straightforward, and easy to modify as the battle unfolded.

The blocking force was in position by last light on 27 July, and 4RAR's rifle companies began manoeuvring into their locations next morning: B Company at 0730hr, C Company at 0830hr and D Company at 0930hr. Timings were staggered to ensure that there were no friendly clashes during these preliminary moves in the thick undergrowth. At 1400hr on 28 July, B and C Company crossed the start line and began their advance.

For the rest of that day the companies had little to report. A few old foot tracks, none of them used recently, were located and reported. B Company found a number of old tunnels, and C Company several L-shaped weapon pits, but the tunnels didn't seem to go anywhere, and the weapon pits were in poor condition and had not been used for twelve months. But at 1615hr on the south bank of the Suoi Ca, B Company found newly cut tree stumps camouflaged with mud. Cut timber meant bunkers, and the company carried out a detailed search of the area, but by mid-morning next day, 29 July, they had found no bunkers or any other sign.

Then at 1105hr, 9 Platoon north of the Suoi Ca found a pile of freshly cut logs with diameters up to 25 centimetres; and 20 minutes later the platoon located thirteen unoccupied bunkers and 403 rounds of AK47 ammunition, though no enemy soldiers. But an enemy suffering acute supply problems does not just forget to pick up 403 rounds when they leave a bunker system, unless they leave it in a hurry. By 1345hr the company had completed their examination of the bunkers but had found nothing else. They continued their advance.

During the afternoon Lt Andrew's 7 Platoon were:

> . . . in thick jungle with good overhead canopy, re-entrants in the area were steeply banked. The Platoon was following a track which led from an unoccupied bunker system found by 9 Platoon [just mentioned]. The track crossed a steep re-entrant and the forward section had just crossed it when a bunker was seen. When the section commander went to investigate, an enemy came out of the bunker and the contact was initiated. Small arms fire was received from within the bunker system and [homemade] claymores in trees were fired. RPGs were used by the enemy after about fifteen minutes from the start of the contact. After about one hour the platoon withdrew using fire and movement. During the contact at least three enemy were heard to cry out from wounds and a commander was heard to take charge early in the contact from within the system.[1]

Lt Andrews also commented that throughout the contact about half of the M79 rounds fired by the platoon failed to detonate. In addition, two of the platoon's M60s had mechanical stoppages, including a broken extractor in the forward gun. But true to his exhaustive training, the gunner stripped the weapon under fire, replaced the broken extractor and got the gun going again.

An added problem for the platoon was that M72s were not available for this operation because they had been found to be malfunctioning on a regular basis and had been withdrawn from service pending technical investigation. They would have been invaluable on this occasion.

During the contact and subsequent withdrawal, 7 Platoon brought artillery fire down onto the system. However many rounds failed to detonate because, logically enough, the fuses had been set to 'delay' so that they would dig in before initiating. But heavy rain had made the ground very soft and some rounds failed to explode. The problem was remedied by setting the fuses to 'quick' so that they detonated on impact. Despite this initial setback, artillery coverage of the bunker system was very good, and the enemy could only have moved about within it at considerable risk of injury or death.

Contact between C Company and 274 was broken off at 1550hr, and 7 Platoon were able to extract their three wounded while artillery fire continued to keep the enemy confined.

As soon as 7 Platoon made contact at 1440hr, two troops of C Squadron, seven Centurions in all, commanded by Lt Cameron, were ordered to leave their NDP, join D Company and move south as planned to attack the bunkers. But it was very slow going, and an airborne liaison officer from C Squadron was dispatched in a light helicopter to assist the tanks in navigation and to facilitate the marry up.

Even so, it was not until 1715hr, two and a half hours later, that marry-up was achieved. Time was getting on, and if the attack did not go in before last light, 274 would slip away in the dark following their standard operating procedure.

As usual on the west of Route 2, visibility was about fifteen metres and the trees varied in height, girth and density. The men of D Company had to keep close enough to the vehicles to ensure that enemy tank-hunting parties could not get a shot at them, but not so close that the infantrymen would be hit by falling trees and branches as the tanks pushed their way forward. And, as Lt Andrews had observed, the going was broken by steep sided re-entrants; while those were not major obstacles for tanks, care was still needed in negotiating them. At one point the advance was completely halted when a nest of red ants was dislodged from a tree and fell through a driver's hatch. Several crew members received minor injuries from falling timber. But at 1810hr D Company and the tanks estimated they were about 200 metres north of the bunkers, and quick orders were given.

For the attack, D Company would adopt the conventional warfare formation of two up, one back. Everyone knew what that formation entailed, and the concept was easy to visualise in the mind's eye, so time was not wasted on complicated orders. Besides, orders for an attack which was only minutes away needed to be kept simple as each man's thoughts turned inwards on himself as the knot of fear began to tighten. But fear was a good thing because it made men careful.

2/Lt Byrne's 10 Platoon would be left assault; 2/Lt Spinkston's 12 Platoon, right assault. The OC's Tac Party would move between 10 and 12 Platoon to coordinate forward movement and control the battle. Behind them would come the rest of CHQ, then the tanks; and behind them again would be 2/Lt McKay's 11 Platoon in reserve, from where they could protect the tanks, or manoeuvre quickly to left or right as the situation demanded.

The problem, as usual, was flank security. An attacking force in such thick country was always vulnerable to an aggressive enemy who believed that the best form of defence was attack. And, as Lt Campbell's 2 Platoon had experienced during Hermit Park, it was not unusual for the enemy to send troops out of a defended position to probe an attacking force from one or both flanks. In this case though, left flank security would be guaranteed by Maj Boxall's C Company, while Maj Hogarth's B Company were across the creek and could prevent enemy reinforcement or withdrawal from or to that direction. It was D Company's right flank, the western one, that was open and vulnerable. Therefore artillery fire was brought down onto it, and the attack got under way. The time was 1840hr.

It was a very slow advance. The two leading platoons edged forward a metre at a time as they minutely examined every leaf, shadow and fold in the ground. The trees here, close to the creek, were smaller but more dense, visibility less. The light was beginning to fade too, so now there was shadow on shadow. But the bunkers were there just ahead, and the enemy were in them.

And then with tropical suddenness the light had gone. It was 1930hr, and contact had not yet been made. OC D Company had to tell the CO that the attack would have to be postponed. This was disappointing, because it meant almost inevitably that the enemy would withdraw from the bunkers in the night, taking their equipment, weapons and rations with them. But it would have been foolhardy to press on. An attack in such close country, in the dark, with tanks, into bunkers, would have ended in farce. More to the point, the risk of friendly clashes, and hence unnecessary casualties, was just too great.

An NDP was put in with the tanks occupying part of the perimeter, and their 20-pounders were loaded with canister. Orders for tomorrow were confirmed. The attack would recommence at 0700hr.

Just after midnight, 5 Troop C Squadron reported sounds and movement on the perimeter from south to north and fire was opened, but with unknown results.

D Company and the tanks reached the bunkers at 0710hr next morning. They had been abandoned in the night, and the rest of that morning was spent in destroying the system, a task much facilitated by the Centurions, whose drivers simply placed a track on the roof of each bunker and slewed left, then right. At 1345hr D Company reported the system destroyed, and the tanks were ordered back to their leaguer to refuel and remain in reserve. B Company was ordered to continue searching along the south bank of the creek. D Company took over the task of searching the north bank from C Company, who would now shadow the advance in reserve. It was 1422hr on 30 July, Day 3 of Operation Iron Fox. Twenty minutes later 10 Platoon came under very heavy fire from a second bunker system.

The enemy initiated the contact with small arms, machinegun and RPG fire, and 10 Platoon's leading scout, Pte Lawton, was hit in the left forearm. He immediately went to ground, crawled *forward* to a convenient bamboo clump and, despite his wound, opened fire on the enemy.

Private Meehan, an M60 gunner in 12 Platoon recalls:

> I had a forward scout [Private A. C. Ottway], and he turned around and gave me the enemy sign and pointed which way they were going. By the

> time I was just about to yell out, 'Gun's going right', to let Spingo [Second Lieutenant Graham Spinkston] know exactly where I was going, all hell broke loose off to our left. 10 Platoon had hit the enemy. I took off anyway and when I hit the ground there was a bunker in front of me and thank Christ no one was at home. The next thing I know, I'm copping rounds across the top of my head and I could hear an M60 going. So I thought, 'Shit, I have walked into our own people', and I held my fire as did the other machinegunner in the platoon, because initially for the first couple of seconds we thought we had walked into each other. We then found out the enemy had an M60, and so I went forward again. I found another bunker which was occupied, so I put as much firepower through as I could, and I was copping rounds, but really I never heard them. So I was just doing my job and trying to get the enemy but I was also trying to put down so much fire so that none of our blokes got hit—but we got word that one of our other blokes [Pte C.D. Sedgwick] who was a couple of hundred metres back, copped a round through the calf muscle, and here I am up the front, I'm not getting hit, but the blokes down the back are getting hit. So bullets don't stop, they just keep going until they find something to hit.[2]

As soon as the battle started, B Company halted where they were and prepared to assist D Company if necessary. OC C Company was ordered to move north and then west round D Company's right flank, and to be prepared to attack the bunkers from that direction. C Squadron's two troops, still under the command of Lt Cameron, who would subsequently be awarded the Military Cross for his leadership and gallantry, were ordered to return and link up with D Company. They arrived at the same moment that Bushranger 71 and 72 reported themselves on station. But by that time the company's forward observer, Lt Gilbert, had brought artillery fire down onto the bunkers and the Bushrangers were asked to stand off for the time being.

It was now 1515hr, and 10 and 12 Platoon with the Tac Party between them, were pushing forward into the bunker system. Meanwhile Lt Gilbert 'walked' the artillery fire back towards D Company in order to bring it as close as possible to the company's front and flanks. This prevented the enemy from 'hugging' the company in order to escape the artillery, and it would also break up any flanking counter-attack they might try to put in. In fact the gambit worked very well, although there were one or two minor shrapnel wounds from tree-burst rounds.

As 10 and 12 Platoons worked their way steadily forward, they were able to identify the exact location of each bunker. Having done so, the tanks were called forward, one or two to each platoon. Then, as soon as the crews were given the target indication, they fired an HE or APCBC round to lift the top off the bunker, followed immediately by a canister round and heavy machinegun fire. It was a devastating tactic, and its simplicity and effectiveness was all the more remarkable when it is remembered that D Company and the crews of C Squadron had not worked together before. Nor had there been time to rehearse for this attack or discuss how bunkers might be neutralised. But Maj Bourke's men had learned much from their previous bunker battles with 3RAR and Victor Company. On this day again, the ANZAC Battalion received splendid and unstinting support from C Squadron, and it has never been forgotten.

Nevertheless, progress was very slow. At the end of an hour the company and the Centurions had advanced less than 100 metres. Ammunition, too, was beginning to run low. And again the irrepressible Capt Earle and his men brought ammunition up in the APCs, and later assisted in the extraction of D Company's wounded.

2/Lt McKay, commanding 11 Platoon, remembers:

> I went forward with some of my men several times to resupply the forward platoons with gun ammunition and to try to see how the battle was going. At about this time an incident occurred as a result of the enemy firing a captured M60 machinegun. Often the only way we could tell where we had advanced to in thick undergrowth was by the noise of our own weapons. Weapon types have their own individual sound; and between D Company and C Company there was the constant fire of an M60. The sound of this weapon led our company headquarters, which was travelling centrally, to believe that 10 Platoon was doing quite nicely. As I was forward I was asked by Peter Schuman (2i/c D Company) to take more linked ammo to 10 Pl; but after I had failed to locate his flank in the bush, the OC asked both platoons to throw a coloured smoke grenade. After a delay of a minute or so orange smoke began drifting upward through the dense foliage. The only problem was that it was to company headquarters' rear, and they in fact were way out in front of the assault line. Peter Schuman made the suggestion that they get their backsides out of where they were and let the platoons do the attacking.[3]

In fact the enemy were still resisting fiercely. Several Centurions received RPG hits, but although the infra-red basket on Lt Cameron's tank, and some ancillary equipment on others, was damaged, no crewmen were injured, even though the tank commanders and their drivers had their hatches open as an aid to better visibility. Moreover, as had been experienced previously, the enemy were firing their RPGs into the tree canopy, which maximised shrapnel splash onto the crew and infantrymen beneath.

Getting and passing information at every level was also very difficult. The closeness of the going and the noise generated under the canopy by machineguns, RPGs and small arms, the impact of artillery rounds, and the bellowing muzzle-blast of the Centurions' 20-pounder guns, all made speech and hearing almost impossible. Yet the passage of information remained vital, almost always coming down to commanders crawling forward to give and receive information. Communication between the infantry and tanks could be by radio or via the tank telephone, which was housed in a metal box at the rear of the vehicle, or by climbing onto the tank itself and speaking directly to its commander. OC D Company and the platoon commanders were also using their given names instead of their usual radio callsigns, which helped to minimise the confusion caused by the noise of battle.

The Battalion used a system whereby the OCs fought their platoons over the company command net, while the company 2i/c or the CSM manned the Battalion command net radio, over which he passed a running commentary of events and progress to the CP on Courtenay Hill. This ensured that the OCs were able to devote their full attention to the immediate demands of the battle, without depriving the CO and his Ops staff of vital moment-to-moment information.

11 Platoon was now passed through 10 Platoon to continue the assault. At this stage the company's devoted and courageous RAAMC medical assistant, Cpl O'Sullivan, moved forward with a stretcher-bearer Pte Pengilly to assist some of the wounded. As the two men were working over one of the casualties, a burst of machinegun fire hit Pte Pengilly in the chest, killing him instantly. Despite this, Cpl O'Sullivan continued treating his patient, and eventually removed him, and all the wounded, to safety. For his work this day, and on others like it, Cpl O'Sullivan was to receive the Military Medal.

It was now nearly 1700hr, and for a moment it seemed as though the enemy resistance was slackening. But almost at once 12 Platoon came under intense RPG and machinegun fire from their half-right. Again the tanks moved forward, located their targets, and instantly destroyed them. And fifteen minutes later C Company, who had just completed their manoeuvre round D Company's northern flank, reported that they could now see 12 Platoon, and were in a position to give covering fire if it was needed. It was, but almost at once the enemy, realising that they had been out-flanked, withdrew. By 1740hr resistance had ceased, and D Company began, finally, to check the bunkers and report the system secure. But not quite yet.

As 11 Platoon moved through the left (south) side of the system, movement and talking was detected from one of the bunkers. The engineer splinter team went to investigate, receiving a burst of AK47 fire for their trouble, but luckily no injuries resulted. There were two enemy in the bunker and they refused to surrender despite all attempts to coax them out. Nobody in the company spoke Vietnamese and there were no interpreters readily available. Time was getting on, the light was starting to fade, and there was still a lot more to be done.

There were two options. The two enemy could be neutralised at once, or sentries could be placed at the entrance to the bunker all night and an interpreter brought in next morning in the hope that the two enemy could be persuaded to surrender. But would it be wise to have armed enemy inside the perimeter at night? What if the two tried to break for it in the dark? What if, as a consequence, a fire-fight broke out, and the company had thus taken casualties? OC D Company therefore ordered 11 Platoon to throw a Claymore into the bunker and detonate it instantly. Inspection showed that the two VC were dead.

Like the night before, the company and the tanks went into a combined NDP, and the loose ends were tidied up. Orders for the next day; a quick walk round the soldiers; locstats, contact reports, casualty reports, maintdems, opdems, and all the rest. It had been a long day, and for much of it the rifle companies, 1 Troop and C Squadron had been running on the high edge of adrenaline. Now it was over, and that adrenaline began to wash back into everyone's system, causing immense weariness. But sleep was slow in coming. For much of the night trees and branches, hit by artillery and tank fire, crashed down onto the forest floor, jolting everyone instantly awake. But as luck would have it there were no injuries.

The CO's orders for next day were that D Company was to destroy the system using the tanks, and construct a helicopter LZ. The tanks would then be refuelled. B Company was to continue with their present task of searching the south bank of the Suoi Ca to the west. C Company was to resume the search along the north bank. The Tracker and Pioneer platoons at Courtenay Hill were placed on fifteen minutes and one hour's notice to move, respectively. Their tasks were to assist the searching companies as necessary.

The next day, 31 July, Day 4 of Iron Fox, the bunker system was searched again and then demolished. Twelve enemy bodies were located, but there were undoubtedly more inside the bunkers which the Centurions had crushed during the attack.

It had taken just over three hours for D Company and the tanks to fight through the system, which comprised 23 bunkers in an area about

200 metres square. The infamous M60 which had caused Pte Meehan and his section so much trouble, and 460 rounds of linked belt, was among the captured weapons, as were two RPG2s, eleven rockets and four AK47s, together with an assortment of equipment, food and medical supplies. Captured documents identified the enemy as C1 1/274 Regiment.

With his customary concern for the men under his command, Brig McDonald visited D Company. As he spoke animatedly with them, the soldiers watched fascinated as, totally unaware, the Task Force Commander sank slowly into a shallow grave containing several VC bodies. He was hurried away to another part of the battlefield, still unaware.

On 1 August, Day 5, B and C Company continued their search along the river. D Company, after completing the demolition of the bunker system, was placed under operational control of A Squadron to take up blocking positions further west. And it was in that vicinity that 3RAR located a bunkered hospital which had recently been evacuated by C24 (Convalescent Company) of 274 Regiment. But apart from that there were no further significant results to be had. Therefore at midnight on 5–6 August, Day 9, Operation Iron Fox concluded.

The overall intelligence assessment of the operation stated:

> As a direct result of IRON FOX the HQ and some company elements of 1/274 Regiment were forced to withdraw from their base area on the Suoi Ca to an area west of the BRIMSTONE Trail. With the 1Bn Sanctuary area destroyed, the VC will have to secure and reconstruct further systems, probably in the tri-border area of Bien Hoa, Long Khanh and Phuoc Tuy Provinces. Basic training scheduled for recent reinforcements to the unit will have been disrupted.
>
> And planned offensive action for the unit, or its companies, is certain to have been adversely effected by Operation Iron Fox.[4]

The cost of the operation to the ANZAC Battalion was one man killed, Pte Bernard Pengilly of D Company, and five men wounded.

Two weeks later, on 18 August, while the ANZAC Battalion was taking part in operation North Ward, Prime Minister, Mr William McMahon announced that 1ATF would cease operations in Phuoc Tuy Province in October. The outline plan, which later came through the command chain, was that 3RAR would leave Vietnam aboard HMAS *Sydney* on 6 October, and 4RAR would go the same way on 8 December, except for D Company. D Company would remain in theatre for another three months to secure the 1ALSG complex at Vung Tau. Finally all 1ALSG personnel would be withdrawn, and D Company would leave aboard *Sydney* on 29 February 1972.

One of the first sub-units to be earmarked for withdrawal was C Squadron 1 Armoured Regiment, and the ANZAC Battalion was disquieted to hear this news. Just before the squadron left, LtCol Hughes wrote to Maj Bourke:

> It was indeed a sorry day when your tanks ceased to be operational. The effort and outstanding esprit-de-corps of your unit have truly been a major factor in the operational success of 1ATF combat units. There is no doubt in my mind that casualties would have been much greater without your unfailing support and willingness to accept calculated risks to assist my men, especially in bunker contacts, and therefore carry the day in the true spirit of armoured/infantry cooperation.
>
> So much has been achieved in again proving the worth of armoured forces in jungle warfare, that even the most doubting Thomas must now be a staunch believer. Certainly this is true in the case of 4RAR/NZ (ANZAC) Battalion. I do not believe there is one man under my command who would not feel a great sense of personal relief and pride in Australian arms when observing C Squadron press home the attack with typical aggression and determination.
>
> Without you our task is obviously more difficult, but should we ever be committed to war again—as we probably will be—then the infantry could ask for no better comrades in arms than C Squadron 1 Armoured Regiment. I ask you to pass onto your men our gratitude for the professionalism and skill they have displayed and assure them that they are held in the highest esteem by the ANZAC Battalion. You and your men are welcome in our messes any time should you have the opportunity to renew friendships.[5]

Over the years there has been a good deal of discussion about the withdrawal of C Squadron before operations had finished in Phuoc Tuy Province, and it's worthwhile pausing here to consider the decision.

Tanks are a fearsome weapon of war. They are big, solid and relatively fast moving, and their appearance on the battlefield raises the morale of those they support and lowers that of the enemy they oppose. A tank has a large accurate gun, and this main armament is backed up by several heavy machineguns and a plentiful supply of ammunition. Tanks have powerful radio sets and thus maintain excellent communications. Mobility, firepower, shock action and communications: these are the tank's particular strengths in the advance, attack and withdrawal and, used wisely, in defence too.

Their principal weakness is that they are vulnerable in thick country, where an enemy can get very close to attack them, and therefore need almost constant infantry protection. Moreover, in thick country tanks will usually have to move at infantry pace and sometimes less, and tank crews are not overly comfortable with that. And if, during battle, tanks have their hatches closed, the crews are to some extent 'blind' to what is happening immediately around them, which adds to their vulnerability.

For these reasons armoured purists might say that tanks were unsuited to operations in much of Phuoc Tuy. They might also quote the military axiom, which was still valid in 1971, that 'the best way to kill a tank was to use another tank'. The purists would then go on to conclude that because the VC and NVA did not have tanks, at least not until the closing stages of the war, there was no need to include C Squadron on the Task Force orbat anyway. But if we pursue that line of logic, we would have to agree that because the enemy did not have air support the Allies did not need it either, and that would be an absurd suggestion.

It was certainly true that Phuoc Tuy Province did not provide much 'good tank country'. But war seldom provides ideal operating conditions for every Arm. The trick is to adapt to prevailing circumstances and make the best use of all available resources. So the advantages of having tanks on the orbat far outweighed the disadvantages. And, too, 3RAR, the ANZAC Battalion and C Squadron had already demonstrated very forcibly during Overlord, Hermit Park and Iron Fox that with determined leadership and an acute awareness of the limitations of using armour in close country, there was no reason why tanks could not be used to excellent effect even in the densest forest.

It must also be stressed that the withdrawal of a formation like 1ATF from a theatre of war, while that war is still in progress, is always a potentially dangerous manoeuvre. As is seen in Chapter 13, units and formations making a tactical withdrawal must thin out their sub-units until right at the end of the manoeuvre only a single rifle company might remain in location. For that reason, tanks and APCs are ideal weapons in the withdrawal because of their speed, armoured protection, plentiful firepower and good communications. Therefore many tacticians would argue that C Squadron should have been retained on the orbat for as long as possible.

However, with the withdrawal announced, the logisticians were faced with the considerable task of back-loading a vast amount of equipment to Australia over a wide sea gap in a relatively short period of time. The Centurions particularly posed a problem because of their size and weight. So tactical necessity would have to be tempered by logistic constraints. In short, there were compelling reasons for keeping C Squadron ready for battle; and there were equally compelling reasons for withdrawing them.

Nor was it a question of deciding the order of withdrawal randomly by pulling units out of a hat. Commander AFV, MajGen Dunstan, an infantryman himself, was one of Australia's most astute and highly respected soldiers. He would have been well aware of the dangers facing 1ATF, and he and his staff, assisted by Brig McDonald and his staff, would have studied the implications of the withdrawal of each combat and supporting unit at length. Every factor would have been rigorously considered and assessed before the decision to withdraw C Squadron was made.

Such decisions are never easy, except of course for those who don't have to make them.

Iron Fox finished at 2400hr on 5–6 August, at which moment Operation North Ward commenced. Indeed, because each operation followed instantly on the heels of the last, some men in the rifle companies were not aware that a new operation had started, or that it had a new title. It probably didn't matter much to them anyway, because 'at the sharp end' one operation was very much like another. It was all about searching, and if you didn't find the enemy today you might find him tomorrow, and in the sections and platoons it was immaterial whether the enemy was 274 or Chau Duc or D445. It all came down to the same thing in the end.

All the rifle companies, now in mid-August, had been under fire to a greater or lesser degree, and so had many of Support Company. And because of it there was a new-found confidence about 4RAR. Each man had a clearer idea of the commitment he had to make to himself, to his mates and to the Battalion, and many had already tested the margins of their courage. Each man now realised that to face death was to learn something new about himself. And because the Australians and New Zealanders did not wear steel helmets or flak jackets on operations, those who had attacked bunkers had also confronted the chilling reality that between them and the fatal bullet lay only the thickness of a green shirt. And most men had undoubtedly been tempted by the thought that under fire, safety lay to the rear, but had instantly faced down that thought with the more compelling notion that duty and self-respect beckoned from in front. This was a vital piece of self knowledge, and because of it the brash or arrogant man had become more introspective, more tolerant, less critical of his peers; while those already given to introspection now found within themselves a greater depth to contemplate

But it was probably too early yet for a man to realise that he had been changed forever. That would come later, on return to Australia or New Zealand when, on meeting civilian friends, he would realise that he now had little in common with them, and that they could never comprehend the things that he had seen and done and thought. The young man who had left Sydney or Wellington or Brisbane or Christchurch only months ago would from now on regard civilians with less tolerant eyes. Perhaps that was why, later, he would join a veterans' association. It was only in the close confines of those exclusive groups that he could be understood without having to explain himself. And it would also be why, in future, he might find himself embarrassingly moved by the melancholy notes of the 'Last Post', or the piper's lament for the dead, 'The Flowers of the Forest'.

The wet season was in full swing. In the mythology of the infantryman, ice-cold rain deluged down every afternoon precisely at 1500hr, soaking everyone to the skin. It was as near as the rifle companies got to a regular shower, but the beneficial spin-off was that a hastily rigged hoochy could replenish empty water bottles in a few minutes. The fact that everyone went to bed wet was of no consequence: you went to bed wet from rain or wet from sweat or wet from a combination of the two. In any case, sixteen months of training and now three months of active operations had accustomed everyone to such minor discomforts, and perpetually damp clothing was no longer noticed. Occasionally fierce electrical storms accompanied the rain, and when they came close the hair on head and arms stood up and the air tasted of copper. There was no point in continuing to search because the rain reduced visibility to the length of a man's arm, and it was too easy to become disoriented and then lost. But such downpours seldom lasted long, and when they had passed, everyone shook himself and moved on again.

There were other novelties too. For example there was the 'Fuck-You bird'. In fact the Fuck-You bird wasn't a bird at all, but a small grey lizard which inhabited the trees and had a triangular flap of skin in its throat. When it expelled air, the flap popped open, and the lizard emitted the first syllable of its distinctive call very loudly and with absolute clarity. The second syllable came when the flap closed again. It was an engaging little creature which looked as though it might have been designed by one of Walt Disney's artists.

There were other things that were not so appealing. Scorpions and millipedes marched across the jungle floor and at night often sought sanctuary inside a vacant boot or in equipment placed beside a hoochy or under a hammock. So it was always wise to tap boots together and upend them before putting them on in the morning.

There were also wolf spiders, with bodies slightly smaller than a squash ball and legs as thick as a man's little finger. Pte Gilpin, OC D Company's batman and an amateur entomologist, captured one, declaring that he would put it in an empty ration tin and take it back to Nui Dat as a pet when the operation ended. But his plan was instantly terminated by a well-placed combat shovel.

And there were leeches, particularly here in the Chau Pha valley. An hour's patrolling yielded usually 15 or 20 small leeches on each leg, which had to be removed during the ten-minute navigation check. When a leech was removed, or if it was surfeited and just fell off, the puncture point continued to bleed messily for up to 48 hours, but otherwise did no permanent harm. But it was found that invasion by leeches could be minimised by soaking boot tops and laces with mosquito repellent.

Bull leeches were another matter. It was an untested theory that eight bull leeches could suck a man's blood system dry. Men checked themselves very carefully for the black and grey shapes, which when empty were as thick as a pencil and 6 or 7 centimetres long. Bloated, they could be the size of an average sausage. One outraged member of CHQ D Company found a bull leech firmly attached to his penis, and although the Australian infantryman exhibits extreme compassion to any of his comrades who are wounded or injured, an occurrence such as this engenders no sympathy at all. The bull leech, still attached, was examined with great interest, and several members of CHQ were of the opinion that it was difficult to tell which was leech and which was penis. Others said it wasn't difficult at all: the leech was better looking. And bigger too, most thought. The next discussion centred round how to remove the creature. Some suggested that a vigorous shaking might do the trick. Others eagerly produced Zippo lighters. Yet others thought that greater benefits might accrue if the penis was removed and the leech substituted for it. The final consensus was that both should remain; the distraught soldier would have 'two for the price of one'. Eventually mosquito repellent was liberally applied and the leech fell off. No damage had been done, except perhaps to the young man's dignity.

When operation North Ward began there was no specific intelligence suggesting the presence of any sizeable enemy units or sub-units in northern Phuoc Tuy. But this was hardly surprising, considering that throughout June and July the ANZAC Battalion and 3RAR had devoted themselves to continuous operations in the area, operations which had inflicted significant losses of men and material on 1/274.

However, it was known that enemy supply services were continuing to operate in and around the tri-border region to obtain and build up stocks of all kinds, and especially food and money. And if the enemy was concentrating on resupply, it must mean that they were also contemplating subsequent offensive operations. It was also known that reconnaissance elements from HQ Ba Long Province, 274 and 33rd were present in the area. Meanwhile Chau Duc were back in their bases in the Nui Dinhs and along the Suoi Chau Pha valley, and they were engaged in resupply activities too.

As usual, the enemy supply services were targeting the rubber plantations and villages along Route 2, always reliable sources of food, money and recruits. But now, at the beginning of August, this resupply activity seemed to have redoubled in intensity. And the question was, why?

As has already been explained, COSVN was responsible for planning all VC and NVA activity in South Vietnam and issuing general directives for the implementation of those plans. And after his election in November 1968, President Nixon had begun peace negotiations with North Vietnam in January 1969. As part of those negotiations, 115 000 American troops had been withdrawn from the South by April 1970. In May and June, COSVN had set themselves the task of assessing the extent of further US withdrawals. If, by 30 June, they considered those withdrawals to be significant, COSVN would order VC and NVA units to mount a general offensive throughout the South similar to Tet 1968. However if the withdrawals were not sufficiently extensive, COSVN's alternative plan was to mount large-scale sapper attacks and attacks by fire onto military and civilian targets. This, COSVN reasoned, would inflict casualties on American, Allied, ARVN, RF and PF forces, intimidate the civilian population and further destabilise the Pacification Programme. The overall objective was to apply pressure at the peace table and speed American and Allied withdrawals from South Vietnam.

Sapper attacks and attacks by fire had proved to be very effective because they were relatively easy to mount, required few resources and resulted in few own casualties. So since May 1971 the communist sapper high command had been infiltrating additional instructors into the South, and they were now running both basic and refresher courses on tactics and techniques, and sapper attacks were starting to increase in frequency. For example, there had been seven major sapper attacks in Binh Duong and Tay Ninh provinces, just north of Bien Hoa Province, in June and July. These had inflicted casualties on the Allies of seventeen dead and 57 wounded, with four helicopters destroyed and two others, plus two trucks, damaged, with the cost to the enemy of nine killed. The effect of these successes on South Vietnamese political, military and civilian morale had been profound. Coming close was 19 August, when the communists commemorated General Revolution

Day, the day the Viet Minh seized power in Hanoi in 1945. Not only that, but elections for the South Vietnamese Lower House of Assembly were due to begin on 29 August, when sapper operations and attacks by fire would be especially productive.

At the local level in Phuoc Tuy, similar operations would involve most enemy units in and adjacent to the tri-border area. Most significantly, 274 Regiment and 33rd were ordered to coordinate their operational activities.

Therefore Operation North Ward was mounted to counter these enemy plans, the concept being to maintain an aggressive presence in the north of Phuoc Tuy, east and west of Route 2. Particular attention was to be paid to enemy resupply and courier routes. 2 Troop A Squadron, under operational control of the ANZAC Battalion, would ambush these routes in the rubber plantations adjacent to Courtenay Hill.

For the period 6–15 August, V Company was to operate east of Route 2 in an area bounded by Xa Bang on the west, Courtenay rubber to the north, and the line Nui Le–Suoi Youert on the east. C Company's AO would be four kilometres west of Xa Bang and north of the Cu Bi rubber. D Company would be four kilometres north-west of C Company. All companies would search and ambush, and the direction of search was to be generally from north to south. Meanwhile, from 2–9 August, B Company would be under operational control of 1ATF as Ready Reaction Force.

Because of the possibility of contact between the Battalion and the civilian population throughout the area, liaison and radio communication would be maintained with District Headquarters at Xuan Loc, and with the Cam My RF unit.

Operation North Ward commenced at 0001hr on 6 August, and results came quickly. At 0905hr on Day 1, Cpl Templeman's section of 8 Platoon was patrolling through light scrub when the forward scout heard movement to his front. On investigating he saw one enemy in black carrying an AK47, and immediately killed him at fifteen metres' range. A second enemy was engaged but escaped.

On the morning of 10 August in a harbour position that Sgt Panui, temporarily commanding 3 Platoon, had established on a VC staging camp, enemy soldiers:

> . . . fired several shots as they approached the platoon position between two sentry locations. Fire was returned with small arms and Claymores. The VC were moving off the track. In fact a soldier was just outside the platoon position answering a call of nature when the contact was initiated.

> Soldier returned fire immediately though enemy definitely fired first. After firing several shots the soldier pulled back into the enemy position.

1800 rounds of small arms and eight Claymores in two banks of four were expended by the platoon, and although one VC was killed, Sgt Panui commented: 'Results would indicate that too much ammo etc was expended, however at the time it seemed quite justified because movement was being reported from the east, south and south-west. Looking back on the contact now, however, I would venture to say that a good deal of the reported movement was imagined.'[6]

Maj Monks added drily, 'The contact emphasises the importance of tactical crapping. In this case the soldier saw the enemy first but refrained from firing as he initially thought the person was the company interpreter. Soldier fired when the suspect adopted a firing position with an AK47, killing the enemy.'[7]

As a consequence of this incident, the rules for the siting and use of field latrines were restated throughout the battalion. Latrines were to be sited to suit the length of halt, with short halts requiring one latrine. Long halts of one or two nights required an inner latrine for night use and an external latrine for day use. To guarantee the safety of men who might otherwise be caught, quite literally, with their trousers down, the approaches to the external latrine and the latrine itself were to be covered by observation and fire by a minimum of one sentry, and preferably two.

The next day, 11 August, at 1108hr, Sgt Panui's platoon made contact again, this time with two or three enemy soldiers who were constructing a camp close to the Suoi Tam Bo. This area seemed to have been specially selected for the very swampy condition of the ground. Although the enemy escaped with their personal weapons, they left behind an SKS, five RPG rounds, clothing, webbing and a quantity of documents. Among these last were found instructions on how to attack tanks. The selection of swampy ground for the camp lent weight to the assessment that, since Iron Fox, the enemy had become more tank-conscious, and were now starting to select ground for camps and bunkers that offered a degree of anti-armour defence.

Other documents suggested that some of those who had escaped Sgt Panui's assault were from C2 Engineer Company of HQ Ba Long Province, and that others were ex-members of the disbanded D65 Engineer Battalion. This tended to bear out the assessment that the enemy were planning sapper attacks along Route 2.

On the afternoon of 15 August, Lt Fry's 1 Platoon surprised eight enemy in the Suoi Le, a non-perennial creek which ran off the north-eastern slopes of Nui Le. The enemy had been engaged in building a small bunker system, and although they fought a spirited withdrawal they nevertheless had to abandon their equipment. Documents found by the platoon indicated the enemy to be members of C5 (Purchasing and Requisition Company) of J85 Transportation Battalion. They were known to assist 1/274 with resupply.

Then on 16 August 2/Lt Byrne's 10 Platoon, two kilometres west of Route 2 and opposite Xa Bang, sprang an important ambush. During the afternoon the platoon had come across a depression in the ground filled with pumpkins, and it was decided to ambush this cache. The ambush went in at about 1730hr, and at 1927hr three enemy were seen approaching from the north-east. The country was relatively open with high grass, scattered bamboo, and generally good visibility. But despite the fact that it was 90 minutes after curfew, the springing was delayed until the enemy could be positively identified. Then, expending 100 rounds of linked belt and 20 rounds each of M16 and SLR, the platoon severely wounded two of the enemy. The third man escaped after firing a burst from an automatic weapon, and the platoon immediately swept through the area and brought the two wounded enemy into the ambush perimeter.

Although a Dustoff helicopter was initially arranged to evacuate the two wounded men for treatment and subsequent interrogation, it was eventually aborted. This was because the third member of the enemy party was thought to be close by, and he might fire on the platoon as they moved to the helicopter LP in the dark, or at the Dustoff helicopter as it came in. As a consequence, the two enemy died of their wounds in the night. It was later established from the documents they were carrying that they were senior cadre staff members, one from HQ Ba Long Province, the other from HQ Chau Duc. The documents which identified them also stated that 2700 kilograms of rice and VN$50 000 had been collected from tappers and villagers in the area. A further 300 kilograms of rice and a quantity of pumpkins and tobacco were recovered from the cache which 10 Platoon had ambushed.

On 22 August, Day 16, at a point five kilometres south-west of their last contact, 1 Platoon, now commanded by Lt Harris, shot and killed an enemy soldier and wounded a second. Lt Harris related:

> Own troops were situated on a low spur rising from a re-entrant in the west to high ground in the east. There was a shallow depression on the southern front of the spur, with thick, tangled vegetation. Vegetation on the spur consisted of fairly clean jungle.

> At approximately 1000hr patrol found tracks made in the past 24 hours by about 10 enemy moving south to north. Moved again after about 1 hour and harboured 200m further on for lunch. Warned out by Coy HQ that 3 enemy, about 3 metres apart were then seen moving north along a track about 20m in front of the platoon. 1 gun and 1 SLR opened fire. Other weapons along south flank of harbour then gave suppressive fire.

He went on to point out:

> The enemy showed uncharacteristic stupidity in travelling along a track that had been used by a large number of our troops a short time previously. Apparently the enemy element was familiar with the track and had not bothered to examine it carefully before using it. Quietness rather than tactical deployment was the decisive factor that made for a successful contact on our part.[8]

Documents found on the body indicated that these enemy, too, were from C5 (Purchasing and Requisition). It appeared that they had been lying up close to the plantation villages to maintain liaison with the inhabitants and local guerrillas. All these contacts reinforced the intelligence assessment on which the operation had been mounted. Obviously the enemy were vigorously engaged in resupply, and the corollary was that this was a preliminary to offensive operations.

In addition, throughout Operation North Ward, village officials from Cam My reported that tappers had been approached by five VC in the western and central parts of Courtenay rubber. The VC had demanded that those working in the plantation donate a day's wages each month together with food. Patrols were sent out from Courtenay Hill to investigate, and on 27 August at 1050hr Cpl Darlington's section of the Assault Pioneer Platoon contacted four enemy soldiers in the north-west of the plantation. One fled north and was killed by machine-gun fire, but the others, who went east, got away. The dead man was identified as a member of the Cam My guerrilla unit. He turned out to be a somewhat ambiguous figure, who either by accident or design was a double agent, because he was known to have given information on VC activities to the Americans at Black Horse. By day he legitimately tended a garden to the west of Route 2, so he had been ideally placed for liaison between villagers, guerrillas and VC resupply services.

National Police Field Force units from Duc Thanh district also carried out frequent searches of the villages in the plantation areas, resulting in the arrest of a number of illegal residents. They were taken away to District HQ for interrogation.

There were five more contacts before the end of Operation North Ward. At 1025hr on 7 September, Day 32, L/Cpl McCloskey's patrol from 6 Platoon sighted one VC moving through the northern end of the Cu Bi rubber. The patrol fired six shots and received one in return, but the enemy soldier escaped.

Next night, at 2215hr, 9 Platoon were ambushing in light timber with chest-high secondary scrub. The platoon were six kilometres north-west of Xa Bang and near the Suoi Soc. Lt Grecian later recounted:

> The gun position at the rear of the ambush heard talking and saw torchlight approaching from the south-east. The enemy then at a range of 40m from our position changed direction towards the west. The rear Claymores were fired and the M60 fired 150 rounds into the area and along the suspected withdrawal route of the enemy. Search at first light found a track 45m out leading to the north.[9]

And on 11 September, at 0625hr, L/Cpl Philp's section initiated an ambush set by the Tracker Platoon on the north-west edge of Courtenay rubber. 2/Lt Murphy related that:

> Four personnel were seen to enter the killing ground of the platoon ambush point. Because of low scrub in rubber it could not be seen if they were carrying weapons. They stopped and appeared to be looking towards a bank of Claymores. L/Cpl Philp challenged with, 'Stop'. They immediately bolted and the area was swept with Claymores and small arms fire. Two bodies were on the track in front of the Claymores and a third about 10m into the scrub on the other side of the track, and the fourth escaped leaving a heavy blood trail. An AK47 and two SKS were also recovered.[10]

On 12 September 9 Platoon had another contact with an enemy soldier dressed in black and carrying an AK47. But the platoon's sentry was badly sited and he had to move before he could get a clear shot. As a result he was seen by the enemy soldier, who escaped.

At 1132hr on 14 September, Day 39 of Operation North Ward, 2/Lt McKay's 11 Platoon, just east of the 265 feature of Nui Le, made contact with an enemy squad; although Cpl Kennedy's section moved quickly into extended line and opened fire, the enemy withdrew. Artillery was brought down onto their likely withdrawal routes, with unknown results.

But the next day, about 400 metres south-east of their previous contact, 11 Platoon wounded an enemy soldier who was scrub bashing (not using a formed path). 4 Section opened fire, went to ground, and provided covering fire for 6 Section's immediate assault into the contact area. The wounded enemy attempted to open fire and was instantly killed. Artillery fire was brought down onto the east and south-east of the contact area to cut the enemies' likely withdrawal routes, but in the end only the one body was found. The man was wearing a green uniform and navigating with an American compass, both of which occurrences were unusual. He also had an AK47 and a gas mask, but no documents or maps. It was later assessed that the man was almost certainly part of a reconnaissance element from 33 NVA Regiment. So the question that had been posed by 3/33rd's reconnaissance around Nui Le earlier in June still remained: what were they recceing, and why?

Operation North Ward had lasted from 6 August to 18 September, a period of 43 days. There had been thirteen contacts and numerous other sitings, and eleven enemy soldiers had been killed by body count, though more had undoubtedly been killed and wounded. The list of weapons, ammunition, equipment and foodstuffs which had been captured by the Battalion ran to two closely typed pages. The operation had aimed to disrupt enemy supply services in their efforts to obtain food and money from the civilian population and to cut their lines of communication. That aim had been achieved, and a number of important rear services links had been severed, particularly around Xa Bang and through the Courtenay and Cu Bi rubber. The ANZAC Battalion had suffered no casualties.

The final two paragraphs of the Battalion's overall assessment of the operation says this:

> The sign located and the contacts in the area of NUI LE during the final stages of the operation confirmed the presence of an unidentified force having recently moved into the area.
>
> There was firm indication during the final phase that enemy initiated activity was increasing in the area, with an ABF on BLACKHORSE of 6 x 107mm rockets early on 14 September. As a result, Operation IVANHOE was mounted to counter the threat to the security of PHUOC TUY Province, and in particular, the civil population of DUC THANH District.[11]

12

The flowers of the forest

It's probably true to say that most battalions that served in Vietnam had one operation or battle that for various reasons became indelibly stamped on everyone's memory. Some operations became enshrined in Australia's military history, and have been carried ever since as battle honours on the Regiment's colours. For 6RAR it is Long Tan; for 1RAR it is Coral and Balmoral; and for 5RAR, Binh Ba; all names which add lustre to the Regiment's already bright fighting record.

But although most battles were neither widely known nor proudly quoted, they are nonetheless significant to those who fought in them. And for the members of 4RAR/NZ (ANZAC) Battalion it was Operation Ivanhoe, and particularly the events of 21 September 1971, that became the focal point of the second tour.

Throughout early September, during Operation North Ward, 'people-sniffer' missions flown to the east of Nui Le and around Nui Sao indicated the presence of an unidentified enemy force. These indications were to some degree confirmed from contacts by V, D and Support Company operating in the vicinity. Intelligence assessments were strongly of the opinion that these enemy elements might be from 33 NVA Regiment. In addition, a visual reconnaissance mission flown over the area on 10 September reported seeing a number of new tracks leading into the province from Long Khanh. And American forces had experienced numerous contacts with RHQ 33rd around Nui Hot, 20 kilometres east of Courtenay Hill, but these contacts had suddenly ceased on 16 September. And it will be remembered that 3/33rd had made a reconnaissance into the same area in May. All this activity indicated that

33 NVA Regiment were now in the Nui Le–Nui Sao area, and that they were probably establishing a base there for operations against the northern villages and outposts along Route 2.

The strength of RHQ 33rd and all the regimental support companies was currently put at 378 all ranks, with 2/33rd numbering 270 all ranks and 3/33rd at 300. 1/33rd had been ordered to remain near Bao Binh eight kilometres east of Route 2 between Xuan Loc and Black Horse. Their strength was 300.

So Ivanhoe was mounted to find and confront 33 NVA Regiment. The operation would be controlled by the Task Force CP at Nui Dat; and the ANZAC Battalion's mission was to 'redeploy east of Route 2 and locate 33NVA Regiment'.

The CO's concept of operations was to deploy three rifle companies into the north of the AO between the suspected locations of 33rd and their probable sanctuaries in Long Khanh Province. The companies would then search from north to south. Support Company would be deployed in block and ambush positions north of the searching companies in the Courtenay rubber. 3RAR would be operating to their north-east. Meanwhile 1 Troop A Squadron, again under operational control of the Battalion, was to maintain a presence west of

Maj Keith Towning, the Battery Commander, at his fire planning map in the Battalion CP on Courtenay Hill. It was the outstanding commitment of 104 Battery 12 Field Regiment that did so much to ensure the survival of B and D Companies on 21 September 1971. (*The Fighting Fourth*)

Route 2 and north of the province border, and would ambush in those areas by night.

This meant that the enemy would either have to fight their way north through the rifle companies to escape into Long Khanh or alternatively go south to evade the companies before turning north and heading for the border. In either case, if the enemy got clear of the rifle companies they would still have to fight their way through the Support Company, 1 Troop and 3RAR blocking positions before gaining the sanctuary of Long Khanh. Once again it was a simple plan, and it would put maximum pressure on the enemy while leaving the CO ample opportunity to redeploy Support Company and 1 Troop if necessary.

Although the operation was scheduled to begin at midnight on 18–19 September, there would of necessity be some coming and going within the AO for the first two days. V Company were in Nui Dat as Task Force Ready Reaction Force, and were not scheduled to be released back to the Battalion again until 22 September. C Company would be taken to Nui Dat for R & C at 1600hr on 19 September and would not be available again until 24 September. And B Company were to be redeployed from Nui Dat into their AO four kilometres south-west of D Company at 1000hr on 20 September. However, D Company,

A M2A2 Gun Howitzer of 104 Battery fires in support of the Battalion during Operation Ivanhoe in September 1971. (*The Fighting Fourth*)

who had been in the AO at the end of Operation North Ward, would begin their search at 0800hr on 19 September.

In practical terms this meant that the CO only had D Company clear of any other commitments in the AO when the operation began. Therefore Brig McDonald placed D Company 3RAR under operational control of the ANZAC Battalion from 1000hr on 19 September, and they were inserted into their AO just east of Courtenay rubber by helicopter at 1510hr on that day.

The operation began tragically.

D Company 4RAR moved off with two platoons forward to begin searching their AO at about 0800hr on 19 September. 2/Lt Byrne's 10 Platoon was on the left (north) of the company's axis of advance, and 2/Lt McKay's 11 Platoon was on the right. 2/Lt Spinkston's 12 Platoon trailed CHQ centrally in reserve.

After the company had been moving for about ten minutes they received an encoded message from Courtenay Hill telling them that a Task Force signals intelligence intercept put the company within 500 metres of an enemy radio set. The OC ordered a halt and made a quick contingency plan with the platoon commanders, then they got moving again.

Courtenay rubber was a kilometre to the north, and the company was heading roughly south-east towards Nui Sao. Visibility here was up to 50 metres, and many of the trees were tall and heavy and going was not difficult. But it was a gloomy place.

Twenty minutes later a second message was received amending the first. D Company, it said, were within 500 metres of *two* enemy radio sets.

The texts of the messages were not recorded in the operations log, but the CO and all the principal staff in the CP that morning—the OPSO, the adjutant, the IO and the RSO—are certain that the wording of the first message was 'within 500 metres of an enemy *radio set*'. However, after receiving this information, OC D Company decided to make a worst-case assumption that, because the enemy were usually short of radio sets, those they did have would probably not be deployed below battalion HQ level. From this he drew the conclusion that the presence of two radio sets might indicate the presence of two enemy *battalions*. He did not discuss his assumption with Courtenay Hill, but based on it he kept the company more concentrated than usual.

As might be expected after receiving the information that they were in close proximity to two enemy battalions who might very well be North Vietnamese regulars, D Company was tightly wound and all their senses were focused forward. So when at 0900hr the leading scout of 11 Platoon saw an armed black figure moving on a track 75 metres to his front he immediately opened fire, and his bullet struck the figure in the head, wounding him fatally. A brief fire-fight ensued, and then it was realised that this was a friendly clash between 10 and 11 Platoon. Both platoons ceased fire. The company was told to remain where it was, and HQ 1ATF mounted an immediate investigation. Subsequently the Task Force Commander concurred that no one was to blame for this terrible event which, he agreed, had been caused by a series of adverse circumstances coming together at this particular time and place. The leading scout, who had fired first, a resourceful and dedicated young soldier, was completely exonerated.

There were no other incidents that day.

At 0705hr next morning, 20 September, four APCs under the command of 2/Lt Lawrence from 1 Troop A Squadron were ambushed on Route 2 about three kilometres south of Xa Bang. The vehicles were travelling north, 75–100 metres apart, when the lead APC, c/s TA11A, was engaged with RPG7 fire. More RPG rounds and small arms fire were then directed at the first two vehicles, but only a few small arms rounds struck their targets and none caused casualties. The vehicles immediately returned fire with 50- and 30-calibre machineguns, and then charged into the ambush, which caused the enemy, estimated to be 20–30 strong, to withdraw rapidly to the east in two groups. When the vehicles swept the area they found the body of one enemy soldier and retrieved his AK47. The only friendly casualty was the commander of c/s TA11A, who was slightly cut over the right eye by stone chips when the first RPG detonated on the road in front of his vehicle.

The enemy ambush position was about 150 metres long and 250–300 metres back from the road, though the RPG which had initiated the contact was much closer. Weapon pits and sleeping bays had been prepared and occupied, probably during the night.

At 1010hr, Maj Hogarth's B Company were inserted into their AO south-west of D Company. He recalls:

> We were inserted into our area of operations by APC after a break in Nui Dat. We travelled north along Route 2 and then east (using the track 500 metres north of the ambush on 2/Lt Lawrence's section at 0705hr). Immediately we left Route 2 the APCs transported us initially into quite open country but I became increasingly uneasy as the vegetation became more dense and so I had the company dismount a little short of our intended destinations.
>
> I don't recall expecting to meet North Vietnamese regular soldiers. We may have been so briefed but in most operations the threat always seemed to be painted more severely than actually transpired. It seemed to me to be a routine operation.[1]

Later the same day, at 1330hr, 2/Lt McKay's 11 Platoon engaged a fifteen-man enemy group about a kilometre north-east of Nui Sao and

> . . . 11 Pl opened fire; killing one VC instantly, and then went to ground. The enemy deployed speedily and returned rapid fire. They were then ordered to withdraw by verbal orders from their commander. The enemy withdrew east then north. Artillery was fired onto their withdrawal route, and a Pink Team [c/s Fox White 26] assisted.

But the enemy were too close to 11 Platoon to allow Fox White 26 to engage with safety. However when they withdrew the Cobras pursued them and opened fire, but without discernible results. Shortly after, 10 Platoon had a brief fire-fight with, probably, the same group as it withdrew, but there were no casualties on either side.

When 11 Platoon searched the contact area they '. . . Located one enemy KIA and an AK47, pack and two Chicom [Chinese communist] grenades. He was dressed in greens. A follow-up failed to locate more enemy, and the platoon formed an NDP. A second enemy KIA was located in the area on 21 September.'[2] It was noted at the time of the contact that the enemy were wearing dark olive green uniforms and navigating with maps and compasses. This was unusual.

At 1625hr 11 Platoon D Company 3RAR, three kilometres east of Courtenay rubber, reported hearing the sounds of chopping. They went to investigate, but by 1810hr they had found nothing. And at 1812hr Fox White 26 reported finding a well-used east–west track not far from 11 Platoon 4RAR's previous contact. Movement on the track, said the pilot, had been heavy in both directions.

Then at 1832hr the CO's Possum reported blue smoke rising from the trees 300–400 metres south of 11 Platoon, but the pilot considered that it was probably from the impact point of the Cobras' rockets earlier in the day. At 1856hr Possum also noted smoke rising from the trees 400 metres south-east of B Company. This was curious, because there had been no airstrikes or artillery in that location. It was almost certainly smoke from a cooking fire, but there were no civilians legally in that area, and no other friendlies either.

There was an uneasy feeling throughout the Battalion on 19 and 20 September 1971. At this distance in time some might say it was hindsight after the events which were to occur next day. But even before 21 September, many felt a sense of foreboding that was difficult to put a finger on but was nonetheless profound. Perhaps it was because some men, after months on active service, developed, or more correctly redeveloped, senses that have their origins in our primaeval beginnings. Intuition, sixth sense, heightened perceptions, or the instinct for danger that comes with training and experience—whatever it was and whatever its origins, there were many in those first two day of Operation Ivanhoe who felt that 'something was going on'. The usual grins and whispered wise-cracks were absent, and in the NDPs eyes moved constantly to beyond the perimeter, and the gun sentries needed no reminders to stay alert.

From 0120hr–0531hr on 21 September, the RF unit at Cam My reported incoming 60mm mortar rounds, and the 105s and 81mm mortars at FSB Debbie fired ten rounds each in support. But as the liaison officer at Xuan Loc did not have direct communications with Cam My, the reports received at Courtenay Hill from the village were confused, and the exact details of the ABF were not known until two days later.

B and D Company were on the move by 0730hr on 21 September. D Company were much more concentrated, but instead of continuing with the search to the south-east, the company now turned north-east. 12 Platoon were on the left, and 11 Platoon on the right. 11 Platoon was also ordered to find a place where they could take a quick helicopter resupply of ammunition to replenish that used the day before.

At 0745hr 11 Platoon located a curving track running south-west to south-east which had been used in the last twelve hours. They began paralleling it in an easterly direction. Meanwhile 12 Platoon were on a separate branch of the same track, 200 metres west of 11 Platoon. 2/Lt Spinkston decided to reconnoitre the north side of the track, and put his men into a quick all-round defence position. Then he set off, taking with him his platoon signaller, Pte Gorringe, the commander of 7 Section, Cpl McKenzie, and his machinegunner, Pte Duff. After going no more than 20 metres the group came under heavy fire from bunkers to their north, and they withdrew back to the platoon and went to ground. At that moment an RPG round impacted in a tree just above Pte Jimmy Duff's head, killing him instantly. More RPG rounds wounded 2/Lt Spinkston and seven other men. The platoon moved back another 20 metres to the south side of the track to be certain they were out of the enemy killing ground, and they then called for artillery fire.

When 2/Lt Spinkston and his men came under fire, 11 Platoon was ordered to move back towards them and to secure D Company's eastern flank. At the same time CHQ and 10 Platoon began moving up towards 12 Platoon. But as they moved, their radio communications with the CP on Courtenay Hill became increasingly tenuous. By 1000hr, CHQ and 10 Platoon were at a location which became known as the Winch Point

Here communications were just workable, and the clearing was the only one big enough to facilitate ammunition resupply and casualty evacuation. As soon as 11 Platoon could be brought back to a position just south-east of 10 and 12 Platoon, the company would be properly balanced and better able to counter whatever moves the enemy might make. But just then 11 Platoon came under very heavy ground attack from the east, which continued with increasing ferocity for the next two hours.

The OC's immediate problem was therefore whether to go to the assistance of 11 Platoon, and risk becoming heavily committed without reliable communications; or to remain relatively firm here around the Winch Point and provide 11 Platoon with a base to withdraw to if the enemy attacks became too heavy. It was decided to remain at the Winch Point, and 2/Lt McKay was told to notify the OC as soon as he felt the odds against him were too great.

Now that it was obvious that the ANZAC Battalion had a substantial fight on their hands, American aircraft seemed to come from everywhere wanting to join in. In fact OC D Company found himself oversupplied with air support and having to fight his platoons over the company command net while at the same time controlling enthusiastic gunship pilots over the admin/air net. But by 1030hr a US Navy FAC, Lt Rodriguez (c/s Jade 07), had come on station and taken over the coordination and control of the air effort. He remained overhead all day and well into the night, returning to base only periodically for more fuel and marker rockets.

Just after 1100hr, air observation and pilot reports indicated that D Company had struck a bunker system of considerable size. Indeed it appeared that it was a complex consisting of several linked systems. The OC therefore decided to put maximum air and artillery onto the complex, and then, if and when confirmation was received from the air that the enemy were withdrawing from the system, the company would advance into and through it in pursuit.

Between 1130hr and 1530hr the bunkers were pounded by successions of Iroquois, Cobras, Pink Teams, Broncos and Phantoms, using pintle-mounted M60s, mini-guns, cannons, rockets and napalm. Hard bombs were not used in the early stages of the battle because of D Company's close proximity to the bunkers. But whenever the aircraft went off-station their place was taken by the guns of 104 Battery, so that the system was subjected to almost continuous bombardment.

It's worth noting here, in the light of what was to happen later, that throughout the day the aircraft on station over B and D Company totalled seven Cobra teams (two aircraft each), four Pink Teams (three aircraft each), two Dustoff pairs, seven pairs of A37s and four FACS. Between them they expended 967 HE rockets, 120 flechette rockets,

US Airforce F4 Phantom attacks with napalm. (*The Fighting Fourth*)

5300 40mm HE rounds, 143 500 mini-gun rounds, 28 pods of napalm and four 500-pound bombs. 9 Squadron RAAF flew sixteen Bushranger sorties, nine Dustoff sorties and five opdems, and expended 115 HE rockets, 79 500 mini-gun rounds and 12 500 M60 rounds. The guns of 104 Battery and A Battery 12 Field Regiment expended a total of 2074 HE rounds.

Meanwhile B Company 'was moving generally east and south, dispersed as single platoons. We had a few minor contacts and saw sign that indicated somewhat larger enemy parties. There were inconclusive indications that the enemy were North Vietnamese. I recall thinking it would be prudent not to be so dispersed'.[3]

However, the CO's first air reconnaissance that morning had been in the vicinity of B Company's advance, and

> The pilot and I clearly picked up tracks in the dew going from north to south into a tree verge that formed an L-shape. The tracks went in, but there was no sign of them exiting. Not being trackers we estimated a platoon to company strength. The fact that Bob [Hogarth] advanced on a

> wide front was fortuitous. As 104 Battery was firing in support of D Company, I called in Bushrangers to attack the L-shaped tree area.[4]

But then at 1128hr 2/Lt McDaniel reported:

> The platoon had discovered a telephone wire and had begun to follow it. A short halt position was adopted prior to recommencing the follow up. Two enemy approached the position from the north-east observed by the sentry and engaged. One NVA was KIA and the other withdrew north-east. The enemy appeared to have been checking the wire.[5]

Six minutes later Lt Willis's 5 Platoon reported that they had found fresh foot-tracks heading east and south, about 1500 metres north-east of 6 Platoon. B Company were now moving carefully because they could hear D Company's battle off to the north-east, and they had been listening to its progress over the Battalion command net. Now their own platoons were making contact and finding sign, and at 1311hr, following searches of enemy bodies and their equipment, Maj Hogarth was able to confirm to the Battalion CP that his company was in contact with NVA troops. Although no unit identification was yet possible, the enemy could only be 33rd.

As 2/Lt McDaniel's platoon followed the telephone wire that had been discovered during their previous contact, they saw an enemy soldier rolling it up. When they engaged him the wire was cut and the man withdrew east. The platoon was still following up.

At 1146hr, USAF Phantoms, directed by Jade 07, put napalm onto the bunkers in front of D Company. Over time, napalm has acquired a fearsome reputation because it either suffocates or incinerates its victims or at least causes terrible injuries. But often in Vietnam, as was the case now, it was very useful for taking the canopy off the forest so that FACs and pilots could get a clearer view of what lay beneath. Having targeted the preliminary runs to achieve this, Jade 07 directed his pilots to expend the rest of their pods onto the bunkers themselves.

As soon as the last pods were gone, Bushrangers and Pink Teams engaged the system almost continuously until 1240hr, at which time more napalm was put down. Most of these pods were dropped a little too far to the east of the bunkers. At this stage the full extent of the bunker complex was not known, and perhaps Jade 07 thought the napalm strike had not been effective. However, it probably helped to discourage further attempts by the enemy to mount a major outflanking movement from the east. Whatever the case, after the napalm strike at 1250hr, Bushrangers, Cobras and more Pink Teams returned and the pounding of the bunkers continued.

Nevertheless, ten minutes later, despite the intense assault from the air, 12 Platoon reported enemy to be probing round their right (eastern) flank; and Fox White 26 reported a large concentration of enemy forming up at the rear (north) of the bunkers. Simultaneously, a Possum pilot reported another enemy concentration on the high ground 600 metres north-east of D Company. But concentrating for what purpose? A coordinated attack on the company, or a mass withdrawal to the north?

11 Platoon, who had not been under attack for over an hour, were now closing up to the rest of the company, and they married-up just east of the Winch Point at 1345hr. The company was now concentrated, and although not dug in, was in a far better position to give a good account of themselves if the enemy put in a major attack. Conversely, if the enemy were about to withdraw, the company was well placed to pursue them. But fresh supplies of ammunition would be required first.

The OC got the platoon commanders together, gave them a quick sitrep, and told them that the plan was to attack through the bunker system if the enemy started to withdraw. The company would again assault two up: 12 Platoon left, Tac Party centre and 11 Platoon right. The leading platoons would move in alternating bounds of 25 metres, with the Tac Party coordinating forward movement. 10 Platoon was to remain at the Winch Point as the firm base and reserve, but was placed on one minute's notice to follow the rest of the company on the OC's order. Because of the possibility of pursuing the enemy, D Company would wear their large packs in the assault. In the meanwhile, helicopters brought in a resupply of ammunition, and the casualties were evacuated.

Just after 1500hr pilots reported that the enemy were withdrawing from the bunkers in large numbers to the north-west, north and north-east. Therefore, as planned, D Company less 10 Platoon moved forward to their start line and shook out into attack formation.

A curious silence descended over the battlefield. The aircraft had departed to refuel and bomb up, or to stand off so that the guns could fire immediately if D Company needed them. The shadows were beginning to lengthen, but the insects were silent, and the air was thick with the pungent stink of burnt napalm. On Courtenay Hill those not on duty stood in small groups looking to the south-east; and at the FSBs the artillerymen eased their shoulders as they stood to the guns. In D Company, during these last few moments, each man's thoughts turned inwards on himself. At 1540hr 12 Platoon crossed the start line.

The platoon completed their first bound unopposed, and went to ground. Now 11 Platoon moved forward. They had been going for about ten minutes when their left-hand section was hit by a tempest of automatic fire from several mutually supporting bunkers. Unknowingly, 6 Section had been advancing along a skilfully sited and camouflaged firelane. Pte Brian Beilken and Pte Rod Sprigg were both killed instantly. Pte Ralph Niblett was hit in the chest, and despite everything that Cpl O'Sullivan could do he died of his wounds about 30 minutes later. After the initial burst of enemy fire, Pte Keith Kingston-Powles brought his M60 into action but he, too, was killed a few moments later. Nevertheless, the last surviving rifleman in the section, Pte Casson, a national serviceman from Western Australia, crawled forward to each of the casualties in turn because 'it looked like they needed help'. When he had satisfied himself that there was nothing he could do for them, he retrieved the M60 and its ammunition, and crawled out of the killing ground.[6]

Private Hannah later recalled:

> We advanced and then all hell broke loose. I was on the far left flank with [Sgt] Daryl Jenkin as the platoon sergeant at that time, carrying an extra radio we had got into the platoon. Right beside us was 6 Section and the gunner was Private K.M. Kingston-Powles. I remember as soon as the fighting started him hitting the ground and getting about 50 rounds away. Then Daryl got hit. He was approximately 10 feet in front of me. I looked across again at Kingston-Powles and there was no movement from him whatsoever. He was just slumped with his head on the butt of the gun. And then Daryl asking me to get him back because he had been hit.
>
> At that stage I turned and said to Daryl, 'What?' And he said to me, 'I've been hit.' I can remember saying, 'What do you want me to fucking do about it?' And he saying, 'Mate, you've got to get me back.' I then crawled forward, got him back to where my pack and radio was and he said, 'Mate I need to be bandaged up.' So I took up my knife and cut his sleeve off and started to put a field dressing around it. I remember him saying to me, 'Watch over there.' I watched, and there was movement to our left front. It was the enemy coming out of a bunker and using two big trees with buttress roots as a route from that bunker to wherever they were going. Once Daryl's arm was bandaged, he laid there and I saw him personally kill, well, hit, four. I don't know whether he killed them, but they didn't move anyway. As they got out of the hole and ran for this buttress tree he just knocked them off.[7]

11 Platoon fought back with M60 and rifle fire, but it was obvious that if four hours of intense aerial and artillery bombardment had not broken the enemy's resolve, it was highly unlikely that riflemen, however

determined, would do much better. Moreover, the company's M72s had been withdrawn just before the operation began because of continuing malfunctions. This meant that the company had nothing other than rifles, M60s and M79s with which to attack the bunkers. OC D Company therefore gave the order for 11 Platoon to withdraw through the Tac Party/12 Platoon position, and thence to the Winch Point. But 11 Platoon found it almost impossible to move back while wearing their packs because they kept becoming entangled among foliage and fallen timber. They were therefore ordered to drop them. The OC also ordered 2/Lt McKay to leave the bodies of his three men where they were. They were dead, and there was no point in taking more casualties to get them out.

At the Battalion CP, Capt Sayce reflected that,

> Unlike most previous contact locations, the general area of Nui Sao/Nui Le, where D Company were engaged in the heaviest fighting, was visible from Courtenay Hill and it became the focal point of everyone's gaze who were not immediately preoccupied in supporting the Battalion HQ's efforts in some way. US helicopter gunships, FACs, fighter ground attack aircraft, our own Possum and RAAF helicopters circled the area. There was an element of frustration apparent in that the individual could not go and physically commit to the battle, particularly when our own casualties began to mount and the companies were clearly under considerable pressure.
>
> The CO spoke more and more on the Battalion Command Net, seeking information and assessments and also providing strong support and advice to his company commanders who were under considerable pressure. Very clearly he had grasped the enormity of the situation as the most testing time the Battalion was likely to face, knowing that this would be a decisive battle as the campaign came to a close.
>
> The strain of command was apparent, but the CO's demeanour instilled a firm and purposeful resolve among the staff that were stretched to their limits organising the commitment of the resources placed at our disposal by the TF Commander. In particular, the BC [Maj Towning] co-ordinated the fire support available with professional skill. Both the Battalion and Intelligence staffs worked well under pressure.[8]

Maj Hogarth, to the south-west, now reported:

> 6 Platoon continued to follow the track made by the enemy and at 1600hr conducted a recce for their night loc. The recce party observed the enemy to their east, south-east and north, engaged them and withdrew to the main

> body. The main body were at this time engaged by SA fire and by a light [60mm] mortar north of their position. 6Pl sustained considerable casualties from the mortar [including 2/Lt McDaniel]. They continued to engage the enemy. 6Pl was ordered to withdraw west and 4Pl [Lt Ballantyne] was sent to their assistance to endeavour to hit the enemy from the north. As 6Pl withdrew they engaged the area of the suspected [mortar] base plate with M79 and continued to engage the enemy. They, formed a defensive position round a winch point.[9]

The Battalion was now heavily committed in two locations four kilometres apart. To the north, D Company's attack had been repulsed, and their situation could best be described as precarious. In the south, Maj Hogarth was of the opinion that 6 Platoon had bumped the rear of a prepared enemy ambush position, though for the time being he was unable to gauge its size and extent, or what the enemy's intentions were. But he was in no doubt that his company was taking casualties at the hands of an aggressive and well organised enemy force.

Of the Battalion's uncommitted companies, D Company 3RAR were in their blocking position north-east of Courtenay rubber; V Company were still in Nui Dat as Ready Reaction Force; and C Company were down at Vung Tau on R & C. There was plentiful air support, however, and the guns of 104 Battery were within range and had almost unlimited ammunition. Maj Towning recalls:

> Both sections of guns were within range of both companies, and A Battery was also within range. The allocation of artillery resources is always a difficult problem to solve. In this case it was possible to allocate one section to B Company and the other section to D Company.
>
> At no time during any action in Vietnam did we ever experience any problem with gun ammunition supply. Although I often had hard words with Arty Tac about ammunition usage rates, Jim Hughes always backed me. On this occasion we did run a bit low on ammo, but the Americans delivered direct to the gun platforms by Chinook. I think it worthy to note that we of 104 Battery hold those Chinook pilots in high esteem.[10]

It was 1637hr when D Company was once more concentrated round the Winch Point after their attack on the bunkers. Here they were able to extract the wounded and receive a much-needed resupply of ammunition. OC D Company discussed the situation over the radio with the CO, and it was decided to resume the bombardment of the complex, but this time with hard bombs. However, the use of hard bombs meant that, for safety reasons, the company would have to move at least 300 metres south. All platoons were also now reporting that groups of enemy were moving through the trees towards the Winch Point. Clearly, if the company were going to relocate they'd have to do it very soon. However it was essential to break clean (to withdraw while not under fire or attack), otherwise the company risked getting into a running fight as they moved south, and with the numbers now opposing them such an occurrence could only end one way. Some method would have to be found to make the enemy keep their heads down as the company quit the Winch Point and made for a new defence position.

The OC therefore spoke to Lt Rodriguez and asked him to get FGA aircraft on station as quickly as possible. He said he wanted napalm put down on the company's present location, the Winch Point, but that he did not want to be there when it arrived. It was absolutely critical, therefore, that Jade 07 gave the company three minutes' warning when the aircraft were inbound and ready to drop. Could he guarantee that? Lt Rodriguez replied that he could.

In fact OC D Company would have preferred to use the guns, because they could shoot at his command, and their fire could keep pace with the company as they headed towards the new position. But with so many aircraft over the AO it would have been impossible to get air clearances without a long delay, and time was the thing that D Company had least of at this moment.

10 Platoon was therefore ordered to move 400 paces south and put in the 10–2 o'clock sector of a defence position. 11 Platoon were to follow and take the 6–10 sector. It was emphasised to the platoon commanders that it was vital to get onto the ground quickly. Almost as soon as 10 and 11 Platoon were on their way, Jade 07 called to say the aircraft were three minutes out and ready to drop, and the Tac Party and 12 Platoon immediately abandoned the Winch Point.

Withdrawing the company in single file and under these circumstances was a risk. But it was a calculated risk, because it was vital to break contact with the enemy, and that could only be done by moving quickly. The only other alternative was for D Company to remain where they were at the Winch Point and face a coordinated attack on ground well known to the enemy.

Even so there was so much that could go wrong at this stage. 10 and 11 Platoon could be attacked while they were strung out in, essentially, a thin green line at the new defensive position. The Tac Party and 12 Platoon could be attacked while they were moving towards the NDP, of necessity faster than was advisable. Or the napalm might be off target and impact among the withdrawing infantrymen. But in fact it all went like a well-rehearsed script. 10 Platoon reported themselves to be in the new defence position; a moment later 11 Platoon were on the ground too; and a few minutes after that CHQ and 12 Platoon joined them.

The napalm hit the Winch Point at 1808hr.

In B Company's location the situation was also precarious, and Maj Hogarth reported:

> 4Pl enroute [to assist 6 Platoon] engaged a party of three enemy who were rapidly withdrawing north. One body was found but no detailed search was made. Artillery was used to the east of the contact area and three Pink Teams in turn engaged the area. They reported seeing 'many enemy' and engaging them. They indicated they 'got some'.
>
> On completion of the airstrike the Pink Teams conducted armed reconnaissance to the east. 6Pl who had used the airstrikes to complete their withdrawal were now reorganising and 4Pl were ordered to proceed to their winch point and conduct the [casualty] evacuation. Enroute they again engaged one man, no results are known.
>
> Medevac aircraft were called in from a holding area once 4 and 6 Pls had married up and secured the winch point. 12 casualties were evacuated by winch and the company concentrated after dark.[11]

CHQ, 4 and 6 Platoon were now concentrated in an NDP and the last of the serious casualties were being winched out. Three more lightly wounded men elected to remain on duty. At 1730hr, when Lt Willis's platoon arrived at the NDP, the company was finally complete, and although they were not yet safe they were at least in a better position to defend themselves.

By 1830hr the last of the casualties were being evacuated under the supporting cover of a Pink Team, and a light observation helicopter was trying to hover close enough to the ground to enable two less seriously wounded men to climb aboard, but the attempt had to be aborted.

With the Dustoff aircraft clear of the area, Maj Hogarth brought artillery fire down onto the likely enemy reinforcement or withdrawal routes, coordinated with the movements of light fire teams which were also still supporting the company. The enemy seemed to be withdrawing, but the day had already cost B Company fifteen wounded.

By 1841hr D Company were complete at their new defensive position, and at once they started to get themselves organised. They urgently needed to be able to fight as a cohesive company from nothing less than shellscrapes, but preferably from weapon pits. The move south had also caused CHQ to lose radio communication with Courtenay Hill, and it was vital to get a 292 aerial up. But almost at once an enemy squad came charging into the north side of the perimeter, though before they could withdraw they had fallen to 10 Platoon's judiciously sited M60s. A moment later 11 Platoon opened fire from their sector on the south-west side of the perimeter. The worst had happened: the move south had brought D Company up against yet another bunker system.

Lt Gilbert, the FO, remembers:

> I had just got my map out to work out where we were when all hell broke loose with rifle fire. So I can remember lying there and seeing all the green tracer going over my head about eighteen inches away. I couldn't put a light on and it was too dark to see my map and I couldn't talk to the company commander because he was maybe 20 feet away and as soon as he and I tried to talk to each other we drew aimed fire, so we couldn't talk. I then had to get the artillery in, so I had to try and remember what the grid reference was where I was during the day, and try to remember how far I had walked, what direction I had walked, and I was lying there with all this rifle fire going on trying to do a trigonometrical equation in my head: I was doing a right-angled triangle saying, 'If I had walked this far, this would be the hypotenuse, so I could be this far down and this far across', and working out this is where I think I am. We were out of range of most artillery [sic], except for the three guns of Lt Brian Steven's section, which were just within range. We were at the extreme end of the zone of the gun, which means there was quite a large error factor. I then called in the artillery, put it out a little from where we were and then was absolutely terrified when the rounds were on their way as to where they going to land. But they landed out, and then I brought them in until we started copping the shrapnel on ourselves and I reckoned that was close enough. Then I just tried to move it around the perimeter a bit to cover it as best I could.[12]

But before the guns could fire they needed ground and air clearances from Arty Tac at Nui Dat. There was no difficulty in obtaining ground clearances, but there had been so many aircraft overhead throughout the day that keeping track of them was almost impossible. Nevertheless it was a golden rule: no clearance, no artillery. And Maj Towning was greatly frustrated by the situation:

> The problem with getting air clearance was associated with the air support that the TF Commander had laid on. However the guns were loaded and ready to fire as soon as clearance was given. At the time I was up in the CO's helicopter relaying fire orders to the guns because Lt Gilbert could not put up his big antenna. Eventually our fuel got so low I had to return

> to Courtenay and from then on the task was taken on by the Recce Flight. I was furious that artillery support was delayed.[13]

And now, once again, the question of withdrawal of C Squadron's tanks hung in the air. The Battalion CP duty officer's log entry for 1858hr says: 'D Company requested all possible support. Terrain, distance and darkness prevents APC assistance. (No tanks). D Company unable to mark position for air support, or accept ammunition resupply because of heavy and sustained ground fire. Artillery continuing on Danger Close procedure.'[14]

Capt Sayce was in no doubt that the lack of tanks was unfortunate:

> During two previous battles against 274 Regiment, D and V Company were both able to employ armour in direct support. The CO had APCs but could not deploy them closer to B or D Company to assist because of the terrain, the need to maintain a mobile reserve, and the fact that they could be used as a blocking force to the north of the contact area in the rubber plantation or to the east along Route 2. Unfortunately the tanks of C Squadron were located in Vung Tau [sic], undergoing preparation for their return to Australia as part of the phased withdrawal of 1ATF. Given the terrain in which the contacts were fought and the weather at the time, I am sure they would have been useful.[15]

But in fact the tanks of C Squadron had already left Vietnam. The first troop had been decommissioned in June, the second in July, and after extensive cleaning and preparation for shipping they had been locked in a special security compound at 1ALSG and their crews had flown home. Squadron HQ and the remaining three troops were scheduled to be withdrawn in August, and a Japanese cargo ship had been contracted to take the tanks back to Australia. However when it arrived off Vung Tau it was discovered that the ship's cranes could not lift the tanks. All the vehicles were therefore stripped of their 20-pounder barrels, their tracks, and anything else that would lighten the load. Eventually the *Harima Maru* sailed for Australia with all Centurions aboard on 14 September. OC C Squadron and the remaining personnel flew home next day.

D Company was now down to about 85 all ranks. The CO was organising helicopters to bring V Company, who had been released early from their ready reaction task, as close as possible, but that could not be done until first light, and the New Zealanders' LZ would still be about four kilometres away from D Company. In the prevailing situation that

National Servicemen Pte Kevin 'Fred' Casson (left) and Pte Peter Minchinton went through basic and corps training together and were posted to 11 Platoon D Company. Mentioned in Despatches for bravery on 21 September 1971, Pte Casson's decoration was upgraded in 1999 and he was awarded the Medal of Gallantry. (Courtesy Peter Minchinton)

meant a five-hour approach march, and that might be too late. The APCs could not be committed in the dark in such thick country, and air support could no longer be used because D Company were unable to mark their position, and the pilots could not release their ordnance without precise visual references. So it all came down to the 85 men of the company, with whatever ammunition remained, and the guns of 104 Battery.

OC D Company remembers:

> I think probably the worst thing that can happen to any commander is to experience the feeling that there is no longer very much he can do to influence events during a battle, and that things will just have to take their course. I experienced this towards the end of the battle of Nui Le, and I think it provided one of the bleakest moments of my life.
>
> The battle of Nui Le started for D Company at 0851hr on 21 September 1971, and fourteen hours later we were still at it, having advanced, attacked, and withdrawn. Now, in the dark, with unworkable direct communications to Battalion Tac, no other company closer than five clicks, with five dead and nine wounded, and the guns almost at maximum range [sic], we had forced up against yet another bunker system, and were encircled by elements of RHQ and 2/33 NVA Regiment.
>
> There had been no time to properly coordinate the defence, and certainly no time to dig even a shellscrape. In fact our perimeter now measured 35 metres across, and any attempt by commanders to move about, or return fire, provoked a hail of small arms. I was able to communicate with Greg Gilbert, my FO, who was about 20 metres from me, only

> by an ad hoc airborne relay manned by Captain Greg Shannon, the Battalion's ingenious Signals Officer.
>
> I'd passed the word that everyone should stay still and be quiet; not shoot unless directly threatened; and that the guns would begin firing Danger Close to dislodge the enemy who we could see moving about round us. I had arranged that the guns would fire on the four cardinal points of our perimeter, and that we would 'walk' the fire in until we started to pick up live shrapnel. We'd used this technique against 274 Regiment on the Suoi Ca, and although it had got fairly exciting, it caused no serious own casualties.
>
> Obviously we needed this defensive fire as quickly as possible. We had already skittled with small arms fire an enemy squad that had come charging into the north of the perimeter. Grenades were also landing among us, but most of them failed to detonate. I had the distinct impression that the movement and talking around the perimeter indicated that the enemy were preparing a concentrated attack. However there were difficulties in getting air clearances from Arty Tac at Nui Dat, so that guns were unable to shoot.
>
> And now, on the south-west side of the perimeter, the small arms fire was redoubled in intensity, and it was suddenly obvious that, after everything else that had happened this day, our perimeter had forced up against another bunker complex.
>
> In the gloom I realised that everyone close by was looking straight at me. Nobody said anything, but the message was obvious: 'For Christ's sake do something'. At that moment I realised that apart from bringing the fall of shot from the guns steadily closer to the perimeter, and giving the best possible account ourselves when the enemy launched their final attack, there was nothing else that could be done except hang on.[16]

But if it was possible there *was* still worse to come. At 2105hr, during a pause in the artillery fire, there was a burst of small arms from the south-west side of the perimeter. A few moments later the OC was informed that 2/Lt McKay had been wounded. The indomitable Cpl O'Sullivan crawled over to him, and soon reported that the young officer had been hit in the left shoulder by two AK47 rounds. He was losing blood rapidly, and Cpl O'Sullivan asked for more shelldressings to be sent over. He also reported that he had no morphine left.

2/Lt McKay was filling a shelldressing every 45 minutes. A shelldressing held about a pint of blood (700 ml). The mathematics was simple: he would bleed to death long before he could be evacuated. There was no question of getting a Dustoff helicopter in. With the enemy all around, and in the dark, no helicopter could get near enough even to lower the jungle penetrator that would be needed to get through the canopy.

The RMO, Capt Trevillian, was summoned to the radio in Nui Dat and briefed on the situation. Via the duty officer in the Battalion CP, he passed detailed instructions to Cpl O'Sullivan about how the wound should be managed, and the compelling need to apply a pressure pad. Pressure, the RMO emphasised, would have to be kept on until evacuation could be arranged in the morning. So for the rest of the night Cpl O'Sullivan sat with 2/Lt McKay keeping steady pressure on the pad, while the young officer bit soundlessly down on his identity discs, his only antidote to pain.

At 2200hr, Lt Rodriguez, who had done so much for D Company throughout this long day, was finally given a direct order by his CO to return to base. Promising to be overhead again next morning at first light, he reluctantly left the beleaguered infantrymen with the words, 'You take care down there, you hear.' On arrival at his base, it was discovered that there were fifteen bullet holes in his aircraft, and that several of them were from the top down. He had been flying so low that the enemy machineguns on the high ground overlooking the company had been firing *down* on him. Lt Rodriguez was to receive the Navy Cross for his work this day, and it was a decoration much applauded by D Company.

Working on a worst-case scenario, the OC reasoned that if 33rd was going to attack they would most likely do so at about 2300hr. That would give them time to complete their assault and withdraw north across the border before first light. A message was therefore passed round the company to expect an attack at any time now, and that when it came everyone was to fight like hell with everything they'd got.

At about the same time, the CO and Capt Sayce were with the Task Force Commander at Courtenay Hill:

> Brigadier McDonald, the CO, and myself were huddled in the intelligence CP where we could monitor the Battalion Command Net and the progress of the battle. We were analysing the events of the day and assessing likely enemy action as a result of the heavy fighting. During the discussions the TF Commander quietly advised us that the Prime Minister had passed a message to the Commander AFV, Major General Dunstan, expressing concern about incurring further Australian casualties at such a sensitive time (ie, after the withdrawal of Australian troops from Vietnam had been announced). However, the Commander AFV in discussing the situation with Commander 1ATF had advised that he would deal with the political aspects leaving the TF Commander free to go forward and give his undivided support to the Battalion commander fighting the tactical battle.

In my opinion I witnessed exactly what should be done in such a situation. I have nothing but admiration for the way in which General Dunstan and then Brigadier McDonald shouldered their responsibilities and provided cool, calm, helpful support to the CO and the Battalion.

At the time we were listening to the Command Net with the duty officer in the CP relaying medical instructions. Here we were, involved in the full range of concerns, from the PM and the strategic political level, to the harsh human realities of war, where communications enabled the RMO to guide the medic tending our wounded mates. Needless to say, we were far more worried about our soldiers than the PM.[17]

Maj McIver, who was leading the resupply effort at the ANZAC Battalion's rear position at Nui Dat, recalls:

. . . an atmosphere of serious concern at Nui Dat together with a sense of helplessness at the inability to do more to help. Everyone was on full alert and ready to respond immediately to any call for help. The activity level was very high throughout the operation. I recall we were all extremely concerned about the isolation of D Company overnight. Most members of Battalion Rear and the echelons stayed close to the comms [radios] when they were not actively tasked.

The management of casualty evacuation was a significant task given that casualties were taken by Dustoff helicopters to a range of medical facilities. It took some time to trace those wounded who went to US facilities.

The echelons [CQMSs] were kept very busy preparing resupply. There was no particular resupply issue with which we could not cope except the overriding concern that the operational situation prevented the timely delivery of essential resupply and [casualty] evacuation. We received offers of support, often unsolicited, from units inside and outside the Task Force.[18]

The unsolicited offers of support to which Maj McIver refers gives an indication of the very good spirit which existed within the Task Force in 1971. For example, when it grew dark, 1 Field Squadron RAE sent lighting sets across to Eagle Farm with sappers to set them up. This meant that the filling of magazines and their packing into sandbags for direct drop by helicopter to B and D Company could continue efficiently after dark. Adventurous young men from other Task Force units also arrived at Eagle Farm with their weapons and equipment and reported themselves ready to go out as reinforcements. And members of Administration Company slept at Eagle Farm throughout the night in case they, too, might be needed to reinforce B or D Company.

As soon as Arty Tac gave clearance, the guns began firing Danger Close around D Company's perimeter, and with great skill Lt Gilbert continued to move the fall of shot constantly, making it impossible for the enemy to close in. Within the perimeter, the 'wump, wump-wump' of the guns' primary charges at the FSB could be clearly heard, followed immediately by the sound of the rapidly approaching rounds, and then a thunderous roar as the salvos landed. The effectiveness of this fire was absolute—by 2230hr there appeared to be no further sign of enemy movement round the perimeter, and the guns were ordered to cease firing. 2300hr came, then midnight, then 0100hr, and now it seemed very likely that the enemy had finally withdrawn and that they would not attack after all.

Even so, the day had cost D Company five men killed and nine wounded.

True to his word, as the first light of day turned two dimensions into three, Lt Rodriguez called up on the company command net to say that he was inbound, and immediately began circling the area. He was soon joined by a Pink Team, but their close visual reconnaissance revealed no sign of 33rd.

The company sent out clearing patrols who located one dead enemy with his RPG2 loaded and aimed at the centre of the perimeter: he had been killed at the moment of firing. There were blood-soaked dressings, and drag marks and heavy blood trails leading away to the north, north-east and east of the perimeter. Scrapes on trees and saplings indicated where litters had passed. Another heavily used track went south, but it was impossible to tell if it had been a withdrawal route during the night. Nevertheless D Company began digging in. And now that the area seemed relatively secure, a Dustoff helicopter came in, and at 0842hr, eleven hours after his wounding, 2/Lt McKay was at last winched to safety astride a jungle penetrator.[19] Lt Wellard, newly arrived in the Battalion from the Australian Reinforcement Unit, was flown out from Nui Dat to take over 11 Platoon.

The CO confirmed his orders for V Company to reinforce D Company. The New Zealanders were originally to concentrate at the southernmost point of Courtenay rubber, and then move south on foot direct to the defensive position. But in the event those orders had to be modified, because air reconnaissance and reports from the Americans at Black Horse indicated that elements of 33rd might still be between the two companies. An LZ 500 metres south-east of Nui Sao was therefore prepped by artillery, and V Company flew in under cover of a heavy fire team. However their landing was unopposed, and they were complete on the ground at 1311hr. They immediately began making their careful way north.

Throughout the day there were numerous sightings from the air of freshly cut trees, piles of logs, and foot-tracks heading mainly north and east. Apart from those sightings, and airstrikes onto the 265 feature using 500-pound bombs, there was no contact with the enemy on 22 September.

At 1739hr, V Company married-up with D Company and the whole Task Force heaved a sigh of relief. At the time there were probably few men who thought much about the symbolism of this event. Everyone was too busy, there was still a lot to do, and no one could guess what might happen in the next few hours. But even so, it could hardly have been more appropriate that, whatever might happen, the Australians of D Company and the New Zealanders of V Company would be facing it together.

Next day, 23 September, Day 5 of Operation Ivanhoe, D Company moved forward under covering artillery fire to secure the Winch Point. This was to be V Company's start line for an attack into the bunkers. It was not known if any enemy remained there, but the CO was taking no chances. It took D Company two hours to locate the place exactly because of the heavy damage caused by artillery and airstrikes, but at 1105hr the start line was secured. V Company shook out and began moving forward with two platoons up, using alternate bounds much as D Company had done two days before. Their progress was not helped by torrential rain and ground damage, and it was not until 1725hr that they were at the bunkers and found the first of the packs dropped by 11 Platoon. A few minutes later they found more packs, and at 1802hr they located the bodies of Pte Kingston-Powles, Pte Beilkin and Pte Sprigg. Members of D Company moved forward with litters to bring their three young men away.

V Company had cleared a rough track back to the Winch Point and secured it by placing riflemen at intervals along it. As the three litters passed, the New Zealanders faced inwards, stood to attention in succession, and shouldered arms. It was an eloquent and moving gesture: the tribute of warriors to fallen comrades.

Throughout the next few days the companies set about locating and destroying the enemy bunkers. B Company found two bunker complexes in the area of their battles. Maj Hogarth later recalled:

> I could not at the time discern much pattern to the enemy movements. I certainly had no idea of his intentions. There was no indication on

> 21 September that they were withdrawing to the north-east although that became obvious subsequently. From there, the next few days could only be described as an exciting anti-climax. We found sign of very large forces having moved from south-west to north-east and a number of bunker systems which showed evidence of recent use and of treating casualties. We didn't know whether to feel relieved or disappointed.[20]

In D Company's area, 38 completed bunkers and seventeen incomplete were located. They were laid out in five separate systems in a Y formation, and they were demolished with high-explosive charges. Eighteen enemy bodies were also found and buried. Of these, nine had been killed by ground fire and nine by artillery.

None of the bodies of D Company's three men, nor the equipment left at the bunkers, had been touched by the enemy. In the case of the packs this was particularly surprising, because they contained ammunition, rations, maps and codes, and other personal equipment that would have been useful to 33rd. Equipment dropped by 6 Platoon's casualties was also recovered untouched. Nevertheless, for security reasons all codes were withdrawn and fresh sets issued.

Ivanhoe continued for another week, but there were no further contacts by the ANZAC Battalion. An APC, c/s TA11A, from 1 Section 1 Troop A Squadron, ran over a mine in Courtenay rubber at 1230hr on 25 September; and ten minutes later c/s TA12B hit another mine 400 metres further east. Both vehicles were extensively damaged and three crewmen injured.

D Company was extracted by helicopter to Nui Dat on the afternoon of 26 September. Next morning Lt Willis's 5 Platoon found blood-soaked bandages in bunkers four kilometres south of Xa Bang. B, C, V, and D Company 3RAR, continued to find bunkers, tracks, fighting pits and graves throughout the area of B and D Company's battles. And at 1905hr on 1 October a PF post at Ngai Giao came under a half-hearted attack mounted by local guerrillas and elements of Chau Duc. 104 Battery fired in support from FSB Robin, and at 1355hr on 2 October three bodies were found buried in the area. They were credited to the Battery.

On 15 March 1972 an addendum was issued to the ANZAC Battalion's Ivanhoe after action report. It was based on information given to 3 Cavalry Brigade (US) by Tran Van Cot, an assistant platoon leader of C9 3/33rd, who was captured on 22 November 1971. Under interrogation he said that RHQ 33rd, and 2 and 3 Battalions had entered Phuoc Tuy Province on 17–18 September. He went on to say that it had been an element of 3/33rd that had ambushed [2/Lt Lawrence's] APCs on Route 2 on the morning of 20 September. The aim of the ambush, Tran said, was to set a bait for 1ATF which would result in the deployment of a reaction force. The plan was that 3/33rd would ambush a logging track which ran east from Route 2, three kilometres south of Xa Bang. [It was in fact the track down which B Company had deployed at 1010hr on 20 September]. The enemy assessment was that the Australian infantry and APCs would use this track to attack RHQ and 2/33rd in their depth bunker position around the Nui Le–265 feature. However, 'on day three' [21 September] 3/33rd had been ordered to withdraw from the ambush position on the logging track, and go to the assistance of the main position, which was now under attack itself [by D Company]. The regiment, said Tran, was confused by the fact that the Australians had come from the north instead of the south.

But as 3/33rd were beginning to withdraw they were themselves attacked [by B Company], and had suffered eight men killed and thirteen wounded. 3/33rd had then withdrawn into Long Khanh Province, but Tran did not know how many casualties RHQ and 2 Battalion had suffered.

When a reunion group from D Company returned to Vietnam in 1993, Gary McKay was told during an interview with an ex-33rd officer that the commander of the regiment had been killed by artillery on 21 September.

The final paragraph of the Ivanhoe after action report says:

> There is no doubt that the quick retaliatory reaction by APCs from 1 Tp ASqn 3 Cav Regt when ambushed on 20 Sep; and the aggressive action by D Coy and B Coy, with plentiful close air and artillery support on 21 Sep 71, were responsible in forcing the NVA to abandon their efforts (which had been considerable) to harass the District, and return to more secure surroundings north of the Province boundary.[21]

Even so, there is little doubt that, had it not been for Maj Towning's training and leadership of 104 Battery; Lt Gilbert's cleverness in calculating his position without being able to consult a map, and his subsequent corrections which kept the fire moving about the perimeter; and the splendid commitment of the artillerymen at the gun positions, D Company might well have come under a coordinated attack on the night of 21 September. One can only speculate what the outcome of that attack might have been.

13

Last out

1ATF began its withdrawal from Phuoc Tuy Province at midnight on 2–3 October 1971.

Operation Valiant was the first phase of the withdrawal, and its aim was to redeploy all units of the Task Force which were currently operating in the north of the province back to Nui Dat. The operation was to be controlled from Nui Dat by HQ 1ATF. The ANZAC Battalion would be commanded from Courtenay Hill until 5 October, when the CP and FSB Debbie would close, and thereafter the Battalion would be commanded from its rear location in Nui Dat. If everything went according to plan, the Battalion and all its supporting units would be back in Nui Dat by 1800hr on 6 October.

Current intelligence assessments of the enemy had drawn the conclusion that reconnaissance elements from 33rd might be on the east of Route 2 as far south as Ngai Giao, with an equally small number of Chau Duc on the west of Route 2 south of the Cu Bi rubber. It was considered that the enemy threat, both from 33rd and Chau Duc, would probably be confined to attacks by fire and sapper attacks on the population centres and military outposts in the area.

Although the CO's mission was to withdraw intact, he was determined that the Battalion would withdraw aggressively. At this stage it was not known how many casualties 33rd had suffered on 21 September, but their losses had certainly been significant enough to force them to withdraw from the province. Nevertheless the CO, like any sensible commander, had to be ready for a worst-case situation. The assessment that the enemy presence in the province was confined to reconnaissance elements may or may not have been correct, but 33rd had demonstrated repeatedly that they could move long distances and infiltrate and exfiltrate rapidly. The CO's concept of operations was therefore that the Battalion would give the appearance of normal operating activity in and around the north of the province up to and during the withdrawal to Nui Dat.

To achieve the aim of withdrawing intact, C Company and A Squadron would operate west of Route 2 to the north and south of Courtenay Hill. At the same time, Support Company would maintain a presence east of Route 2 in the Courtenay rubber. V and B Company would begin moving south on foot and by APC, searching and ambushing in their AOs on both sides of Route 2. D Company would remain at Nui Dat as the Task Force Ready Reaction Force.

Then, on 4 October, C Company would be extracted by helicopter to Nui Dat and would occupy 3RAR's base defence perimeter on the night of 5–6 October. This would leave 3RAR free to make final preparations for their fly-out to HMAS *Sydney*, which would be standing off Vung Tau on the morning of 6 October.

4RAR and all supporting units were to be south of an east-west line through Ngai Giao by nightfall on 5–6 October. V Company would be in AO Otago, an AO north and east of Nui Dat, on 4 October; and B Company would move into AO Kingsgrove, an AO north and west of Nui Dat, on 6 October. Both companies would then patrol back through those AOs to the Task Force base during 6 October. 12 Field Regiment would close FSB Robin that same day.

As soon as 3RAR were clear of their area in Nui Dat, 4RAR BHQ/CP, C, Support and Administration Company would transfer stores and occupy the 3RAR lines, and thereafter be responsible for their defence. D Company, and the rear details from V and B Company, would be responsible for the defence of 4RAR's original lines in Nui Dat from 0600hr 6 October.

The preliminary manoeuvres of Operation Valiant went according to plan. By 1100hr on 4 October C Company were back at Nui Dat, and immediately began packing and transferring stores from their lines to 3RAR's. At 1201hr, V Company and 1 Troop married-up, and they had completed their combined move south to AO Otago by 1503hr. The troop then returned to Courtenay Hill for further tasking.

At 1630hr a group from HQ 18 ARVN Division arrived at the Battalion CP to examine the feasibility of positioning 105mm howitzers on the Hill, also checking to see what stores might be left next day when the CP closed. However, at 2035hr that evening a message from 18ARVN said that they would *not* require the use of Courtenay Hill after all, and orders were therefore issued that all stores were either to be back-loaded to Nui Dat or destroyed next day. The ANZAC Battalion's CP then settled down to its 114th, and last, night of operation on Courtenay Hill.

At 0745hr on 5 October, Day 3 of Valiant, elements of A Squadron began checking south along Route 2 for mines and ambushes, and the road was picketed ready for the convoy which would carry personnel and stores from Courtenay back to Nui Dat. And at 1200hr, while taking up a position 500 metres west of Route 2 and 1.5 kilometres south of Xa Bang, an APC from 1 Section 1 Troop detonated an M14 anti-personnel mine. The APC was not damaged, nor were any of the crew injured, and it was learned later that the area had been used some years previously by the Allies. The mine was believed to have been part of a defensive minefield which had not been properly cleared subsequently.

Before that, at 1055hr, 2 Platoon were taking a short break in a quick harbour when they made contact with three VC three kilometres east of Binh Ba. The enemy approached from the west, but the section which made the initial sighting could not be sure if the three were enemy or civilians, and did not open fire. But then the enemy caught sight of the New Zealanders and bolted, and it was seen that one of them was carrying an M1 carbine. Fire was opened and an immediate search made, but only a jungle hat was found.

At 1205hr the ANZAC Battalion's CP on Courtenay Hill closed down, and from that moment command of the Battalion was exercised from the Rear CP in Nui Dat. Five minutes later HQ 18ARVN advised that Courtenay Hill *was* required after all, and that any remaining stores and installations should be left intact. FSB Debbie came out of action at 1600hr and closed; and at 1615hr Support Company's rear party handed the Hill over to a platoon from 177 RF Company. They then left Courtenay for the last time and were back in Nui Dat by 1745hr.

Early on the morning of 6 October 3RAR were ready to begin their fly-out to the waiting *Sydney*, and 4RAR completed the transfer of stores to 3RAR's lines. By 1105hr the CP had moved yet again and was in its new location and operating smoothly. Fifteen minutes later B Company reported that A Squadron had begun ferrying their platoons into AO Kingsgrove. The company at once started patrolling towards Nui Dat, while V Company continued to search AO Otago as they moved south. FSB Robin came out of action and closed at 1200hr, and by 1800hr 4RAR and all their supporting units were safely back in Nui Dat.

Operation Valiant, the first phase of the withdrawal from Phuoc Tuy Province, had gone almost without a hitch. Apart from a few small incidents there had been almost no contact with the enemy, and the Battalion had suffered no casualties. 3RAR's withdrawal had also gone without a hitch, and they were now heading home aboard *Sydney*.

Of the original three-battalion Task Force, only 4 RAR now remained in Phuoc Tuy Province.

The next and final operation to be carried out by Australians and New Zealanders in the Vietnam War was Operation South Ward, and it was the second phase of the withdrawal. The operation would be controlled by HQ 1ATF from Nui Dat until 16 October, and thereafter HQ 1ATF would exercise control from its new location in the 1ALSG base at Vung Tau.

Reports reaching the Task Force suggested that Chau Duc had been ordered to carry out a close reconnaissance of Nui Dat. This would make sense, because Chau Duc's old base areas were situated in the vicinity of Nui Nghe and the eastern foothills of the Nui Dinhs, which were just inside AO Kingsgrove. It was also known that the northern edge of AO Otago had been crossed in the past by the Binh Ba guerrillas and elements of D445. Although a significant threat to the Task Force base itself was not now considered likely, it was possible that the enemy might carry out sapper attacks, or attacks by fire onto Ap Suoi Nghe or Ngai Giao. If that happened, they might also mount a limited diversionary attack onto Nui Dat to disrupt any deployment by a reaction force. But in any case the latest assessments of HQ Chau Duc, C41, C2 D445 and C36 Sapper Reconnaissance Company, who were with them, put the total strength at 176 all ranks, and a force that size could not threaten Nui Dat significantly.

But even though 1ATF was now in an essentially defensive posture, Brig McDonald and the CO agreed that it should be an aggressive defence. Therefore the concept of South Ward was that all companies, including Support and Administration Company, would each patrol their TAORs with a minimum of one platoon at all times, while securing their company base areas with a minimum of CHQ and one platoon. APCs and FSVs would deploy to key points within the Nui Dat perimeter in order to thicken up the defensive firepower. And A Squadron was ordered to maintain a minimum of one night ambush within the Task Force TAOR. This meant that at least nine platoons, and elements of A Squadron, were deployed in the Task Force TAOR 24 hours a day. Their task was to ensure that enemy units could not get close enough to Nui Dat to mount either a ground attack, sapper attacks or attacks by fire.

For added flexibility of fire support, one section (two tubes) from 4RAR's Mortar Platoon was positioned with D Company on Nui Dat Hill, while the remaining three sections occupied 3RAR's former baseplate position. Moreover an appearance of normal activity was to be maintained in and around Nui Dat when HQ 1ATF and support and administrative units withdrew to Vung Tau on 16 October. This would be achieved by maintaining daily Caribou flights in and out of Luscombe Field by 35 Squadron RAAF; by the use of visual reconnaissance and sniffer missions; and by simulated SAS insertions and extractions by 9 Squadron RAAF.

All resupply to Nui Dat would be by Caribou, and road convoys from and to Nui Dat could be approved only by the Task Force Commander himself. Those road convoys which were approved would be provided with escorts from A Squadron and aerial cover as far as the Green road, south of Baria, to Vung Tau. Bushrangers and artillery would also be on call for each road convoy.

The ANZAC Battalion's final withdrawal from Nui Dat to Vung Tau would be in two phases. The first would be the withdrawal by road of all bulk and heavy equipment and stores by 6 November. On that day the Battalion's advance party would also position at Vung Tau.

The sequence of events for the second phase, which would start and finish on D Day, 7 November, would be:

- The deployment of one section of 104 Battery to a fire position south of Baria.
- The deployment to Vung Tau of V and C Company by Caribou as an administrative move; and the movement of four road convoys with Support Company and any remaining stores and equipment.
- As soon as the last of the four convoys left Nui Dat, Luscombe Field and the area north of it would be abandoned.
- The remaining force, consisting of the Battalion Tac CP, B and D Company and 1 Troop A Squadron, would concentrate in the Hornbill–Pelican Heights–Nui Dat Hill area.
- D Company, on Nui Dat Hill, would be relieved in the line by 946 RF Company, and would then be extracted by helicopter. Concurrently the Battalion Tac CP would be extracted from Pelican Heights.
- With 1 Troop A Squadron maintaining security, B Company would also be extracted from Pelican Heights by helicopter.
- As soon as the last elements of B Company were clear, 1 Troop would withdraw to Vung Tau. Nui Dat would thus be abandoned by 1400hr on 7 November 1971.

The administrative plan to support the tactical plan from 6 October to 7 November would be based on:

- The continued use of all facilities normally available in Nui Dat up to D-3, 4 November. These included electricity, refrigeration, water, fresh rations and canteen supplies.
- The pre-positioning of sufficient non-perishable supplies before the Task Force Commander's restriction on road convoys came into force on 6 October. These supplies included stocks and reserves of all types of ammunition, together with canteen supplies, clothing, equipment, defence stores, petrol, oils and lubricants.
- The resupply of all perishable items including fresh rations, maintdem items, laundry, and the movement of personnel in and out of Nui Dat, was to be by air.

This administrative plan could be achieved by two Caribou sorties each day for rations, maintdem items and laundry, supplemented by a Caribou lift and Iroquois tasking for passengers as required. At the same time the Battalion's AQ cell would position in 1ALSG for liaison duties and to handle and secure stores and equipment being back-loaded from Nui Dat.

In order to meet the requirements and constraints of the final tactical withdrawal on D Day, the normal services and facilities had to be gradually closed down. This included:

- The removal to Vung Tau of all non-essential personal items and individual steel trunks, using Caribous, by 1 November.
- The move by road on D-4, 3 November, of all heavy non-essential stores in metal shipping boxes and connexes.
- The cessation of fresh rations and canteen items on D-3, 4 November, at which time all refrigeration would be turned off and back-loaded to Vung Tau on semi-trailers. From then on the Battalion would use combat ration packs.
- And finally, on D-1, a second major road convoy to take the remaining stores and equipment to 1ALSG, and the fly-out of the Battalion's advance party.

For the conduct of Operation South Ward, the Battalion would be retitled 4RAR/NZ (ANZAC) Battalion Group, and its task organisation would include:

a detachment 104 Signal Squadron
1 Troop and FSVs from A Squadron
104 Battery, and a gun section LAD RAEME
one troop (-) 1 Field Squadron

one DS Possum, 161 (Indep) Recce Flight
elements of 161 (Indep) Recce Flight
elements from 8 Petrol Platoon
elements from 176 Air Dispatch Company
elements from 11 Movement Control Group
detachment Communication Zone Postal Unit

Elements of 9 and 35 Squadron RAAF, an Air Transport Operations Control Centre RAAF, and a platoon (three guns) from B Battery 5/42nd Battalion (US) Artillery would also be in direct support.

Although patrol activity in that last month was intense, there were almost no sightings or contacts in the Task Force TAOR. The duty officers' log in the Battalion CP records the constant comings and goings in and out of 'the wire' by patrols and ambushes. Fictitious locstats were sent to maintain the appearance of normal radio traffic as part of the deception plan. HQ 1ATF authorised the use of one platoon from the Ready Reaction Force to be used for TAOR patrols, but that platoon had to be within one hour's recall. And the Australian Embassy in Saigon required soil samples from around Nui Dat. Lt Willis's 5 Platoon were given the task, and they duly reported that the samples had been successfully 'captured in action' on 13 October.

At 1448hr on 16 October HQ 1ATF was clear of Nui Dat and on their way to their new location in 1ALSG. At 1800hr the same day, the ANZAC Battalion Group assumed responsibility for Luscombe Field and all air operations in and out of it.

On 17 and 18 October Lt Ballantyne's 4 Platoon found Claymore mines rigged as mechanical ambushes (booby traps). The platoon destroyed one and a splinter team from 1 Field Squadron dismantled the other. It turned out that the Claymores had been set by PF troops from Ngai Giao, and they were ordered to immediately clear any other such random set-ups.

During the 32 days between 6 October and 7 November there were only three incidents that could be classed as contacts with the enemy. On 12 October at 0047hr an APC section from 1 Troop A Squadron sighted one, possibly two, enemy with a torch approaching their ambush position. However the enemy spotted the APCs and fired one shot, which was answered immediately with machinegun fire and illumination. A search in the morning revealed no result.

At 2040hr on 18 October, 6 Platoon, now commanded by Sgt Fairley after the wounding of 2/Lt McDaniel on 21 September, were in an ambush position in their TAOR. A sentry heard movement to his front, challenged, and fired, but without any apparent effect. Thirty minutes later more movement was detected; the sentry fired again, and this time moaning was heard. Nevertheless a search revealed no further result.

And on 2 November at 0830hr, 5 Platoon was patrolling to the east of Route 2 opposite Suoi Nghe, when they came under automatic M16 fire. The platoon made a search, and the DS Possum and 3 Section 1 Troop were reacted into the area. But although the platoon, the Possum and the APCs worked together for some time searching, they found nothing.

On the evening of 5 November, D Company held a memorial service on Nui Dat Hill for their eight men who had lost their lives since May. At 0830hr on 6 November the Battalion's advance party, under the command of Maj McIver, flew out to 1ALSG in the Caribous of 35 Squadron; and at 1000hr the advance party from 946 RF Company arrived at Nui Dat Hill to begin the handover from D Company. A member of the company recalls:

> We watched them toiling slowly up the hill towards us. They wore an assortment of uniform, civilian clothes, and webbing, all in varying degrees of shabbiness and disrepair. One of them had the torso of a monkey wired to the foresight of his M16: his evening meal presumably. They might have been figures of humour or ridicule, but I felt overwhelmingly sorry for them. I think we all did, because nobody said anything and nobody laughed.[1]

It's possible that other members of the ANZAC Battalion who saw the RF platoon that morning felt the same way. And it's possible, too, that the uncomfortable thought occurred to many that these unfortunate people were about to be abandoned to their fate.

At 1910hr all the Battalion's unserviceable ammunition, which had been collected together outside the wire, was destroyed by high explosive. Patrolling and ambushing continued until the morning of D Day, 7 November, when at 0617hr Victor Company's 1 and 2 Platoons entered the wire. Then 7 Platoon came in; and at 0640hr Lt O'Brien's 8 Platoon closed the gap in the wire behind them and reported themselves safely back.

At 0700hr 1 Troop began moving south to Baria, checking and picketing the road. The Caribous commenced the Victor Company fly-out at 0715hr, and they were complete at Vung Tau by 0812hr. At 0730hr the Battalion Main CP closed, and the Tac CP began operating from D Company's position on Nui Dat Hill. At the same time the Mortar Platoon came out of action, except for the two tubes with D Company. The gun section from 104 Battery that would support the move south departed for its position at Baria at 0804hr. C Company began flying out by Caribou, and were complete in Vung Tau at 0907hr;

and the road convoys departed in succession, and by 1230hr all were safely arrived at Vung Tau. At 1012hr Luscombe Field closed down and was abandoned; and at 1048hr, 946 RF Company relieved D Company on Nui Dat Hill. The Tac CP and D Company flew out from Pelican Heights at 1115hr, at which moment the CP at Vung Tau opened. The Tac CP and D Company were complete at Vung Tau by 1225hr.

Maj Hogarth's B Company commenced their fly-out from Pelican Heights at 1225hr. They were the last rifle company to leave Nui Dat, and they were complete at Vung Tau at 1332hr.

1 Troop A Squadron 3 Cavalry Regiment was the last sub-unit to leave Nui Dat. They abandoned the former 1ATF base at 1341hr on 7 November 1971, and were complete at Vung Tau by 1445hr. At 1500hr the Task Force command net closed down for the last time. The withdrawal of Australian and New Zealand troops from Phuoc Tuy Province had been a textbook operation, and had been achieved with no battle casualties.

At 1530hr 4RAR/NZ (ANZAC) Battalion's command net closed down for the last time. The final entry in the duty officers' log reads '1800. Op SOUTH WARD concluded. End of operations'.

The month in Vung Tau was an anti-climax. Metal trunks were repainted and addressed; equipment was scrubbed and re-scrubbed to remove the pink dirt of Phuoc Tuy, and if that didn't work it was burnt and replaced. Malarial eradication courses started, and the Battalion was required to provide numerous work parties for the preparation and loading of stores. There were several parties at which the Battalion said goodbye to the many friends they had made throughout operations. And a memorial service was held in the Badcoe Club gymnasium at which the New Zealand and Australian chaplains, Father John Carde and Chaplain Alan Switzer, officiated.

As the time approached for Victor Company to return to Singapore, and for the Battalion, less D Company, to go aboard HMAS *Sydney*, many messages of farewell were received. The Chief of the New Zealand General Staff, MajGen L.A. Pearce wrote to his Australian counterpart, LtGen M.F. Brogan:

> In a short time, the last of the NZ Army personnel who have been serving with 1ATF and 1ALSG will withdraw from the Republic of Vietnam.
>
> Since this will mark approximately six years of close association of Australians and New Zealanders within these two formations, I would not wish the event to pass unrecorded. In looking back over the statistics I find that we have had some 3000 soldiers serving in the Republic of Vietnam over the period. However statistics mean little.

Victor Company during the Battalion's farewell parade at Vung Tau in December 1971. Behind Maj Brian Monks are *(from left)*: Lt Greg Campbell, 2 Platoon; Lt Mick Harris (obscured), 1 Platoon; and Lt Chris Mullane, 3 Platoon. (*The Fighting Fourth*)

What has meant a great deal is that once again our soldiers have served alongside Australians. Again they learned to appreciate the staunch qualities of the Australian soldier and, in operating towards common goals in an exacting environment, gained much from the mutual experience.

While it is of some regret that we were not able to contribute a New Zealand battalion, I know our Infantry took great pride in and shared the achievements of the Anzac Battalions in which they served. Our Gunners closely identified with the Australian Infantry they supported, while logistic personnel within 1ALSG units were well integrated with their parent Australian units. Without the logistic support given to NZV Force by AFV, we would have been severely restricted in our ability to maintain the Force. I would like you know that we are much indebted to the Australian Army for this support.

This withdrawal from the Republic of Vietnam sees the closing of yet another chapter in the history of our combined military endeavour which began on the Gallipoli Peninsula. We are proud that we have been associated with you in Vietnam.[2]

The ANZAC Battalion paraded at 1ALSG and was reviewed by Gen Abrams, the supreme commander in Vietnam; President Thieu made a speech of thanks and farewell on *Sydney*'s flight deck. Gen Sir Thomas Daly, Colonel Commandant of the Royal Australian Regiment, signalled the CO:

> Please convey to all ranks of your Battalion my sincere congratulations on the success of your tour of duty in Vietnam. 4RAR is the last battalion to leave Vietnam and as such has written with distinction the final chapter in a splendid story of the Regiment's participation in the Vietnam conflict. A good trip home and good luck in the future.[3]

Aboard HMAS *Sydney*, as the old aircraft carrier headed south for Australia, the CO sent this signal to CO 1RNZIR in Singapore: 'From 4RAR. For CO from Hughes. Today I reluctantly lose V Coy and return them to your command. The ANZAC tradition has been well maintained and added to by V Coy. All ranks 4RAR send greetings to 1RNZIR with special reference to their many friends in V Coy.'[4] Maj Brian Monks' Victor Company was the last New Zealand rifle company to serve in, and leave, Vietnam. And 4RAR was the last Australian battalion out.

But D Company remained behind in Vung Tau, and many members of the company considered that the most difficult part of the second tour in Vietnam was yet to come. This was because the company's aims and objectives were now not as clearly defined as they had been in operations. Moreover, just before the final withdrawal from Nui Dat a large number of NSM had left the Battalion for Australia after the government had foreshortened their two-year commitment. Among them were two dozen from D Company, or around 20 per cent of the company's strength. These were men who had been in all the company's battles, big and small. Their loss was very keenly felt, not only because they were old friends, but also because they were battle-hardened, and in most cases their knowledge and experience could not be replaced. So when it was decided that D Company would remain behind after the rest of the Battalion went home, plans were put in train to reinforce the company with volunteers from within the Battalion.

The company also felt far less comfortable with the environment, and commanders at all levels were worried by the potential for disaster that Vung Tau and the surrounding area presented. These misgivings were intensified when, a day or so before the bulk of the Task Force left to go home, an Australian senior NCO had been stabbed to death in the town by locals, and a number of other men from his unit had been badly injured in the same incident. This was an extremely worrying episode:

it was bad enough to lose young men in battle, but to lose them in such a stupidly wasteful way as this was utterly tragic.

D Company's role in 1ALSG was to be that of a ready reaction force in case the enemy decided to put in a final effort to send the Australians home with a bloody nose. The enemy might do this in one of two ways: sapper attacks against 1ALSG, which was the most likely option, because civilian labourers were employed within the base, and despite security precautions, any of them could smuggle in and set explosive charges. Or else the enemy might try to lure D Company out of Vung Tau and back into Phuoc Tuy. This could be achieved by attacking the AATTV jungle training centre at Van Kiep, just outside Baria, or the AATTV teams located with RF posts in the south of the province. At the time OC D Company considered this to be a likely enemy option, and so it had to be planned for.

A coordinated ground attack against 1ALSG was highly unlikely because of the difficulty faced by the enemy of getting onto, and away from, the Vung Tau peninsula. But it was an enemy option, if only a very faint one, and therefore could not be overlooked.

D Company's concerns were further compounded by the fact that the dedicated systems of command and control of supporting arms were no longer available. The comforting presence of the Battalion CP was gone, as was the intimate support of the other companies and 104 Battery. Command and control would now come from HQ 1ALSG, and it was staffed by officers who were mostly logisticians and heavily preoccupied with planning and implementing the backload of equipment and vehicles to Australia. Nevertheless the question remained: if D Company were activated and found themselves in a fight, where would artillery support come from? Or air? And if these *did* materialise, what would be the liaison and coordination arrangements, especially if they came from ARVN sources, with all the attendant language problems? OC D Company was told that there was very little chance of the company group going back into the province, but even so the company could hardly have stood idly by if the AATTV men came under attack.

The company's role as ready reaction force required them to have one platoon continually at fifteen minutes' notice to move, with the rest of the company to follow within the hour. All three rifle platoons were now up to full strength, and in addition the company was allotted a support platoon consisting of a section of 81mm mortars with CP and MFCs; a pioneer section; and additional signallers and stretcher-bearers. Cpl McGurk, the Intelligence Section linguist, was also assigned to the company.

Lt Bryant arrived to command Support Platoon. He had been 2i/c of the Mortar Platoon and had a sound knowledge of support weapons and their application. The grievously wounded 2/Lt McKay, now recuperating satisfactorily in Australia, had been replaced permanently in 11 Platoon by Lt Wellard, a CMF Full Time Duty officer. At 31 years of age, he was one of the oldest members of the company, and as a consequence 11 Platoon nicknamed him 'Fossil'. However, despite 'having one foot in the grave', he quickly earned the respect and affection of his new platoon. Both Lt Bryant and Lt Wellard fitted in very well.

To complete Delta Company Group, as it was henceforth to be titled, the company was allotted a reinforced troop of APCs from A Squadron 3 Cavalry Regiment, under the command of Lt Stephens. He and his troop were old friends of D Company, having worked together several times on operations, and the company were very pleased to have them alongside again now. And in addition to the normal establishment of APCs, the troop had a section of mortar carriers, and a section of FSVs with their 76mm guns and coaxially mounted machineguns. So the company group would be able to bare a formidable set of teeth if necessary.

It seemed likely that life in 1ALSG would begin to wear somewhat thin by the time D Company left in February 1972 and that morale, and then discipline, might eventually begin to suffer. The best way of getting through those next three months was to keep everyone gainfully employed. Despite the excellent facilities at the Badcoe Club, where D Company were now permanently quartered, the OC was concerned that boredom might soon set in unless aggressive steps were taken to prevent it.

So it was decided that the company's routine, five days a week, would be training from 0800–1230hr daily; lunch, then sport until 1600hr. There were movies every evening, and for those so inclined, two hours of Tae Kwon Do in the gymnasium under Captain Kim, a charmingly homicidal little officer from the Army of the Republic of Korea. Supper, consisting of two 'hepatitis' rolls per man filled with fresh salad, was available at about 2200hr. The combined company officers' and sergeants' mess, and the diggers' canteen, closed at around 2230hr, and lights out was about 2300hr. Whenever possible Saturday was a general administrative and make-and-mend day; and Sunday was stand-down, insofar as anything was stand-down, given the company's constant state of readiness to move.

The daily training programme consisted of three courses: mortar, signals and a general course which was a refresher on skills like combat first aid, TsOET, shooting, physical fitness tests, and similar subjects. All platoons bullringed through the three courses, the aim being that everyone would qualify as a mortar crew member and as a signaller, and be up to date with personal proficiency tests, by the time the company left for Australia.

Each afternoon volunteers were also sent to help with the construction of a local orphanage run by Roman Catholic nuns. And towards the end of the withdrawal, D Company were employed as stevedores to load the ships taking stores back to Australia: work which continued round the clock, and which everyone found novel and usually enjoyable.

Sporting facilities at the Badcoe Club were excellent. The South China Sea was 50 metres away, and the company had the use of a surf rescue boat and a ski launch. There was a full-sized gymnasium with weights and other instruments of torture; and a swimming pool, which none of the logistic units seemed to want to use, fearing presumably some sort of sinister pollution from such a large contingent of infantrymen. A swimming carnival was held during which L/Cpl Dowell won the diving competition by removing his bathers while performing an intricate and beautifully executed forward pike. Volleyball was popular;

HMAS *Sydney* loads off Vung Tau just before leaving for Australia with 4RAR on 8 December 1971. (*The Fighting Fourth*)

and the company also regularly sent a combined rugby and cricket team to Saigon, where they played against the British, French and Australian High Commissions.

A variant of touch rugby was devised to get over the fact that there were many avid players of all codes of football, but no pitches at Vung Tau. The game was played on the beach by two teams consisting of any number of people, and it sometimes resembled a mix of the deciding game of a State of Origin series and the Zulu attack on Rourkes Drift. The use of a ball was frequently incidental. The whole procedure was further complicated by the fact that people on both sides could be in shirts or 'skins' at the same time. OC D Company was invited to referee one of these tournaments, and he said that while he was happy to do so, he was not entirely certain of the rules. But as it turned out this didn't matter, because nobody ever took any notice of referees anyway.

Overall though, the company got the mix of work and play right, and nobody became lost in the alleys of Vung Tau, at least not permanently. There were some minor disciplinary infringements, but nothing very serious, and the company was fortunate to have Capt Hoban and his Military Police detachment at 1ALSG. They did a splendid job in the town and with a combination of commonsense and good humour scooped up any D Company soldiers who wanted to take on the world, bundled them into paddy wagons; and brought them safely back to the admonishing gaze of CSM Huish.

And then, just before midday on 29 February 1972, 1ALSG closed down and D Company Group went aboard *Sydney*. Later that afternoon,

The last of the last. D Company left Vietnam on 29 February 1972, three months after 4RAR's main body. Behind the OC are (*from left*): CSM Huish (obscured); Lt Bryant, Support Platoon; Lt Wellard, 11 Platoon; and 2/Lt Spinkston, 12 Platoon. (*Army Public Relations*)

'As HMAS *Sydney* got underway, groups of men from D Company gathered at her stern and stood watching as the unhappy coastline of Vietnam receded. After a while it could only be seen as a thin grey line, except where the hills of Phuoc Tuy thrust up. Soon even they had vanished beneath the rim of the sea'.[5]

Of the battalions of the Royal Australian Regiment which served in South Vietnam from June 1965 to December 1971, all were good and some were better. 4RAR/NZ (ANZAC) Battalion was one of the better.

The reasons were various, but their sum was greater than the parts. The first and most important factor was LtCol Hughes' very strong and positive influence over the Battalion, both in preparation for Vietnam and during operations there. From the start of his tenure as CO he let it be known that second best was not good enough and would not be accepted. He was not bombastic or theatrical about this fundamental requirement. He simply laid down the personal and corporate standards which were demanded, and never deviated from them. Nor did he allow his Battalion to deviate from them either. Those who could not or would not conform were first given a fair chance to mend their ways, and if that failed they were removed from the Battalion and replaced by better material.

The CO had not served in Vietnam before, but he had been decorated for gallantry in Korea as a platoon commander, and had raised 2SAS Squadron and taken them to Borneo during Confrontation, so he already had 'the numbers on the board'. Subsequently he proved to be a most able active service CO. His plans were always uncomplicated and capable of rapid modification if the uncertainties of battle showed that to be necessary. He trusted his company commanders absolutely; gave them freedom of decision and action; and allowed them to get on with their jobs without constantly breathing down their necks. But when a fight started, he always found an opportune moment to let his subordinate commanders know that he was there if they needed advice, and that he would provide them with every supporting agency at his disposal. And he was always calm and confident even under the most prolonged pressure.

In all aspects of preparing the Battalion for Vietnam, and throughout operations, the CO was most ably supported, first by RSM Healy and, after his tragic death, by RSM Thompson; and by Maj McIver when he arrived from New Zealand in January 1971 to become Second-in-Command. The quality of these three men, and the leadership and impetus they exerted, was considerable, and is highlighted by the fact that all three went on to achieve extremely distinguished careers subsequently.

The very strong Sergeants' Mess under the leadership of RSM Healy and then RSM Thompson was a powerful force for good throughout the Battalion. The Mess members were men who had been in the service for lengthy periods of time and had gained their experience through successive ranks. Their collective knowledge of soldiers and soldiering was vast, and their pride in the Battalion and its reputation was immense. This sense of pride and loyalty ultimately flowed across to every member of the Battalion.

Maj Stevenson, the Operations Officer, and all the Australian company commanders and their CSMs had served in Vietnam previously. In total, 141 members were returning to Vietnam, many for a second tour with 4RAR. This active service experience was spread throughout all levels of the Battalion, and had a profound effect on it.

Maj McIver and Maj Monks had not served in Vietnam, but they had been on active service in Malaysia and Borneo during Confrontation, and both men had been hand-picked to accompany the ANZAC Battalion to Vietnam. Victor Company were all regular soldiers who had volunteered for Vietnam, and many of them had already served there. The company had been rigorously trained and prepared by Maj Monks, and all members were highly proficient in their primary tasks, and cross-trained in a broad range of other infantry skills as well. As a consequence, their performance throughout operations was of consistent high quality.

By 1970 the training system for Vietnam had been perfected, and it's probably true to say that no member of the Battalion, high or low, was ever confronted by an operational situation in 1971 for which he had not been trained. This solid base of preparation was backed up in Vietnam by a lavish and responsive resupply system, underpinned by the members of Administration Company and the dedication of the CQMSs and their assistants.

The part played in the Battalion's successes by the supporting arms cannot be over-emphasised or praised too highly. Air support was unstinting, and the commitment of the pilots total. The support given to the ANZAC Battalion by 104 Field Battery 12 Field Regiment RAA, by A Squadron 3 Cavalry Regiment and C Squadron 1 Armoured Regiment RAAC, and by 1 Field Squadron RAE was superb, and could stand as a model for any professional army.

The ARA and the Royal Australian Regiment generally, and 4RAR in particular, will always owe a great debt of gratitude to their NSM of the Vietnam years. All national service members of the Battalion were volunteers for Vietnam, and they served with courage and distinction.

This quality was mirrored and intensified by their regular peers; and the proposition advanced at the beginning of this book—that in the end all battles are won by the soldiers—can only be strengthened by the results achieved at section and platoon level during operations in Phuoc Tuy. The war highlighted once again, if such were still necessary, that Australian and New Zealand soldiers, properly led, are among the best in the world.

4RAR's second tour had finished officially on 8 December 1971, as HMAS *Sydney*, bearing the Battalion home, left the territorial waters of South Vietnam. Now D Company, the last of the last, were going home too. The journey to Australia took twelve days: occasionally there were mess duties to be done, but in the main the company passed the time in a delicious idleness of eating, sunbaking and sleeping.

Ahead for the Battalion stretched the uncertainties of peacetime soldiering. Ahead, too, lay the reduction in size of the Regiment. On 15 August 1973, 4RAR was linked to 2RAR during a parade at Lavarack Barracks, after which the 2nd/4th Battalion, Royal Australian Regiment, marched away to its lines under the command of LtCol L.D. Johnson.

In the cycle of time, members of the Battalion would be reposted to perform other tasks throughout the Regiment and the Army. For some there would be United Nations service in the Middle East and Kashmir, or in Rhodesia and Uganda, Papua New Guinea, Somalia, Rwanda or East Timor.

On 1 February 1995, the 31st anniversary of 4RAR's raising, 2/4RAR would be unlinked, and 4RAR's Colours would be sent under escort to Holsworthy, the Battalion's new home. There, under the watchful eye of the CO, LtCol R.C. Smith, and the RSM, WO1 K.R. Kahler, the Battalion would begin to rebuild, and by the end of 1996 would number 300 all ranks.

But in 1997 there would be a momentous change for the Battalion. It would be ordered to quit its traditional role of infantry of the line, and become instead the first regular commando battalion in the Australian Army. Those who passed the gruelling selection procedures would still have to qualify in a range of demanding courses: parachuting, roping, amphibious and many others besides. They would form 4RAR (Commando), and they would exchange the rifle-green beret of the infantryman for the paler green one of the commando soldier, but with the cap-badge of the Regiment still proudly in evidence.

But, on 12 March 1972, as HMAS *Sydney* stood in towards Townsville, and the ship's landing craft began taking D Company ashore to their waiting families and friends, all this was still in the future.

Author's note

The first Face of Battle presentation was given at the Infantry Centre, Singleton, in 1979. The aim of the presentation was to give students an insight into command in battle.

WO2 Bernie Le Sueur, MM, described some of his experiences as a section commander in Vietnam. Col John Essex-Clark, the Commandant, spoke of commanding a platoon of the Royal Rhodesian Regiment during the Malayan Emergency. And I talked about D Company 4RAR during the Battalion's second tour in Vietnam. The presentation was so well received that it subsequently became a permanent part of the Company Commanders course.

Since 1979 I have given the presentation many times at Singleton, and to other units of the Regular Army, the Army Reserve, to RMC cadets newly graduated from the Australian Defence Force Academy, and to cadets at Officer Cadet Training Units. In April 1999 I had the sad duty of delivering the presentation to the last Company Commanders course to be conducted at Singleton, and the pleasure in November of presenting it to the newly instituted Combat Officers Advanced Course at Bridges Barracks, Puckapunyal.

What was most rewarding throughout those years, as it still is today, was to see the intense thirst for practical knowledge shown by every audience. And often their questions began with, 'What was it like when . . .?', 'How did you feel when . . .?', 'What did you do when . . .?' Moreover, from time to time it was suggested that I should document the presentation in a more lengthy and permanent form.

So when MajGen Jim Hughes, AO, DSO, MC, wrote to his former company commanders in April 1999, canvassing their opinion on whether or not a book should be written about 4RAR's second tour in Vietnam, I took the plunge and volunteered to write it. *Last Out* is the result.

I have tried to go beyond making the book just a factual account of the second tour, and to describe for old soldiers, young soldiers, and the public at large, some of the whats, whys and hows that *are* the face of battle.

In writing the book I have been helped by many people. LtGen Don McIver, CMG, OBE, and Col Brian Monks, in New Zealand, have been particularly helpful in providing insights to the ANZAC affiliation and the raising and training of Victor Company.

My thanks go to MajGen Jim Hughes for proposing the book in the first place, for his suggestions and encouragement throughout its writing, and for information on many aspects of the raising, manning, training and command of 4RAR in 1970–71; to Mrs Jan Hughes for background on the 4RAR Wives' Club; to LtCol Bob Hogarth for his perspectives as the commander of B Company; to Maj Keith Towning for his responses to my questions regarding the part played by 104 Field Battery 12 Field Regiment RAA; to LtCol Gary McKay, MC, for allowing me to quote from his books, *In Good Company* and *Delta Four*; to Maj Mike Murphy for detail on his Tracker Platoon; to RSM Wally Thompson, OAM, for his wise insights; and to WO1 Digby Lawrence for his help on a range of matters concerning the Battalion.

I am grateful to Professor David Horner for allowing me to quote from his history of the Royal Australian Regiment, *Duty First*; to LtCol Jeff Sengelman, CSC, CO 4RAR (Commando), for allowing me access to material from *The Fighting Fourth*; to LtCol Greg Pike, CO School of Infantry, for allowing me to access technical information on the 81mm mortar: and to WO2 Joe Linford, the Curator/Manager of the Royal Australian Armoured Corps Memorial and Army Tank Museum, and to his deputy, Tpr David Gibson, for their assistance; and to Gaye Morris for re-keying my manuscript.

My thanks also go to Ian Bowring at Allen & Unwin for his support and advice throughout the writing of the book, and to Emma Cotter for her expertise during its production.

Last, but by no means least, I am forever indebted to Col Bob Sayce, CSC, who has helped me with research and information, and given me his perspectives of events as they occurred in the Battalion Command Post during operations in Phuoc Tuy Province, and who, as 4RAR's Intelligence Officer in 1970–71, had the historical foresight to retain copies of all training précis, standing orders, weekly intelligence reviews, maps, after action reports, and many other documents relating to the second tour; for allowing me unlimited access to them; and for managing to keep them intact throughout almost 30 years of the travels that are so much part of a soldier's life.

Jerry Taylor
Batemans Bay
December 2000

4RAR/NZ (ANZAC) Battalion in Vietnam

A complete nominal roll of the Battalion can be found in, *The Fighting Fourth: A pictorial record of the second tour in South Vietnam by 4RAR/NZ (ANZAC) Battalion 1971–1972.*

Battalion Headquarters

CO	LtCol J.C. Hughes, MC
2i/c	Maj D.S. McIver (NZ)
RSM	WO1 W.T.C. Thompson
OPSO	Maj E.H. Stevenson
IO	Capt R.L. Sayce
Adjt	Capt D.D. McKenzie
then	Capt J.D. McAloney, MC
A/Adjt	Lt R.L. J. Martin
CC	S/Sgt R. Heffernan
UPR	Sgt W.B. Warnes, BEM
Chaplains:	Maj J.E. Carde (NZ)
	Capt A.L. Switzer
NZ Component:	Capt S.J.N. Winton
	WO2 A.D. Nixey

Support Company

OC	Capt J.D. McAloney, MC
then	Capt D.D. McKenzie
CSM	WO2 D.G. Holmes
CQMS	S/Sgt F. Galvin
RSO	Capt G.R. Shannon
Mor	Capt J. Sullivan
Pnr	Lt R.J. Swarbrick
Tkr	2/Lt M.F. Murphy

Administration Company

OC	Maj J.H. Taylor
then	Maj J.H. Robbins
2i/c	Capt M.J. Wadsworth (NZ)
CSM	WO2 D.N. Cook
CQMS	S/Sgt D.B. Lawrence
QM	Lt J.S. Catton
A/QM	2/Lt P.F. Darby
TO	Lt M.D. O'Neill
P/M	WO2 D.A. Thoresen
D/M	Sgt I.W. Fryer
RMO	Capt P.R. Trevillian
Med Sgt	Sgt E.A. Chapman
SB Sgt	Sgt K.B. Miller
WO Cat	WO2 J.N. Ploenges

Salvation Army: Hon Lt G.J. Currie

The Rifle Companies in Vietnam

V Company

OC	Maj	B.R.H. Monks
2i/c	Capt	J.S. Harman
CSM	WO2	R.H. Shepherd
CQMS	S/Sgt	J.M. Richardson
1Pl	Lt	N.J. Fry
then	Lt	M.C. Harris
2Pl	Lt	G.F.S. Campbell
3Pl	Lt	C.B. Mullane

B Company

OC	Maj	R.R. Hogarth
2i/c	Capt	T.W. Roderick
CSM	WO2	T.A. Barnes
CQMS	S/Sgt	C.A. Fletcher
4Pl	Lt	I.J. Ballantyne
5Pl	Lt	S.V.L. Willis
6Pl	2/Lt	D.N. McDaniel

C Company

OC	Maj	R.E. Boxall
2i/c	Capt	C.H. Babington
CSM	WO2	T.W. Smith
CQMS	S/Sgt	P.R. Webber
7Pl	Lt	P.S. Andrews
8Pl	Lt	P.A. O'Brien
9Pl	Lt	A.C. Grecian

D Company

OC	Maj	F.J. Kudnig
then	Maj	J.H. Taylor
2i/c	Capt	P.J. Schuman, MC
CSM	WO2	G.N. Huish
CQMS	S/Sgt	R.J. Hann
10Pl	2/Lt	K.M. Byrne
11Pl	2/Lt	G.J. McKay
then	Lt	R.J. Wellard
12Pl	2/Lt	G.D. Spinkston

Glossary

1ATF	1st Australian Task Force
1ALSG	1st Australian Logistic Support Group
1RTB	1st Recruit Training Battalion
2i/c	second-in-command
AAAvn	Australian Army Aviation Corps
AATTV	Australian Army Training Team Vietnam
ABF	attack by fire
ACV	armoured command vehicle
ADC	aide-de-camp (a general's personal assistant)
AHQ	Army Headquarters
AM	Member of the Order of Australia
AMR	Australian Military Regulations
ANZAC	Australian and New Zealand Army Corps (founded at Gallipoli in World War I)
ANZUK	Australia New Zealand United Kingdom
AO	Member of the Order of Australia
AO	Area of Operations
APC	armoured personnel carrier
AQ	administrative and quartermaster
ARA	Australian Regular Army
Arclight	B52 carpet-bombing mission
Arty Tac	command post controlling all 1ATF artillery support, and coordinating it with air support and manoeuvre
ARVN	Army of the Republic of (South) Vietnam
BC	battery commander
BK	battery captain (the battery 2i/c)

Bombardier	an Artillery corporal
BSM	battery sergeant major
C ration	an American combat ration pack
CMF	Citizens Military Forces
CMG	Commander of the Order of St Michael and St George
C/s	callsign (on a radio net)
CSM	company sergeant major
CO	Commanding Officer
Cobra	US helicopter gunship
COSVN	Central Office for South Vietnam (communist high command in the South)
CQMS	company quartermaster sergeant
CRP	combat ration pack
DCM	Distinguished Conduct Medal
DF	defensive fire (artillery or mortar)
Digger	an Australian soldier
DS	directing staff; also direct support
DSO	Distinguished Service Order
Dustoff	casualty evacuation helicopter
Echelon	a battalion's forward supply area
FAC	forward air controller
FGA	fighter ground attack aircraft
FO	forward observer (an RAA lieutenant or captain)
FSCC	Fire Support Control Centre
FSV	fire support vehicle
GP	general purpose
GSO	general staff officer (grades 1, 2 or 3)
Harbour	to establish an NDP
HE	high explosive
Hexamine	solid fuel blocks for heating food and water
H Hour	the time at which an attack starts
H & I	harassing and interdiction (speculative artillery or mortar fire mission)
hoochy	waterproof sheet used as an open-ended tent
JTC	Jungle Training Centre, Canungra, Queensland (now the Land Warfare Centre)
KIA	killed in action
LAD	light aid detachment (RAEME)
Leaguer	tank defensive or echelon position
LOB	left out of battle
LP	landing place (for one helicopter)
LZ	landing zone (for several helicopters)

M113	a generic term for an ACV, APC or FSV
MC	Military Cross
MBE	Member of the British Empire
MFC	mortar fire controller
NCO	non-commissioned officer
NS	National Service
NSM	National Serviceman
Nui	hill
OAM	Medal of the Order of Australia
OBE	Order of the British Empire
OC	Officer Commanding
OCS	Officer Cadet School (Portsea or Scheyville)
OCTU	Officer Cadet Training Unit
OHP	overhead protection
Orbat	order of battle
PF	Popular Force (militia, less well trained than RF)
PM	preventative maintenance (a US Army term)
Possum	callsign prefix denoting a light observation helicopter from 161 Recce Flight AAAvn
PW	prisoner of war
QM	Quartermaster
RAA	Royal Australian Artillery
RAAC	Royal Australian Armoured Corps
RAAMC	Royal Australian Army Medical Corps
RAE	Royal Australian Engineers
RAEME	Royal Australian Electrical and Mechanical Engineers
RAAOC	Royal Australian Army Ordnance Corps
RAR	Royal Australian Regiment
R & C	rest and convalescence (leave taken in Vung Tau or, less usually, in Saigon)
R & R	rest and recreation (leave taken outside SVN)
RR	recoilless rifle (an anti-armour weapon)
RF	Regional Force (South Vietnamese militia)
RMA	Royal Military Academy Sandhurst (UK)
RMC	Royal Military College Duntroon (Australia)
RMO	Regimental Medical Officer
RNZIR	Royal New Zealand Infantry Regiment
RPG	rocket-propelled grenade
RSM	Regimental Sergeant Major
RQMS	Regimental Quartermaster Sergeant
Sapper	A member of the RAE; also an RAE private
SAS	Special Air Service

Sheep-counter	used to tally paces when navigating
SOP	Standard Operating Procedures
Suoi	creek or stream
SVN	South Vietnam
Tac	tactical
TAC 3	an all-corps tactics course for senior captains and majors
TAOR	Tactical Area of Responsibility, usually applied to the area immediately round Nui Dat
TEWT	tactical exercise without troops
TsOET	tests of elementary training
VHF	very high frequency
WIA	wounded in action
zeroing	to calibrate the sight and barrel of a weapon with the point of aim in order to hit targets at various ranges

Ranks

Pte	private
L/Cpl	lance corporal
Cpl	corporal
Sgt	sergeant
S/Sgt	staff sergeant
WO2	warrant officer class 2
WO1	warrant officer class 1
2/Lt	second lieutenant
Lt	lieutenant
Capt	captain
Maj	major
LtCol	lieutenant colonel
Col	colonel
Brig	brigadier
MajGen	major general
LtGen	lieutenant general

Endnotes

Chapter 1

1. Author, letters to LtCol Gary McKay, 1993.
2. MajGen Jim Hughes, letters to author, 1999–2000
3. ibid.
4. LtCol Bob Hogarth, letters to author, 1999–2000

Chapter 3

1. 4RAR Standing Orders, issued 14 January 1970.
2. WO1 Digby Lawrence, letters to author, 1999–2000.
3. Col Bob Sayce, letters to author, 1999–2000.

Chapter 4

1. WO1 Wally Thompson, audiotape and letters to author, 1999–2000.

Chapter 5

1. Maj K.E. Newman, *The ANZAC Battalion in South Vietnam 1967-68*, published by the Battalion, 1968, p. 7.
2. Col Brian Monks, letters to author, 1999–2000.
3. ibid.
4. ibid.
5. ibid.
6. ibid.
7. ibid.
8. ibid.

9. LtGen Don McIver, letters to author, 1999–2000.
10. MajGen Jim Hughes, letters to author, 1999–2000.

CHAPTER 6

1. LtCol Bob Hogarth, letters to author, 1999–2000.

CHAPTER 7

1. Mrs Jan Hughes, letters to author, 1999–2000.
2. Author, letters to LtCol Gary McKay, 1996.
3. Maj Keith Towning, letter to author, 2000.
4. LtCol Gary McKay, *Delta Four: Australian Riflemen in Vietnam*, published by Allen & Unwin, Sydney 1993, pp. 239 and 241.
5. Author, letters to Gary McKay, 1993.
6. LtCol Hughes, 4RAR Training Precis 35/70, 8 December 1970.
7. LtGen Don McIver, letters to author, 1999–2000.

CHAPTER 8

1. 1ATF Battle Intelligence Section, Order of Battle, D445 VC Local Main Force Battalion (Ba Long Province), dated 6 May 1971.
2. ibid.
3. Major K.E. Newman, *The ANZAC Battalion in South Vietnam 1967–68*, published by the Battalion, 1968, p. 64.

CHAPTER 9

1. David Horner, *Duty First: The Royal Australian Regiment in War and Peace*, Allen & Unwin, Sydney, 1990, p. 261.
2. Author, letters to LtCol Gary McKay, 1993.

CHAPTER 10

1. Col Bob Sayce, letters to author, 1999–2000.
2. 4RAR/NZ (ANZAC) Battalion, After Action Report, Operation HERMIT PARK, dated 16 September 1971
3. ibid.
4. ibid.
5. ibid.
6. ibid.
7. C Squadron Combat Operations, After Action Report, Operation HERMIT PARK, dated 15 July 1971.

8. 4RAR/NZ (ANZAC) Battalion, After Action Report, Operation HERMIT PARK, dated 16 September 1971.
9. ibid.
10. C Squadron Combat Operations, After Action Report, Operation Hermit Park, dated 15 July 1971.
11. 4RAR/NZ (ANZAC) Battalion, After Action Report, Operation Hermit Park, dated 16 September 1971.
12. Maj Keith Towning, letter to author, 2000.
13. 4RAR/NZ (ANZAC) Battalion, After Action Report, Operation Hermit Park, dated 16 September 1971.

Chapter 11

1. 4RAR/NZ (ANZAC) Battalion, After Action Report, Operation IRON FOX, dated 29 September 1971.
2. LtCol Gary McKay, *Delta Four: Australian Riflemen in Vietnam*, Allen & Unwin, Sydney, 1996, p. 83.
3. LtCol Gary McKay, *In Good Company*, Allen & Unwin, Sydney, 1987, p. 116.
4. 4RAR/NZ (ANZAC) Battalion, After Action Report, Operation IRON FOX, dated 29 September 1971.
5. Captain R. L. Sayce and Lieutenant M. D. O'Neill, *The Fighting Fourth: A pictorial record of the second tour in South Vietnam*, published by the Battalion, 1972, p. 146.
6. 4RAR/NZ (ANZAC) Battalion, After Action Report, Operation NORTH WARD, dated 20 October 1971.
7. ibid.
8. ibid.
9. ibid.
10. ibid.
11. ibid.

Chapter 12

1. LtCol Bob Hogarth, letters to author, 1999–2000.
2. 4RAR/NZ (ANZAC) Battalion, After Action report, Operation IVANHOE, dated 4 November 1971.
3. LtCol Bob Hogarth, letters to author, 1999–2000.
4. MajGen Jim Hughes, letters to author, 1999–2000.
5. 4RAR/NZ (ANZAC) Battalion, After Action Report, Operation IVANHOE, dated 4 November 1971.
6. Pte Kevin Casson was Mentioned in Despatches for his bravery. In 1999 the award was reviewed and upgraded, and he received the Medal of Gallantry.

7. LtCol Gary McKay, *Delta Four: Australian Riflemen in Vietnam*, Allen & Unwin, Sydney, 1996, pp. 104–5.
8. Col Bob Sayce, letters to author, 1999–2000.
9. 4RAR/NZ (ANZAC) Battalion, After Action Report, Operation IVANHOE, dated 4 November 1971.
10. Maj Keith Towning, letter to author, 2000.
11. 4RAR/NZ (ANZAC) Battalion, After Operation Report, Operation IVANHOE, dated 4 November 1971.
12. LtCol Gary McKay, *Delta Four: Australian Riflemen in Vietnam*, Allen & Unwin, Sydney, 1996, p. 110.
13. Maj Keith Towning, letter to author, 2000.
14. 4RAR/NZ (ANZAC) Battalion, After Action Report, Operation IVANHOE, dated 4 November 1971.
15. Col Bob Sayce, letters to author, 1999–2000.
16. LtCol Gary McKay, *Delta Four: Australian Riflemen in Vietnam*, Allen & Unwin, Sydney, 1996, pp. 106–8.
17. Col Bob Sayce, letters to author, 1999–2000.
18. LtGen Don McIver, letters to author, 1999–2000.
19. 2/Lt Gary McKay was a National Service officer. He was awarded the Military Cross for his leadership and gallantry throughout 21 September 1971.
20. LtCol Bob Hogarth, letters to author, 1999–2000.
21. 4RAR/NZ (ANZAC) Battalion, After Action Report, Operation IVANHOE, dated 4 November 1971.

Chapter 13

1. David Horner, *Duty First: The Royal Australian Regiment in War and Peace*, Allen & Unwin, Sydney, 1990, p. 277.
2. Capt R. L. Sayce and Lt M. D. O'Neill, *The Fighting Fourth: A pictorial record of the second tour in South Vietnam*, published by the Battalion, 1972, p. 201.
3. ibid.
4. ibid.
5. David Horner, *Duty First: The Royal Australian Regiment in War and Peace*, Allen & Unwin, Sydney, 1990, p. 280.

After Action Reports

- 4RAR/NZ (ANZAC) Battalion, After Action Report, Operation BHOWANI JUNCTION/OVERLORD, 3–14 June 1971, R569/1/80 dated 31 July 1971.
- 4RAR/NZ (ANZAC) Battalion, After Action Report, Operation HERMIT PARK, 14 June–27 July 1971, dated 16 September 1971, R569/1/82.

- 4RAR/NZ (ANZAC) Battalion, After Action Report, Operation IRON FOX, 280001 July–052400 August 1971, R569/1/83.
- C Squadron Combat Operations, After Operations Report, Operation HERMIT PARK, dated 15 July 1971, R569/1/27.
- 4RAR/NZ (ANZAC) Battalion, After Action Report, Operation NORTH WARD, 052400 August–182400 September, R569/1/84.
- 4RAR/NZ (ANZAC) Battalion, After Action Report, Operation IVANHOE 182400 September–021800 October 1971, R569/1/89; and Addendum, dated 15 March 1972, R569/1/89.
- 4RAR/NZ (ANZAC) Battalion, After Action Report, Operation VALIANT, 030001-062400 October 1971, R569/1/87.
- 4RAR/NZ (ANZAC) Battalion, After Action Report, Operation SOUTH WARD, 061800 October–071800 November 1971, R569/1/88.

Index